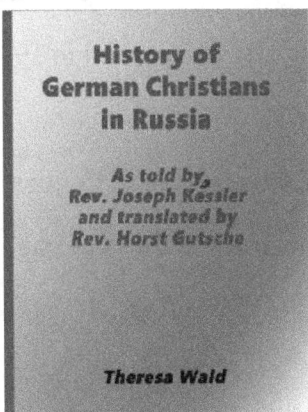

Original title written in German: *History of the Diocese of Tyraspol,*

by Joseph Aloysius Kessler, Titularr Archbishop of the Bosphorus, previously Bishop of Tyraspol

Translated by Rev. Horst Wilhelm Gutsche, Barrhead, Alberta, Canada

1930 – Published in German by the Publishing House of the Rev. George Aberle, Dickinson, ND, USA

2019 - Published in English by Husky Publishing, East Grand Forks, MN, USA

Cover Design © 2019 Jayne Flaagan

ISBN: 978-1-944410-24-7

This book was composed in German by Joseph Aloysius Kessler, and was originally titled "*History of the Diocese of Tyrasol*," (English translation of the German title). It was printed in 1930.

The book was then translated from German to English by Rev. Horst Gutsche of Barrhead, Alberta, Canada and made available via the "Heritage Review" in a long series of articles from Kessler's book.

From GRSH Heritage Review Editor: *"Rev. Gutsche initiated contact with me nearly six years ago about his translation of this book composed in German by Archbishop Kessler and printed in 1930. Around this time, Rev. Gutsche expressed to me his intense desire that as many readers as possible will enjoy his translation series."*
The articles began with volume 47 #1 and they continue through 2020.

From Theresa Wald: *"This book is a remarkable account of Catholic German life and events in the Soviet Union at about the time of my parent's residence in the Kutchergan areas of Russia, now known as the Ukraine. It deserves to be published to retain its availability for all Germans from Russia and their descendants. The information in this book tells of both the trials and tribulations, as well as the many joys found only in our Catholic faith. It deserves to be published to retain its availability for all Germans from Russia and their descendants."*

Preface

The idea of writing a history of the diocese of Tyraspol took hold of the heart of the author for the first time while he was residing in Germany, where he had lived in exile since 1922. So far away from his homeland, not all of the facts and events which had occurred in and to the diocese could be described because all of the sources and the archive, which today perhaps have been removed or have been destroyed, were unavailable to the author. Because he had researched through the diocesan archive in Saratov before the World War, he was able to record all the important historical facts from memory. Other sources of aid, which were available to him, were: "the papal document of establishment: "universalis ecclesiae cura" (Translator's note: "For the Care of the Universal Church"), the charter of the dean and the chapter of the Tyraspol Cathedral, Pastor Gottlieb Beratz: "The German Colonies on the Lower Volga," Pastor Konrad Keller: "The German Colonies in the Black Sea Region," Alois Zottmann, Franz Xaver von Zottmann, Professor Godlewski: monumenta historica ("Historical Annals"), in the same annals, diarium archiep. Siestrzencewicz ("Diary of Archbishop Siestrzencewicz"). All of the other facts, which this book reports, originate from the oral reports of the members of the diocese, from the clergy in the diocese and from the author's own experiences and views. Because the traditions of the people are being forgotten more and more as a result of the very stormy times which they have lived through and the clergy, who are more or less familiar with the fate of the diocese are slowly dying out as time passes, it was imperative that everything which accumulated in the memory of the author be recorded, so that it could be saved for posterity. Since the author was himself the head of the diocese for a quarter of a century, which was without question the most troubled and most fatefully difficult period of time for the German colonists in Russia and for the diocese of Tyraspol, he could not pass over this period of time in silence. He also was cognizant of the fact that some people who played a prominent role in the diocese were still living. For this reason the author had to record everything with consideration for these people and in the spirit of Christian love so that it would not be lost.

When recording the historical facts the author, by using many words of scripture, did not neglect to point out how the history of the religious and church life of the faithful people in the diocese evolved through the guidance of divine providence, so that also in this it was reaffirmed what the divine Redeemer once said to his disciples: Matthew 10:30 "Why, every hair on your head has been counted."

St. Ottoheim near Zinnowitz on the Baltic Sea, February 10th 1930
Joseph Kessler, Titular Archbishop of the Bosphorus

1. The word Tyraspol, that is Tyras City, is spelled Tiraspol in all ecclesiastical and government documents and manuscripts. This spelling is not correct. It originates from Russian which renders the word Tyras with a double i. This i is the same as the Latin or German i. However, the ancient Greeks named the Dniester Tyras, from which the small city of Tyraspol got its name. The author chose the proper spelling and not the ministerial or official spelling. (Translator's note: for this reason, I have followed Archbishop Kessler's example.)

Table of Contents

A. Early History of the Diocese of Tyraspol

1. Natural resources and peoples settled upon the territory of Tyraspol - Page 6
2. Christianity prior to the establishment of the bishopric -Page 8
3. The religious conditions among the Volga colonists -Page 9
4. The Jesuit pastoral care of the Volga region-Page 10
5. The German colonists and their pastoral care in the Black Sea region- Page 13
6. The expulsion of the fathers of the Society of Jesus-Page 14
7. A ravenous wolf in sheep's clothing-Page 16

B. History of the Diocese of Tyraspol

8. The visit of Czar Nicholas I to Pope Gregory XVI -Page 17
9. The apostolic charter "universalis ecclesia cura" -Page 19
10. The trip of the apostolic nunctio/delegate to the south of Russia-Page 22
11. The separation of Cherson from the archdiocese of Mohilev -Page 23
12. The Roman Catholic Church in Theodosia - Page 25
13. The appointment and the consecration of the first bishop of the diocese-Page 26
14. The cathedral chapter-Page 28
15. Transfer of the episcopal see to Tyraspol-Page 30
16. Opening of the diocesan seminary-Page 32
17. Bishop Ferdinand's administration and his death-Page 34
18. The consistory - Page 3 7
19. The bishop's chancellery -Page 3 9
20. Franz Xaverius Zottmann -Page 40
21. The reorganization of the Tyraspol seminary - Page 42
22. Suffragan Bishop Vinzenz Lipski, curate of the chapter-Page 48
23. The seminary for priests under German administrators-Page 50
24. Franz Xaverius Zottmann -Page 54
25. Bishop Zottmann's concern for a good ministerium-Page 57
26. The Tyraspol seminary under Rector Boos-Page 61
27. Supervisor Antonius Zerr, suffragan bishop ofTyraspol-Page 67
28. Johannes Antonov, supervisor and professor of the seminary-Page 69
29. Bishop Franz Xaverius Zottmann' s work - Page 7 6
30. The construction of the cathedral in Saratov-Page 79
31. Bishop Franz Xaverius Zottmann' s resignation and words of farewell - Page 81

32. Suffragan Bishop A. Zerr, bishop of Tyraspol -Page 86
33. Rector Boos's removal from office and farewell-Page 93
34. Eduard Baron von Ropp, bishop of Tyraspol - Page 96
35. Johannes Antonov, rector of the seminary for priests in Tyraspol -Page 100
36. The religious life of the colonists under the clergy who were members of orders -
37. The religious life under the German curates of souls -Page 107
38. Church, parish and school-Page 118
39. Transfer of Bishop Eduard von Ropp to Vilna-Page 121
40. The Priests and believers of the diocese - Page 122
41. The Catholics and the middle schools - Page 125
42. The religious life of the Catholic urban population-Page 128
43. The inner missions of the diocese-Page 129
44. Attendance at chapel and prayer processions- Page 132
45. Pilgrimages of the colonists -Page 133
46. Church hymnody- Page 135
47. The relationship between the government and the church - Page 138
48. Relationship of the different language groups of diocesans and clergy to each other. - Page 143
49. The relationship between the Catholics and their Lutheran compatriots-Page 145
50. The construction of Catholic houses of God- Page 148
51. State "methods of conversion" among the Catholics of Tyraspol - Page 151
52. Church property and its administration - Page 154
53. Immigration to America-Page 156
54. The Catholic military chaplaincy- Page 158
55. Huge problems in regard to pastoral care-Page 160
56. Menacing dangers for the way of life of the German colonists and for the bishopric - Page 167
57. Establishment of the "Deutsche Rundschau/German Review" and the "Deutschen Stimmen/German Voices" - Page 170
58. Two memorandi sent to the diocesan bishop- Page 173
59. Transfer of the bishop's see to Odessa- Page 175
60. The persecution of the vicar general of Tyraspol - Page 177
61. The clergy martyrs of the diocese - Page 179
62. The persecution of Christianity and the church - Page 182
63. The great famine among the colonists - Page 190
64. The value of the church assets which were stolen by the Bolsheviks- Page 192
65. Directory of the bishops of the diocese of Tyraspol-Page 195
66. Directory of the parishes and filial congregations in the diocese - Page 195
67. Directory of priests who graduated from the Tyraspol seminary-Page 201

A. Early History of the Diocese of Tyraspol

1. Natural resources and peoples settled upon the territory of the Tyraspol

The diocese of Tyraspol consists of a geographic region with about 14,000 square miles. It is three times larger than Italy and, second to the diocese of Mohilev/Mogilev, is larger in terms of area than all the dioceses of Europe. In the east its borders extend to about 100 kilometers west of the Ural River down to the Caspian Sea and it includes its northern and western coasts together with the Caucasus. In the south it borders on Persia and Turkey and includes the Sea of Asov and the northern coast of the Black Sea. Today, after the separation of Bessarabia (since the fall of 1921), its western border is formed by the Dniester, called the Tyras by the ancient Greeks. The diocese got its name from the little city of Tyraspol which is located on the left shore of the Dniester. The northern border ends on the borders of the provinces/governments of Cherson, Yekaterinoslav, the Don Basin, Saratov and the county of Nikolayevsk in the government of Samara. Within these borders, the by far largest area consists of a high plateau which, because of its rich humus soil, is very suitable for agriculture. Since the days of their settlement, this is where the German immigrants planted the most suitable kinds of grains which were loaded on to European ships in the harbours of the Sea of Asov and the Black Sea and were transported to Western Europe. European steamboats conveyed the finest wool from sheep which the German farmers raised in the thousands and hundreds of thousands. Just one of these German colonists, for the sake of emphasis, owned about one million sheep and 500,000 hectares of land and sold 750,000 rubles worth of wool in the year i894 to European factory owners. His name is Falz-Fein. The silk manufacturers of Germany and Austria got their raw materials for their fabrics from the German colonists.

Meanwhile, not only was there excellent production achieved in the area of grain crops and wool in the area of the subsequent diocese of Tyraspol. The German colonists, especially those of the Volga region, planted a superior type of tobacco, which was processed in the large factories belonging to Staff, Asmoloff, Kuschnaryeffs and which often won first prizes at international exhibitions. The wines produced by the German colonists of the Black Sea region were sought after in all of Russia and those from the Crimea and from Bessarabia were often exported to Western Europe where they often competed with the better products of the vine present there.

Baku is world famous for its never-ceasing oil wells. During the World War, all of Russian daily newspapers reported that a well drilled by the member of the diocese named Subaloff, the donor of the beautiful church in Batum, produced 500,000 pails of petroleum per diem! If Baku is immeasurably rich in regard to oil, then the Caspian Sea and the Volga are not to be surpassed in terms of the most superior varieties of fish. On an annual basis, millions of rubles worth of caviar are exported from Astrachan to all the countries of the world. In the area of Yekaterinoslav, large reserves of bituminous coal are located within the bosom of the earth. Should this resource be mined, it will serve as fuel for industry for centuries. In close proximity to the coal deposits, we find large iron deposits in the plains of Yekaterinoslav which the largest companies in Russia manufacture and then export the products which have been produced by their diligence to distant lands. The diocese even owns a second Weliczko in closest proximity to Bachmut: Here salt from the mountain is mined which seasons half of the meals in Russia.

As there are various climatic zones within the territory of the diocese, nature also produces the most varied kinds of fruit which are consistent with the climate. Among these there are some which are so superior that Western Europe has no knowledge of them: the incomparable water melons, which actually have their real original home in the lower reaches of the Volga in the region of the German colonists. There are also the most varied of southern fruits such as pomegranates and lemons which grow outside next to palms and bamboo, Chinese tea, and coffee plants on the other side of the Caucasian mountain range. The southernmost coast of the Crimea, the eastern coast of the Black Sea, from Novorossyisk to Batum is endowed by nature with similar beauty which can only be found on the French or the Italian Riviera. The mountain range covered with year-round snow, which separates Ciscaucasia from Transcaucasia is higher and naturally wilder than the Swiss mountain range. Its highest peak ranges 800 meters above Mont Blanc. If someone wants to take a pleasure trip upon a "floating palace", he can do no better anywhere than on a large Volga steamship. Many places in this gigantic river, which surpasses the Danube and the Mississippi in terms of the amount of flowing water, remind one of the most beautiful rivers in the world, ie. the German Rhine. The powerful river within the eastern region of the diocese of Tyraspol rolls its deluges downstream to the Caspian Sea, providing an unusual, nice variety to the monotony of this region and thus enriches the population.

Nature has also taken care of restoring health in the bishopric of Tyraspol. Without even mentioning the healing baths in the sea, there are fresh air resorts in the Crimea and in the mountains of the Caucasus for those suffering from illnesses of the lungs.

Russia's most beneficial mud-baths are near Sochi and in the Caucasus; the four health spas are in close proximity to one another. Essentuki, with its 23 mineral springs is efficacious for the most varied of illnesses and infirmities known to man. What would the rest of Russia be without this blessed territory of land upon which the diocese of Tyraspol was founded?

According to the report given in the Holy Scriptures, Noah's arch rested on the Ararat mountain chain after the Great Flood. This mountain range lies within the southeastern reaches of the diocese of Tyraspol. From there, from the borders of Tyraspol, the peoples streamed out in all directions under the heavens. Various peoples of Europe moved through the Caucasus at various times. Some of them, such as the Huns, laid waste the nations which had been established before they came on the scene.

The diocesan area of Tyraspol is also very noteworthy in terms of ethnography. Prior to the World War, about one and one-half million German colonists, 70,000 Poles, 7,000 Lithuanians, 50,000 Armenian Catholics, Grusinians/Georgians, Frenchmen, Greeks, Persians, Jews, Tartars, Turks, Kurds, Kalmucks, Cossacks, Kyrgyz, Mordvinians, Ossetians, Circassians and others lived in this territory.

2. Christianity prior to the establishment of the bishopric

In the first century, Christianity already had believers residing in the area of the present diocese of Tyraspol. During the first century of the Christian era, the Crimean Peninsula was a place to which criminals were exiled by the Eastern Roman and Western Roman emperors. Among others, the Roman Pope Clement I, a student of St. Peter and Pope Martin I suffered a martyr's death. For this reason the former was chosen to be the patron saint of the diocese.

History also records that the Causcasus was in the arena of apostolic activity. The apostles Philipp and Matthew preached here. In the documents pertaining to the Council of Ephesus, it is noted that among the bishops who participated, that the signature of the Bishop of Sebastopol is found which is proof that during the fifth century, there was a Catholic diocesan see in Suchum-Kale which was the old city of Sebastopol. Perhaps this see was of apostolic origin. For according to the witness of history St. Andrew the Apostle preached the gospel in Suchum and vicinity. On his missionary travels of conversion, the apostle visited the entire eastern shore of the Black Sea which was then known by the name of Chersones. He is even supposed to

have gone as far as the present city of Kiev. During the fourth century, Christianity had already spread a lot in the Crimea. In the city of Chersones, one kilometer southwest of present-day Sebastopol, there was a Catholic diocesan see in existence which for a period of time was led by St. Aeterius. While on a trip from Constantinople to his home city, the saint was taken prisoner by sea robbers, dragged to the island of Beresany and murdered. His bones were interred right there by Christians. Bishop Bruno, together with many missionaries, was martyred in the northern Black Sea region during the first century by the barbaric Petschenegs. He had won many of their related peoples for Christianity. The Russians later procured the bones of these sainted martyrs who had met a violent death, constructed a church with a monastery over their graves, and publicly honoured them.

The situation of the Christians during the later middle ages developed in a more positive manner. After the conquest of Constantinople by the crusaders, the Venetians and Genoans founded colonies on the southernmost shores of the Crimea in order to establish trade relations with the Eastern peoples. At the same time as Italian merchants, Catholic missionaries also made their appearance and worked with blessed success. During the thirteenth and fourteenth centuries, several Catholic mission dioceses were in existence in the Caucasus and north of the Black Sea where our German colonists reside today.

After the advance of the Turks to the Crimea in the year 1475, the cross had to withdraw and the half moon took over again. All of the bishoprics were abolished and the churches were destroyed or turned into Turkish mosques. The few Catholics who remained behind were left to carry out a very sad existence in terms of their religious situation.

3. The religious conditions among the Volga colonists

The first pastoral care workers who accompanied the Volga colonists to their new homeland, were the Franciscans and the Capucins from the mission prefecture of

Polozk. They were completely fluent in the German language, preached on Sundays and holidays, instructed the children and maturing youth in religion. In the true sense of the word, they were the spiritual fathers of those who had been entrusted into their care and with whom they shared poverty, misery and distress. The disciples of St. Francis, because of their love for poverty and renunciation of the world, had been chosen on purpose to be the first pastoral care workers for the settlers. As the disciples of the poor of Assisi, they made small demands upon life. The holes which were created in their ranks by death were filled with Dominicans and Trinitarians. These regular clergy were, to be sure, very pious, but they did not know the German language. Added to this was that a priest had to be the pastor of several parishes.

Empress Catherine II proclaimed, after the annexation of large areas of Poland, that the mission prefecture of Russia was abolished and founded as equally good by herself one sole "archdiocese" with the see of the archbishop in Mohilev with the name: "Bishopric of White Russia" which the czarina thereupon soon elevated to an archdiocese. She appointed Bishop Siestrzencewicz as the new "archbishop." He had formerly been an officer of the hussars and an adherent of Calvinism and, perhaps without deep convictions, accepted the Catholic faith. That this bishop was not correctly Catholic is proven, besides various facts; by this especially, that he, one day upon the passing by of the emperor excitedly pointed toward him and called out: "That is my pope; that is my pope!" The conditions which were created by this "archbishop" were very damaging for the Catholic Church in Russia. By holding tiring negotiations, Pope Pius VI tried to remedy the conditions. Because no other better way was found, Siestrzencewicz was recognized as the legally authorized archbishop. His canonical appointment was registered in Petersburg in the year 1783.

By having moved its adherence to the archdiocese of Mohilev, the religious situation of the Volga Germans did not improve. The clergy who were sent by the archbishop's ordinary were as little familiar with the German language as their predecessors under the mission prefecture. The Volga German historian,

1. Professor Godlewski, Monumenta historica.

Schoolmaster Anton Schneider writes in regard to this: 1. "The parish family heard the Word of God on Sundays and festivals which was read to them with poor pronunciation from the pulpit from a book of sermons. Religious instruction was given by the schoolmasters, who often were forced to miss teaching because they also had to perform the duties of the sexton. Because the clergy could not even supervise the religious instruction because of excessive work, the schoolmasters did not take instruction seriously. The unavoidable consequence of this was religious ignorance and the brutalization of the people and the youth. "The religious-moral life slowly but surely sank so low that one had to be concerned for the future of the people." 2. Immediate aid was needed. This aid soon appeared.

4. The Jesuit pastoral care of the Volga region

At the beginning of 1801, Senator Karl Hablitz, the council member of the tutel-office (Translator's note: guardianship office) of the German colonists in Petersburg came to Saratov for the audit of the German office. He, as the highest official of the German immigrants, could not have been apathetic in regard to the religious-ecclesiastical situation of the colonists. The colonists used his presence in order to hand over a petition to him in which they expressed their complaints in regard to the deficient pastoral care in the Catholic parishes of the Volga region. Senator Karl von Hablitz promised to attend to the situation so that in the place of clergy who were foreign in speech the priests of the Society of Jesus would take over their pastoral care. Although Senator von Hablitz was a Protestant, the conjecture that he sent the Jesuits to mistreat the colonists because of ill will is a fable and a terribly wrongful accusation. Hablitz was an entirely honourable character and had, at that time, truly shared the high esteem of the Russian circles which were ruling at that time against the members of the Society of Jesus.

The Jesuit order had been provisionally dissolved by Pope Clement XIV. Upon the petition of Czarina Catherine II and Frederick II of Prussia this order was allowed to remain in Prussia and in Russia. Under Czar Paul, the fathers were even able to found a college in Petersburg. Catherine II showed how highly she valued the Jesuits and interceded for them in her letter to Pope Clement XIV. She wrote: "Ever since instruction and education have been given over to the Jesuits, I have often, to my great satisfaction, had occasion to experience the pious zeal which fills the souls of these members of the order as well as their clear fortunate success which crowned all of their efforts. I would be treating my subjects in White Russia badly if I would remove such an order which is of such public benefit and I would do this if I did not concern myself for the continuation of the order and then it would also be secured for the future. Time has proven that the order has not, as yet, been properly been replaced in Catholic countries." When the czarina found out that a Spanish minister sent a grievance to Pope Clement XIV against the continuation of the order in Russia, she wrote these very energetic words

1. The great-grandfather on his maternal side of the author of this history.
2. Beratz, Die Deutschen Kolonien (The German colonies)

in favour of the Jesuits to King Charles III of Spain: "I implore your majesty to not send even the slightest complaint to His Holiness in regard to this matter and thus not to bother him in any way for I would have to view this as something which has been directed toward me and I would have to consider myself duty-bound to defend him and would have to thereby also risk losing my crown."

Senator von Hablitz actually, as he had promised, interceded with Czar Alexander I, Paul's successor in order to secure the care of the Catholic Germans with the fathers of the Society of Jesus.

At the beginning of March, the first ten priests of the S.J. came from Polozk and arrived in the colonies of the Volga region. Among them were four Germans, four Poles and two Frenchmen. The latter were fully conversant in the German language, as can be determined by the testimony of their superior, Father Landes, who took up his seat of residence in Saratov.

So that the reader will be able to get a genuine picture of the richly blessed activity of the Jesuits in the German colonies of Russia, we will let a pupil of theirs, the Volga German historian Anton Schneider personally give a testimony. As a student of the Jesuits and long-term schoolmaster in the colonies of the Volga, Schneider had the best opportunity to get to know the activity of the fathers and, since he had enough education, to evaluate the same. That the historian had the desire to report everything truthfully can be certified by the great esteem in which the people in the Volga colonies had for him. In his "Lebensbildem" (Pictures of Life) Schneider writes: "Just as the previous century had ended with its sufferings and in 1803 with the beginning of this age, the fathers, the Jesuits, who had been promised by His Excellency Senator Karl Hablitz, came to our parishes …. Their first action was a moving speech to the gathered people and their words and their first teachings were so full of spiritual power and so impressive that the audience and flock entrusted to them were moved to tears of emotion in their eyes."

"They preserved their purity of heart and conscience much more carefully than their health and their own lives, and this purity was the strongest bond of friendship and of the grace of God ... Emotional comfort, rest and peace filled the hearts of the flock which had been entrusted to them. They were zealous clergy because of the daily sacrifice of the mass which they always held at the appointed time. Even on Sundays and Holy Days they would exchange the masses in that they would, according to sequence, also hold an early mass and then celebrate a high mass in a filial congregation as well as a sermon for which they had received the necessary permission from their superior. They also held a very nice teaching session on moral behaviour in the afternoon which was presented with the nicest examples. The moral teaching session was not only wholesome and beneficial for the youth but also to the older people who often attended ... Through sermons, confessions, encouragement, admonishment and administering the holy sacraments, by visiting the sick and supporting the dying and by countless other spiritual and physical works of mercy they showed themselves to be very excellent in everything. They were feared by their adversaries but were honourable, they patiently cared for the flock entrusted to them and did so with watchful diligence ... They gave the poor and suffering aid, advice and did things for them ... in summary, they carried out saintly duties all the time and lived rightly according to the instruction of the apostle to the gentiles as "an example to the believers in word and deed, in love, in faith and in chasteness." Yes, they gave their lives for their lambs and their example set the best impression upon their activities and might so that one was filled with a showcase of the sainted, so that one was moved to look at oneself very carefully and encouraged to new Christian zeal ... Falsehood and vice were eradicated by their sermons just like wild animals who stroll away at dawn into the woodlands ... The dear, unforgettable, good Jesuits did so much for the salvation of the little sheep that had been entrusted to them. Oh, if only the spirit of these praiseworthy men would still be alive among us now!"

By this the chronicler of the Volga describes the efforts of the fathers in replacing the old, original, poor, little churches by constructing beautiful churches and Houses of God. These efforts were crowned with success. He continues: "At the time of the Jesuits love, joy, and harmony, which pleases God and human beings, reigned among us and the angel of peace lifted its hands over us. Their efforts also raised the earthly standard of living at home, on the fields and everywhere in that they often knew how to lighten the hardest work which often is the lot of the tired farmer... Good seed was thereby sown among the people, so much to be sure, that the colonists improved in all branches of their enterprises which improved cottage industry and agriculture and made that which was secular and that which was religious perfect. The blessing of God came down upon the fields, meadows and forests, over people and animals, so that so to say, everything which was salutary came into our homes in rich measure of blessing. Every year, every day and hour there was joy because of a surplus of the good things of this world and of property and there was no complaint of worry heard in our homes such as we see taking place now (1863)."

We add the testimony of Father von Landes, the Superior of the Jesuits to these words from which we recollect how admirably Loyola's students worked at the school. Because of a lack of space, one example will suffice. Father Superior wrote after his visitation to Mariental on the Great Karaman River, where Father Averdonek ministered, the following in regard to his activity: "Father A verdonek, who I visited during my return trip to Saratov, during Lent, gave religious instruction to the children every day at 10:00 a.m. It is a pleasure to listen to him while he does this. One cannot present the material in a more interesting manner than he does. He is truly a master of this art. I was very surprised by the answers which a child of ten years gave to all the questions of the reverend. On Palm Sunday, Father Averdonek started with the spiritual exercises and on the three first days of Holy Week daily gave three teaching sessions and one meditation. The crowd of believers was very great. The best of praise was given to their preacher by the people in their tears and in acts of repentance ... Father Averdonek is cheerful and satisfied and makes do with every meal which is brought to him. This makes a good impression upon the people. He often distributes alms ... He is a musican and leads the singing. For his schoolchildren he obtained thirty songs to be sung and he associates with the colonists in a kind and courteous manner. But he also understands how to keep his respected character and to be determined and strict without, however, offending anyone. Despite the fact that he is very experienced, he does not neglect, where this may happen, to make use of the advice of the old and the young."

Seldom has a clerical order ever received greater praise from a man of the people than the fathers of the S.J. (Society of Jesus) who were active in the German colonies of Russia. The most capable among them were also active here such as Father von Landes, who subsequently was rector of the Collegium Germanicum {German college) in Rome, Father Meyer, as well as Father Aloysius Moritz, who died in 1805, and who was considered a saint in the colony of Mariental. Today, the people still recount the various miracles which he is said to have brought about. Thus he would suddenly heal the sick by the laying on of hands and prayer. Mariental was special even back then with its many fruit and vegetable gardens. One spring so many caterpillars appeared in the forest and in the gardens that not only orchards but also the beautiful oak forest was in danger of being defoliated. The reverend father went to the gardens and into the forest, said several prayers and sprinkled the trees with holy water. Thereafter the insects fell to the ground dead. The people had kept him in thankful memory. He was buried in the old church yard beside Father Sebastianus, across from the warehouse hill. Even after the deterioration of the cemetery the faithful honoured his grave and built a small vault house over it. Since 1910 there is a beautiful little Gothic chapel which rises above the grave.

5. The German colonists and their pastoral care in the Black Sea region

After the conquest of the Taurian Peninsula and the Black Sea Region by the Russians, Christianity was able to be reestablish itself. The first Catholics who settled on the Crimean peninsula were Armenians in Karasubasar (Translator's note: Today this is the city of Bilohirsk, which means white mountain, and originally was Quarasvbasar which means bazaar on the Black River in the Crimean Tartar language) who, however, were soon driven out again by the Tartars and, at the end of the eighteenth century settled in Yekaterinoslav. They moved back in the year 1800 and built a large church in Karasubasar which was later richly endowed by Baroness von Schuetz. The endowment consisted of a large orchard of fifteen dessiatines, a smaller one of four dessiatines, a water mill, a piece of property upon which, at present, the Catholic churchyard is located together with a funeral chapel which the Baroness constructed for herself and for her deceased husband, General von Schuetz, a large residence near the church and several stores in the city. The will was initially written to be of benefit for the churches of the Latin rite in the Crimean peninsula, but because of the influence of the Armenian priest in Karasubasar, was revised and changed to benefit the Armenian Catholic Church in Karasubasar.

The first Catholics who settled in the region north of the Black Sea were our German colonists. They moved there from 1808 - 1813 as a result of an invitation by Alexander I proclaimed on February 20, 1804. They came from various regions; mostly from the Rhineland Palatinate and from Wuerttemberg. Just as the immigration to the Volga region, the immigration here also took place in several large movements of people. As the route went through Moravia, Silesia, Galicia and the city (Translator's note: actually a village) of Radziwiloff, all Catholic regions, the emigrants did not need their own priests to accompany them as was the case with the colonists of the Volga region which, as is known, traveled via Rostock on the Baltic Sea to St. Petersburg, and from there via Moscow, Petrovsk and Saratov.

Twenty years before the settlement of the colonists in the Black Sea region, the port city of Odessa was founded. The land which was allotted to the colonists lay around this city, around the Sea of Asov and in the Crimean Peninsula. The regions north of the Black Sea conquered under Catherine were given the name New Russia. The governor of New Russia was the French Duke Richelieu. Even today the main street in Odessa bears his name, if the Bolsheviks, who like to turn everything on its head, have left the name the same. The duke was a true son of the Holy Catholic Church. The Catholic German immigrants submitted a petition to him so that he might use it with the church officials to have some clergy appointed. The duke readily agreed to carry out their request. While the Kutschurgan colonists were served spiritually right from the beginning by the clergy of Odessa, those in the Beresan were assigned to the priest in Nikolayev. There had been a congregation there since 1800. Its members were Poles and Lithuanians. Unfortunately, the priest did not know how to speak German. However, because the priest on the estate of the Polish Count Potocki in Severinovka was fluent in German, the Berezan colonists were assigned to this priest until the year 1811. It was however, a great sacrifice that Father Paul Krutschkovksi had to make, as the settlers lived about one hundred versts (kilometers) from his place of pastoral residence. It was also a burden for the colonists themselves, because they had to fetch the priest from such a great distance for the dying and bring the children so far in order to have them baptized etc. Because of this reason alone, one could not consider this to be a proper ministerial work. Pastoral care was reduced to what was absolutely necessary. For this reason, it was an absolute imperative to establish ministerial work right in the centers of the colonies. This already happened in the year 1811. In May of the same year, the following fathers of the Society of Jesus from the mission station of Polozk were sent to the settlers: Andreas Pierling as the priest of the Kutschurgan colonies, with his residence in Selz; and Anton Jann for the Berezan colonies with his residence in Landau. Father Hubertus was assigned to Muenchen and Rastatt and Father Oswald Rausch to Josephstal, Franzfeld and Mariental.

All of the priests developed very blessed ministerial work, which unfortunately was not of long duration; as we will see later.

6. The expulsion of the fathers of the Society of Jesus

In the fall of 1820, the fathers of the Society of Jesus, who had worked with such great blessing, were forced to leave Russia and the Catholic colonies of the Volga and Black Sea regions. The hatred of the schismatic Russian clergy against the sons of St. Ignatius was too great. They feared the influence of Rome and of the Catholic religion upon the Russian upper classes and even upon the government and the czar himself. For this reason, they pulled out all stops in order to get the government to have the emperor give a proclamation by which the Jesuits were to be expelled from the empire. As history recounts, their efforts were successful. The Jesuits were expelled.

When the Russian state law was codified under Emperor Nicholas I, a separate paragraph was included .in regard to opposing the Jesuits which read: "The Jesuits will not be allowed to enter under any circumstances." Through this paragraph by-law and through Protestant influence a wrong view of the Jesuits has developed among many of the

Russian intelligencia, which is even repeated in its history books. The embodiment of everything sinister, cunning, false and deceiving is determined by them to be the Jesuit!

Russia at that time stood at a crossroads just as Israel once did when it was to decide between Christ and Barrabas. The powerless state church which had been in the chains of the state especially since the days of Peter the Great, could not fight against Protestantism successfully, as the leaders of the government were ruled by its destructive principles.

If back then, Russia's responsible leaders had decided for the Jesuits, more clearly stated for the rock, upon which Christ had built his church then the unfortunate people would today not have become the booty of the Bolshevik monster. The words of the prophet in Hosea 13:9 "You are your own destruction, Israel, there is only help for you with me," were thereby affirmed. The leaders of the people did not decide by the representative of Christ for Jesus Christ, but they chose the emperor, caesaropapism (Translator's note: the subjugation of the Church under the ruler of the state). The emperors, under the continual influence of Protestantism since the time of Peter the Great, led the people to Bolshevism; the greatest murderer of people known to history. May the surviving intelligent Russians consider this truth with the proper seriousness and which such an important question deserves; yes, even desperately demands!

Schneider writes: "It was a hard blow for the Catholic colonists both in respect to spiritual and economic matters, to lose such tried and tested spiritual leaders. After the Jesuits, the spiritual care of the Catholic colonists once again was given into the hands of the regular Polish clergy. They only served deficiently and because the Polish clerical administration, to which the Catholic settlements belonged in regard to ecclesiastical matters, did not want to send its more capable and better workers to them. Also, the priests assigned to the colonists for the most part did not have a thorough command of the German language."

The best witness to the blessed activity of the Jesuits is certainly the grateful and reverential remembrance which has remained among all of the people. Since the disciples of St. Ignatius left Russia and the colonies, more than a century has flowed into the sea of eternity. The fathers could not, because of their short period of activity which lasted only a little more than 17 years, and because of the poverty of the population, establish a single institution which lasted. Presently, in the entire region of the Volga, there is only one single church, the church in Katharinenstadt (Translator's note: today this is the city of Marx) from the year 1815 which originates from the time of the Jesuits. This church was built of bricks. All of the other houses of worship in the Volga region, because they were built of wood, no longer stand today. There is also no memorial made of stone or iron to keep the remembrance of these great benefactors alive and yet the fathers continue to influence the colonists. This is to be valued even higher as the same people today have forgotten the regular clergy who took care of their pastoral needs for 50 years. Such a living remembrance even under the most unfavourable of circumstances is the most beautiful memorial. Christian love has imprinted this upon the hearts of the people with writing written by fire. For this reason the words of the Latin poet may be applied to the Order of St. Ignatius: "Monumentum exegit aere perennius/Arrange the action so as to give the narrative shape and momentum." The order has established a memorial which lasts longer than one made of ore/bronze.

7. A ravenous wolf in sheep's clothing

After the departure of the "dear Jesuiters," for which the Catholic people in the subsequent Diocese of Tyraspol afterward shed many a tear, the episcopal leadership of Mohilev, with its seat in St. Petersburg, sent the false mystic Ignaz Lindi to Odessa as the priest and visitor of the Catholic parishes of the Black Sea region. His predecessor in this office in Odessa, Father Nicole S.J., had worked in this office with blessing from 1811-1820. Using wise foresight in regard to the dangers which threaten the faith of the colonists among a schismatic and Protestant population, the Jesuits specifically impressed the teachings which differentiate upon those placed in their care. Father Nicole S.J. and those priests of the Society of Jesus who were placed under his administration were very thorough in regard to this in every way. How wisely they had acted would soon be evident.

The heretic Ignaz Linell was born in Baindlkirch in Bavaria. He had finished his studies in his homeland and was ordained a priest. Soon after his posting in Bavaria, he fell prey to views which were dangerous to the faith and even heretical, which he tried to spread among his circle of influence. The episcopal curia in Augsburg forced him to renounce his errors. However, since he did not want to give them up, he left his homeland, went to St. Petersburg, where he was received into the archdiocese of Mohilev. But here as well he was soon betrayed by his efforts at heresy. In doing so, he understood how to have himself considered an enlightened and acknowledged sanctified priest by the superficially believing Russian intelligencia which had tendencies toward mysticism. He did this in a hypocritical manner. Even Czar Alexander I knelt before him in order to receive his blessing! With his fanatical sectarian sermons, which he held for a period of time in the Catholic Maltese Church, he influenced many of his hearers to accept his teachings. His fanatical zeal allowed him no peace: it urged him to "make happy" the German colonists in the South of Russia with his heresy. Meanwhile, before he left St. Petersburg, he had himself wed to his former maid by Pastor Gossner who shared his views. He was so shameless that he introduced his prostitute as his wife to a large gathering of his admirers!

He knew how to hide his disgraceful relationship to his maid while he was in Odessa. His intelligent manner caused him to do so if he was going to get away with it without being injured by the German colonists and was going to win followers for his false teaching. It was just that he could not continue to play the role of the hypocrite, which he had begun, much longer.

Soon after his arrival in Odessa, Lindl "visited" the Catholic colonies on the Berezany. In Rastatt and Muenchen he was able to delude several Catholic families with his false teaching. In the villages of the Berez.an, at first one listened to him quietly but notwithout a certain suspicion. The courageous farmers in Landau did not let him preach from the pulpit a second time. One even threatened the heretic with death if he came a second time. It did not take long before Lindl was reported to the episcopal curia in St. Petersburg by the members of the congregation in Odessa and by the colonists in the county. The investigation revealed shameful intercourse with his maid (he had conceived several children with her) and his heretical errors. Having been removed from his office, Lindi went to Bessarabia. Several families which had left the congregation in Muenchen followed him. In Bessarabia he founded the village of Sarata He was appointed as the colonizer and chairman of the new village by the Russian government. Then he tyrannized his subjects, which had increased by immigration from Bavaria until he, having been removed from his position by the Russian government, was expelled from Russia. However, the inhabitants of Sarata, lacking a pastor of their own doctrine, accepted Lutheranism after he had departed.

Thus God's providence watched over the little group of German Catholic immigrants so that the wolf in sheep's clothing could not inflict an even greater amount of damage upon them.

B. History of the Diocese of Tyraspol

8. The visit of Czar Nicholas I to Pope Gregory XVI

The Holy Apostolic See received the first news of the deplorable religious and ecclesiastical situation of the German colonists who had immigrated to Russia under

Empress Catherine II and under Alexander I into the South of Russia from the fathers of the Society of Jesus and especially from the subsequent rector of the German College (Collegium Germanicum), Father Landes, who was the superior of the Jesuits in the Volga region from 1803 to 1820. The Holy See, conscious of the pastoral office which had been bestowed by Christ upon St. Peter concerning the entire Christian flock, decided to turn its special attention toward these unfortunate inhabitants of the steppes. If their spiritual state was to be truly solved, then they would have to be united in their own diocese with a German bishop and a German episcopal administration at its head.

Insurmountable problems seemed to be placed before the Holy See in regard to this matter. If the prerequisites for the creation of a new diocese were already very unfavourable in the empire during earlier times when a schismatic Church had very closely allied itself with an absolutist state, when Gregory XVI and Pius IX ascended the papal throne, this seemed to be even more difficult. At that time a man ascended to Russia's throne who used his scepter with an iron fist and, who as a decided enemy of the Catholic Church, a suppressor of religious freedom, persecutor of the unfortunate Uniates (Translator's note: this was the Church which used an Orthodox liturgy but acknowledged the supremacy of the Roman Catholic pope) and of priests who were members of various orders attained infamy. This was Czar Nicholas I.

Emperor Peter I, the Great, had abolished the patriarchate of the Russian Church and declared himself to be the head of the Church in his empire according to the Protestant pattern and established the Holy Synod in St. Petersburg. By using the synod, he wanted to administer his state church and even rule it. The pope has always been viewed by the Russian state as an outside spiritual power which would be able to administer its directive pastoral power in no other way over the Catholics in the empire than through the acquiescence of the emperor and under the control of the state. Because of this, paragraph 17, volume XI of the Russian law for "Foreign Confessions" was introduced. According to this paragraph all of the correspondence by the Catholic bishops and clergy which was directed to the Holy See had to be sent via the Ministry of the Interior. Directives given by the Holy See were allowed to reach the Catholic bishops only via this ministry. If such directives appeared in the official publication of the Holy See: the "Acts of the Holy See," and later in the "Acts of the Apostolic See," which were unpleasant for the government, they were either confiscated or in a blunt way blotted out in red. The continual goal of the rulers of the czarist empire was to also wield the highest spiritual authority over the subjects of the Catholic religious confession. An "outside power" was in no way to reduce the limitless power given by God to the czar of "having power also over their consciences of the people!"

Under these conditions the establishment of a new bishopric in Russia seemed to be completely out of the question, especially since by the establishment of the Catholic College Administration in St. Petersburg in the year 1800, which was an institution subsequently formed miming the Russian synod with a secular procurator of the emperor as the representative of the state, this was the first step in the separation of the Catholics in Russia and Congress Poland from Rome.

Only the wise providence of God found, in these most difficult of circumstances, ways and means of reaching its goal. The words of the scriptures proved to be true: Esther 13:9 "For everything is set under your power and there is no one who is able to stand against your will when you have decided to rescue Israel." Yes, God wanted to make use of the most tyrannically-inclined and despotic ruler of modern times in order to carry out his wise intensions. For another czar would have hardly been able to have enough energy to carry out a task which had as its opponents the entire Russian clergy and population. God ordained that Czar Nicholas I-visited Rome at the end of 1845. Pope Gregory XVI presented very serious complaints describing the persecution of the Uniates, the suppression of so many monasteries/nunneries in Poland and Lithuania and closing of Catholic houses of worship and the secularization of Church property etc. The words of the representative of Christ seem to not have been without a positive influence upon the czar. The czar promised to read the document of grievance, consisting of 21 articles, which was presented to him by the pope. The emperor even visited the pope a second time when he promised to consider the pope's complaints. During the negotiations which were being held between Count Nesselrode, who had been left, and Cardinal Lambruschini, Gregory XVI died. Soon after his election, his successor, Pope Pius IX heard of the czar's willingness to send Graf Nesselrode as a special ambassador of the czar to Rome in order to regulate Catholic issues with the Holy See. The negotiations were therefore continued between Bludoff and Cardinal Lambruschini. The result of these talks was the Concordat of August 3, 1847. In it, 31 articles were set in which the dioceses of Vilna, Samogitien, Minsk, Luck and Cameniez were retained and a new diocese named Cherson (later Tyraspol) was to be established. All of these bishoprics were to belong to the metropolis (Translator's note: archdiocese) of Mohilev. The diocese of Tyraspol was to have two suffragan bishops, a cathedral chapter and a seminary for priests (Hergemoether, Kirchengeschichte/Church History Volume IV Page 445).

It is actually surprising that Emperor Nicholas I himself, after the death of Pope Gregory XVI, took the initiative to resume negotiations with the Apostolic See. It seems as if the good influence of a man upon the absolute ruler of Russia played an important role in this. This man is remembered in tradition and in history with the greatest of reverence and high esteem. This was no other than the suffragan bishop of Mohilev, Ignatius Holowinski, who had the right of succession. At that time he had, as yet, not been appointed to the worthy office of bishop, but he was the first rector of the Catholic Spiritual Academy which Emperor Nicholas had established in St. Petersburg in the year 1842 in the place of the university which had been abolished in Vilna. Rector Holowinski often received visits from the imperial patron when he was in the new institution. There is a tradition which has been maintained among the Poles and the Lithuanians according to which no one like the rector and subsequent Bishop Ignatius Holowinski had enjoyed such favour and goodwill from this ruler of all the Russians. Every time when the czar had again right thoroughly chastised his ministers, as a rule he would add the words: "In the entire empire there are only two sensible men: I and Bishop Holowinski." If the Russian code of laws contained some legal paragraphs which were much more favorable to the Catholic cause than one would have expected then this can be attributed to the influence of the subsequent Archbishop Ignatius, since the legal code was established under Czar Nicholas. Innumerable newer circulatory directives from the state government made the legal paragraphs which were favourable toward the Catholic religion illusory.

9. The Apostolic charter "universalis ecclesia cura"1.

Since time immemorial in Russia, one has made us of the proverb: "The slower you go, the further you get." This proverb was also applied to the matter of the concordat. It was first ratified in St. Petersburg on July 3, 1848. Now it had to be quickly put into force. The decree of establishment soon arrived in St. Petersburg and it was signed by Cardinal Lambruschini and Spinola. In the preface, the decree mentions that "to be sure, because of negotiations with the government of Emperor Nicholas I, many ecclesiastical issues

1. No one ever saw this apostolic founding document "univ. eccl. cura" (Translator's note: this means: the Care of the Universal Church) has several items in it which were not acceptable to the Russian government. The notary responsible for this, J. Antonov had them removed from the bull. The author worked with his copy.

have been regulated, although many others are still waiting to be resolved." Without a doubt, the questions in regard to the religious freedom of the Uniates, restitution for the many suppressed religious orders, the construction of Catholic schools in Poland and Lithuania, and religious instruction in the state middle schools etc. were meant by this.

According to the words of the decree the last organization of the Catholic dioceses in Russia had been attempted in November 1798 under Pope Pius VI by means of the proclamation "Maxime undique pressi" (Translator's note: "Pressed strongly from all sides;" probably because of the religious persecution and changes which had broken out and were implemented as a result of the French Revolution). As is documented from the new organizational document/constitution, there were still six Catholic bishoprics of the Latin rite left in Russia. Now, so states the document, the Apostolic See has come to an agreement with Czar Nicholas I to add and establish a seventh of the same rite to the six existing bishoprics of the Latin rite. The see of the bishop of the new diocese was to be in the port city of Cherson and two suffragan bishops were to be appointed for him so that he could fulfill the duties of his office. The first one was to take up his residence in the city of Saratov on the Volga and the second was to be without any set residence and be "a latere" (Translator's note: this is a suffragan bishop sent to the aid the bishop by the Pope), so that he could always according to his judgment, send him to the parts of the large, extended diocese where the ministry of a bishop was required. In the proclamation the advantages of the city of Cherson are pointed out and these include its beauty, its size, its spacious public buildings, in which one could easily house an episcopal administration together with a seminary and furthermore, and the advantageous position because of it being at a crossroads etc. The aforementioned advantages commended the city of Cherson as the residence of a Catholic bishop. Because of this, the choice of Cherson was made as the see of the bishop of the diocese which was to be newly formed. Then the territories are named which were removed from the archdiocese of Mohilev and which were always to belong to the new diocese of Cherson. Besides the provinces of Georgia and Bessarabia, the gouvernements/regions of Tauria and Ekaterinoslav are mentioned. The region of the Don River is strangely missing without any kind of reference. This may be because there was not a single real parish located in it. There is also no mention of it in the list of assigned regions. Because it had not been assigned, it was always considered a part of the diocese of Tyraspol or Cherson and administered as such. Thus the area of ministry included the gouvernement of Cherson, Saratov, both of the southern counties of the gouvernement of Samara, Nikolayevsk and Novouzensk, and finally the gouvernements of Astrachan and Stavropol. At that time Samara was not, as yet, a gouvernement city and the German Catholics on the left side of the shore of the Volga all belonged to Saratov.

Next to the constituting of the cathedral chapter, the decree encourages the first diocesan bishop to build a seminary for priests "in which young men, who wish to dedicate themselves to the spiritual office be introduced from the earliest age to the virtues of church discipline and subjects of learning in the most diligent way and be trained in them." From time to time the bishop was to send out missionary priests to the far-flung regions of the diocese. Since the state took care of the costs of travel, this sending of missionaries could be carried out much more easily. The decree also mentions that Emperor Nicholas I had promised to have everything established. A dwelling fit for a bishop's station in life was to be acquired in Cherson as well as the necessary residences and rooms for the seminary for priests. If possible, they were to be in the vicinity of the cathedral church. 4,480 rubles were determined for the Mensa episcopalis (support of the bishop - Translator's note: literally "the episcopal table" in Latin). Both of the suffragan bishops were to receive an annual salary of 2,000 silver rubles which was the same as the other suffragan bishops in the dioceses of Russia.

Since according to canonical regulations at the time of the establishment of the dioceses, a suitable tax was to be remitted to the Apostolic See, this action should be mentioned but, at the same time, the Holy Father decreed that this tax should benefit the bishop of Cherson. This was to be recorded in the books of the apostolic chamber. This tax consisted of 33 ½ florins.

The decree also states that the czar had been convinced to promise the return of **all** the assets of the orders and monasteries and nunneries. There were over 100 of these in the Congress Poland and Lithuania. According to the directives of the pope, the person who was to carry this out was given the duty of giving an exact report in regard to the religious orders, their assets, their number, the places where they had been established etc. and the names of the residences of the suffragan bishops who were listed in the bull given by Pius VI which described the diocese.

The newly-appointed Titular Bishop of Karystos (Translator's note: a town on the Greek island of Euboea, a titular bishop is considered to be the bishop of a diocese which is no longer functioning as a diocese within the governance of the pope, the Bishop of Rome), Ignatius Holowinski, was appointed for the implementation of the directives of the Apostolic See. He received the authority from the decree of establishment to delegate one or two ministerial dignitaries as his representatives in those regions which the legate himself could not visit because of pressing reasons. Six months after the separation of the diocese of Cherson had been completed Ignatius Holowinski was to give an accurate report about everything to the Holy Apostolic See. This report was to be filed in the archive of the Holy Consistory Office.

The apostolic decree of establishment only mentions in general terms that for the support of the members of the cathedral chapter, for the proper acquisition of the holy vessels, robes, church instruments and for the support of the seminary for priests, the necessary funds were to be allotted by the Russian state. To be sure, these were to be in the same amounts which were received by the rest of the dioceses in Russia. The decree stated that the disbursement of the funds which were to be given by the state was to be left to the apostolic legate, Bishop Holowinski. The legate then also determined the division of the funds in the various institutions of the diocese which was to be done by him in the document describing the diocese. According to this, the cathedral chapter was to annually receive 1,980 rubles, the seminary for priests 4,500 rubles, and the consistory (for the general budget), 2,500 rubles. The diocesan cathedral church was to receive an annual stipend of 2,500 rubles.

10. The trip of the apostolic nuncio/legate to the south of Russia

The decree of charter/establishment and description of the region served of the Holy See was dated "On July 3 of the year 1848.1." At that time, Pope Pius IX resided at Maria Maggiore in Rome. If one considers the postal services of that time and added to this, the situation that from time immemorial all things moved very slowly in the large empire of the czars; the decree would not have been received in the northern residence before fall. The papal legate was, as we have noted above, firstly appointed as the Bishop of Karystos in advance of his actual diocese. Before he could take his trip into the regions of the present Diocese of Tyraspol, the celebration of episcopal consecration had to take place first, because he had to administer pontifical acts everywhere he would go. The time of year was not favourable for such a long and difficult journey by this prince of the Church. Since besides this, Bishop Ignatius was the headmaster of the spiritual academy and had a professorship at the college/academy, these factors did not allow for him to undertake a trip to the regions of his assigned diocese. He also had to wait for the imperial appointment to this very important mission. For this reason, Bishop Ignatius postponed his departure until the following spring. His first trip was via Moscow and Nishny-Novgorod to the region of the Volga Germans. At that time, the first well appointed steamships (since 1843) of the "Steamship Travel on the Volga" navigated the Volga River. It was on one of these steamships in which the bishop arrived in Saratov at the beginning of May, at his "residence on the Volga," accompanied by several clergy. The Russian Ministry of the Interior, upon the command of the czar, in a timely manner, seems to have informed all of the governors in the southern region in regard to the arrival of the papal legate, who made his visitation trip as an envoy of the czar. In doing so, the ministry did not neglect to point out that the Catholic prince was the recipient of special favour and affection from the czar and this gave the state officials a strict directive to receive the bishop with the highest of honours and to give him and his entourage everywhere an honour guard for safety. The arrival of the papal and imperial legate did not only cause excitement among all the Catholics, but also the entire Russian population. All of the state officials were involved. Everyone wanted to see the illustrious Catholic bishop. He was given a very respectful reception everywhere. The tradition concerning this event has been retained until the present day among the inhabitants of the Volga region. About 80 years have passed since then. The legate won over everyone's heart by means of his commanding appearance and his friendly and kind character. His trip was comparable to a real victory march. The Catholics of the Volga region and also of the Black Sea and the Sea of Asov had never seen a Catholic bishop. And now they saw such a kind and friendly gentleman! All of the parishes received the representative of the Holy Father like an angel from heaven. Many, and not only the women but men bronzed by working in the sun, shed tears of pious emotion and joy, fell on their knees when the bishop appeared, and requested his episcopal blessing. Long columns of an honour guard composed of young riders seated upon high horses, which had been decorated in a festive

I. Thus the date on which the concordat had been ratified in St. Petersburg (see Page 28).

manner accompanied the procession of the papal legate from one parish to another. Every parish waited for the important visitors at the entrance to the village with a nicely ordered procession with flags and pictures of the dear Mother of God and other ~mints carried by members of the parish. Every time when the prelate stepped out of his carriage, he blessed the people and bowed before the cross which had been brought to him by the priest of the parish to be kissed. He walked down the long streets with his retinue to the church, where he chanted the prescribed prayers and gave those present the first celebratory blessing. Even today the tradition story revolving around the "nice bishop" is still alive in the collective memory of the Catholic people. The senior citizens say they were days of indescribable joy and rich blessings from God. Today the diocese of Tyraspol has forgotten its first bishop, but Bishop Holowinski continues to be talked about. A letter of Bishop Ignatius sent from the Volga colonies to his colleague in ministry, Bishop Wolonczewski of Rovno, states in the following section: "You praise the piety of your Lithuanians; here in the gouvernement of Saratov I met 80,000 Germans who surpass your flock in terms of the fear of God and piety."

11. The separation of Cherson from the archdiocese of Mohilev

The archdiocese of Mohilev covered a great expanse. Neither the life nor the physical powers of a bishop sufficed in order to visit every place even once. One could not even think of having a regular administration for the huge diocese in the dispersion. A division of the area into several ecclesiastical deaneries was the concern of the highest shepherds of the Holy Catholic Church. If schismatic Russia had been a land which from time immemorial was closed to the beneficent influence of the Apostolic See as if it were behind the Great Wall of Chin~ Russia's border guards were especially fearful of the invasion of a foreign ecclesiastical power ever since the partition of a large part of Catholic Poland. From that time on, a political policy began in the residence of the czars which attempted, especially in Russia and then in Poland to separate Catholics from the visible Head of the Church. The establishment of the Holy Catholic Council in St. Petersburg was the first great step toward the realization of this plan. In light of these considerations, everyone understands the kind of obstacles the Apostolic See had to overcome in order to reach a decision regarding the separation and the establishment of a new diocese. The visit of the czar had opened the way for this to happen. Together with this the extraordinary affection which the absolute ruler had for Bishop Ignatius Holowinski played a role.

Bishop Ignatius had been given the responsibility of explaining and determining the borders of the new bishopric of Cherson. It must be added that he had received imperial authority to do this. In consideration of the huge area and problematic means of transportation in the empire, the papal legate could hardly have personally visited all of the inhabited places. He will therefore have used his authority to send sublegates to the parishes which were located the furthest away. The report of the bishop to the Holy See shows that he travelled through the entire north of the diocese and in the south, through the regions of Cherson and Tauria. Today, the people in these gouvernements still remember the visitation and confirmation journey of the "first bishop'." The papal legate drew the borders of the diocese to be established in such a way that they included all of the German Catholic colonies. At present, the borders of the diocese by far no longer include all of the German settlements. Because of the great increase of the German Catholic population, it already poured over the old borders at the end of the last century. In 1922, we came upon three dioceses in America (in the States) in which 90 % of the immigrants came from (the diocese) Tyraspol. Not a few German Catholic colonists who came from Russia also settled in Argentina and in Canada. This does not include those who found a new home in Siberia, in the Turgai area and in Akomolinsk. Two German colonies in the gouvernement of Chernigov; Grosswerder and Kleinwerder, were not included by the bishop within the borders of the diocese. They lay too far north and too far from the other German colonies in the south. Separated from the large groups of

German colonists, these unfortunate Germans lost their mother tongue because they did not have German teachers or priests. In close proximity to these colonies, there are two German Lutheran colonies. These saved their German culture together with their mother tongue because they always had German teachers and pastors. Two little villages composed of these people migrated at the right time to the diocese of Tyraspol and thus saved their German culture and mother tongue. With the loss of its mother tongue, every small ethnic group is in great danger of losing its faith because it cannot be convinced to pray in the Russian language. They have their old German prayer and hymnbooks from which they pray and sing without being able to understand the meaning of their contents. Because they do not understand German anymore, the sounds which they utter are no longer similar to German. They are much more an incomprehensible gibberish. What a sad worship of God! Bishop Cieplak, when he visited these villages, was very moved by the misfortune which had befallen the people and advised them to be re-Germanized. For this purpose, they were to endeavour to obtain good German teachers from their own families by sending their boys and girls to German schools.

The directory which was established by the papal legate for the diocese of Tyraspol includes 52 parishes with as many parish churches and lists 40 filial congregations with churches or prayer chapels. The parish church in Theodosia (Feodosia) and the Genoan chapel in Sudak on the southern shore of the Crimean Peninsula are missing from the list. However, the document includes the parish of Tultscha (Tutschkow). Because Russia, after the establishment of the chersonese (tyrasplian) diocese, exchanged land with Romania on the left shore of the branch of the Danube River, the parish of Tultscha/Tulcea was exchanged for Isrnail/Izmail. The bishops of Tyraspol and Jassy/Iasi mutually exchanged the jurisdiction in regard to both parishes; that is regions.

The visitation for the establishment of the diocese made by Bishop Holowinski took the whole of the summer of 1849. It was only at the middle of September that he could return to St. Petersburg where the archbishops of Mohilev had resided since the end of the eighteenth century. The papal legate had accomplished a great and difficult task. He had not only travelled great distances in a wagon, visited the largest part of the diocese, administered the sacrament of confirmation, given the papal blessing, often proclaimed the Word of God which he had translated into German, but held celebrations of pontifical masses. In the same year, at the end of October, he gave an accurate report concerning the borders and the establishment of the diocese of Tyraspol to the Holy See.

12. The Roman Catholic Church in Theodosia

The papal legate did not receive the Church of Theodosia (Feodosia) on the southern shore of the Crimea into the chartered list of parishes. In the report to the Holy See it is quite clear that he did not even visit Theodosia. Without a doubt one had informed him that the church in this city, together with the entire parish, was of the Armenian rite. This was the reason why the priests of this church were always from Armenian orders who were Mechitarists from Venice. The Mechitarists in this seaport city own a monastery with a seminary on St. Lazzaro Island with a beautiful church and an Armenian printing press. In the city proper, there is a High School/College where lads are prepared for entrance to the theological seminary. The abbot of the monastery is, at the same time, also the archbishop of their rite.

At the time of the establishment of the parish of Theodosia the city counted not a few Italian merchants who had settled there. Because of this, the priests had to know the Italian language as well as others. Tue archdiocese of Mohilev, to which the parish belonged at that time, always had a lack of Italian-speaking priests. For this reason, after the dedication of the church building, Archbishop Siestrzencewicz appointed an Armenian Mechitarist as the first priest of this church. In the archbishop's diary, this appointment is mentioned with the specific comment that "by way of exception a clergyman of the Armenian rite was provided." This took place in the year 1789. But the clergymen who succeeded him in this parish were also clergy of the Armenian order which was mentioned. In the structure of the diocese of Tyraspol, to which the Catholics of the Armenian rite were assigned, one of the notices stated that the church had been transformed from a Tartar mosque into a Catholic church and had been dedicated in the year 1789 by Archbishop Siestrzencewicz. The bishops of Tyraspol were always firmly convinced that this church belonged to the Latin and not to the Armenian rite. On the other hand, the Armenians claimed the House of God for the Armenian rite. These claims were validated even then when the papal legate, Bishop Ignatius, journeyed to the Southern Crimea. This explains why the church was missing in the papal description of the diocese. Without a doubt the church and parish in Theodosia were presented to him as one which was Armenian Catholic. However, in reality the church is of the Latin rite.

As long as the bishops of Tyraspol administered the Catholics of the Armenian rite, the question of the membership of the church in Theodosia did not come up. Since the clergy of this parish were Mechitarists even until modern times, with the privilege of celebrating (the mass) in both rites, neither the Armenian nor the Latin members of the flock had a reason to complain about being neglecting in regard to church matters.

However, when in 1909, after the establishment of an apostolic administration for the Armenian Catholics, the Armenian apostolic administrator appropriated the church as an "Armenian Catholic Church," in opposition to the protest of the bishop of Tyraspol, quarrels concerning membership of this House of God arose which even led to fights between the Latins and the Armenians in front of the church building. Tue Armenians based the claim concerning the membership of the church solely upon a notation in the first diocesan description of the diocese of Tyraspol from the year 1857 and upon the fact that until now all the clergy were members of an Armenian order. As a result of the disputes the Russian Ministry.of the Interior sent Petrov/Petroff, the official of the department for "foreign confessions," who right then and there, was supposed to determine the membership of the church. The enquiry ended to the advantage of the Latins.

Following the directive of the diocesan curia, the dean of Simpferopol, Father Scherger, had taken a document from the archive of the Taurian gouvernement and sent it to the diocesan curia in Saratov. This document declared that a mosque had been given to the Latins by Empress Catherine II as a Catholic house of worship and that the same building was dedicated as a church by Archbishop Siestrzencewicz. After the ordinary of Tyraspol, Bishop Joseph Kessler, had made a notarized copy of this document, he sent the original to the department for "foreign confessions" as proof that the church of Theodosia had to belong to his jurisdiction, as it was a church of the Latin rite. In the meantime the Armenians, through their representative in the Duma, sought to have a second investigation done concerning the membership of the Theodosian church. Then the ministry dispatched the official Andreev to Theodosia, who soon returned to St. Petersburg with the news that the church belonged to the Armenian rite! The minister of the interior, Makarov/Makaroff, who was not personally well-disposed toward Bishop Kessler, awarded the place of worship to the Armenians. This happened in the years 1909-1912 when the Poles were still neglected children of the Russian empire (translator's note: the implication is that because the archbishop who dedicated the church was ethnically Polish, this caused the decision to be in favour of the Armenians). If this dispute had taken place after the outbreak of the Great War, when a "great friendship" was established between the Poles and the Russians, then the church would have certainly been honoured as a Latin one by the Russian government! No appeal by the bishop of Tyraspol in regard to this notorious violation of justice helped the situation at all. In vain the ordinary of Tyraspol referred to the authentic document which he had submitted. The head of the department blatantly replied that the department had never received such a document from him.

13. The appointment and consecration of the first bishop of the diocese

With the establishment of its own diocese for the German Catholic settlers of Russia, a desire of the heart was fulfilled. The diocese was the first institution with a German Catholic character. As everywhere, where Lutherans or Protestants and Catholics are so-called guest peoples in countries outside of German lands, so also the former were favoured and preferred. In the area of the diocese, the Lutherans and the Reformed were twice the size in terms of numbers. All of the German state government institutions were in the hands of the Lutherans or the Protestants. This applies equally to the secondary educational institutions which were collectively established by the colonists. A so-called tutelage/guardianship chancellery was located in St. Petersburg as the highest administration for the colonies. Both of the German offices in Saratov and in Odessa were under its leadership. Barons from the Baltic Sea were at the head of these institutions and they had little sympathy for the Catholic settlers. An official was in the office in Saratov, who, to be sure, grew up German, but who was married to a Russian lady. The only thing which he had in common with his German fellow compatriots was his name. He was Russian in his manner of thinking. He name was Klaus. His history, with the title "Our Colonies," gives proof that he was hostile toward the German colonists. Abnormal phenomena such as this are very rarely found among other ethnic groups or not at all among Germans outside of Middle Europe. This weakness of character seems to be a result of the religious division of the German people. This division caused and still causes today, suppression of the Catholics in the political arena by their non-Catholic fellow compatriots in whichever country these form the majority.

The history of the German people provides classic examples of this. This superiority complex of the Protestants over their fellow Catholic brethren was taken along by the Protestant settlers from Germany to their new homeland. In the diocese of Cherson all the higher officials of the civil service, all of the teaching positions in the central school were occupied by Lutherans and Protestants. The superior court judges were all Lutherans, all of the secondary educational institutions which were established and supported by colonists of both confessions were, without one single exception, located in Lutheran villages. Because of this situation, the joy which the Catholic population publicly expressed concerning the founding of it own diocese, could be justified even more. Since the diocese was an ecclesiastical institution, the Catholics could, at least, not be taken advantage of by their Lutheran and Protestant brethren. On the other hand, at the beginning, the seminary and the curia mainly had to be led and administered by Polish clergy because of the complete absence of German priests. Nevertheless, since the diocese was supposed to be German, at least its first bishop had to be a German. But it was not easy to find a gentleman of the clergy who was of German extraction, had German education and, at the same time, in religious scholarly terms, fulfilled all of the requirements which such a high post had.

The then archbishop of Mohilev, Kasimir Dmochowski, and the papal legate Holowinski, seem to have pointed the imperial Russian government in the direction of the prior of the Dominican province in Riga, Father Ferdinand Helanus Kahn. He was a German by birth. Born in Galicia in the year 1789, he joined the preaching order there while he was still very young, and completed his studies in the humanities and in theology with them. After the completion of his studies, he received ordination as a priest in the Order of St. Dominic. Unfortunately, too little is known about his life. This meager information comes from the pen of the very honourable Bishop Antonius Zerr, which was published in the Reichert Calender in the year 1897. As a young member of the order, Father Ferdinand was sent by his superiors in the order to Grodno in order to lecture in t\le German and Russian languages there. Probably it was a matter of lectures in the Ukrainian (Little Russian) language, which Father Ferdinand had been able to learn in Galicia. From here, Father Ferdinand was sent as the curate and German preacher to Reva! (translator's note: presently Tallinn in Estonia). However, he had this position for only a few years, for his superiors soon appointed him to the post of religious instructor in the military college in Riga. Here his fellow members of the order had the chance to get to know Father Ferdinand closer and learned to appreciate him greatly. For this reason, after a few years, they elected him prior of their abbey in Riga. The circumstance that Father Ferdinand worked as an instructor of religion at the military college in Riga can probably be ascribed to the false thinking of the Germans in the Volga region that Bishop Kahn had, before his entry into the priesthood, served in the military and was even promoted to captain. Father Ferdinand Helanus Kahn fulfilled all of the requirements which could be expected of a new bishop for the new diocese of Cherson (Tyraspol). Because of this, on May 24, 1850, with the approval of Emperor Nicholas I, he was pre-canonized as the first bishop of Cherson (Tyraspol) and consecrated a few months later in St. Catherine's Church by Archbishop Dmochowski. Shortly before his consecration, genuine doubts regarding the legitimacy of his baptismal certificate and therefore the validity of his baptism appeared. Since without the sacrament of holy baptism, no other sacrament could authentically be received, nothing could be done except to conditionally bestow all of the sacraments from baptism to ordination as a priest upon the elected personage. The following day, the festive Episcopal consecration took place. This was a very unusual case in the history of the Catholic Church!

According to the document of establishment the new bishopric of Cherson (Tyraspol) received two suffragan bishops. The appointment of the first did not follow long after (1856) the pre-canonization of the diocesan bishop. The election of the Holy See fell upon the then supervisor of the Catholic Theological Academy in St. Petersburg, Dr. Vinzentius Lipski, who should be well-known to the Catholic diocesan office in St. Petersburg and also to the important state officials. With the appointment of a Polish suffragan bishop for the bishopric, which included a significant percentage of Poles, these members of the diocese were also satisfactorily cared for Suffragan Bishop Lipski was only eight years younger than the diocesan bishop, for he was born on March 17, 1 797. His bishop's title was Jonopolis. Only little could be ascertained concerning his earlier life. The second suffragan position was never filled. The first one, after the passing of Bishop Lipski, was only filled once by a son of German colonists under diocesan bishop, Franz Zottmann; by suffragan bishop Antonius Zerr. This occurred thanks to the efforts of the ill bishop, Franz Xaverius, and on March 3, 1883.

14. The cathedral chapter

According to the papal decree of establishment, a chapter was to be established at the cathedral in Cherson. It was to have nine members. Two dignitaries: a) High prelate b) High archdeacon, four canons: a canon of theology, a canon for penance, a canon for the parish and a canon who would be the cantor. The chapter was to give the responsibility of administering the parish connected with the cathedral to the parish canon (dean), as the jurisdiction of the parish had been bestowed on the cathedral chapter by the charter/document of establishment. The statutes of the cathedral chapter were to be drawn up by the papal legate, Suffragan Bishop Holowinski, and this did, in fact, take place.

According to the wording of the decree, the office of the parish canon was permanent. To be sure, the chapter can elect him from its midst, but cannot remove him from office. Whether this right belongs to the ordinary is not stated in the decree. The members of the cathedral chapter are to be supported by the sacristans who are part of the chapter. All members enjoy the same rights and privileges as the other gentlemen belonging to cathedral chapters in the rest of the dioceses of Russia. According to the statutes, they are to wear, besides a robe of purple colour, a distinct enameled cross with a gold border and rays of gold in the four corners of the cross. The distinctive item is in the form of a Maltese cross, is six centimeters long and just as wide. On the front side, imprinted upon white enamel is a picture of St. Clement with the palm of victory, the patron of the cathedral church and the diocese. As in the rest of the dioceses of Russia, the gentlemen of the cathedral wear the cross and on the back of this there is an embossed figure of a two-headed eagle of the Russian Empire. It hangs from two gold chains. The prelate's robe is a mozzetta (translator's note: a short cape with a small ornamental hood) worn over the rochet (translator's note: a white linen vestment resembling a surplice with close-fitting sleeves) however, that of the canon is a mantoletta (translator's note: a longer cape) worn over the rochet. The latter's clerical garb is also worn by the three sacristans of the cathedral chapter. According to the statutes of the chapter, it is not clear whether they have the right to wear a special cross. They did in fact wear one like that since the year 1874 after Bishop Franz Zottmann allowed it after previous consultations with the then Metropolitan Fialkowski. The cathedral chapter has the responsibility of holding high mass and vespers in the cathedral if the diocesan bishop does not want to celebrate himself, to sing the low mass on weekdays, and on church holidays and some other festivals to hold the office in the chancel. One main duty of the cathedral chapter consists of assisting the celebrating ordinary at festival services according to the rules set forth in the liturgical books. While the prelates and the canons have the right of voting whether present or not, the sacristans are able to vote only when at a meeting. According to the decree of establishment, the statutes of the cathedral chapter of Tyraspol were to be confirmed by the Apostolic See, which was, nevertheless, never carried out.

The first members of the cathedral chapter of Tyraspol were all Poles and Lithuanians. As there were no German-speaking priests in the diocese available at the time of its establishment, clergy of foreign origin had to be received into the cathedral chapter if the ordinary did not want to be without a cathedral chapter. Of course, this was unthinkable. The papal legate himself appointed the first dignitaries and chapter personnel of the new diocese. He had, as we have noted above, been empowered by the decree of establishment to do so. According to the statutes of the cathedral chapter all of the holders of these offices were to have master degrees or degrees of doctors of theology or canon law.

The first cathedral chapter of Tyraspol consisted of the following clergymen: 1. Head Prelate: Zeno Jotkiewicz, 2. Archdiaconal Prelate: Georg Rasutowicz; as Canon 1: Maximilian Orlowski; as Canon 2: Anton Rajuniec; *as* Canon 3: Joseph Szelwowicz; as Canon 4: Gabriel Onoszk:o; *as* Sacristan 1: Vinzenz Snarski; as Sacristan 2: Johannes Rymsza; *as* Sacristan 3: this was vacant.

All of the members of the cathedral chapter had their masters of theology. Since the salaries of the clergymen in the cathedral chapter had not been determined in the bull of establishment, later on there was the sum of 1,980 rubles for everyone. This low salary forced the bishop to fuse several positions in one. The great lack of priests also caused positions to be combined. According to ancient canonical law the ordinary of the diocese appointed all of the canons of the cathedral chapter. The Russian state law demanded their confirmation by the czar himself. The only exceptions were the three sacristans of that which was also called the little chapter. These could be freely appointed by the bishop. After 1907 the officials of the Ministry of the Interior confirmed all appointments. The new legal codex retains the appointment.of the dignitaries; that is of the prelates of the chapters, by the Holy See:l. In any case the bishop of Tyraspol has the right to nominate that person. The first German cathedral clergymen were appointed by Bishop Franz Xaverius Zottmann. With the exception of two Bavarian citizens, who had been given the directorship of the Tyraspol Seminary, and of a West Prussian, Robert Glass, they were all sons of German colonists. The first son of a colonist who was raised to the rank of prebendary/canon was Alexander Boos, who was elected in the year 1876 as a legate of the college for the diocese of Tyraspol by the cathedral chapter. Since this office could only be held by a canon, Rev. Alexander Boos had to first be appointed a canon. Until then Father Alexander Boos was the priest of the Church of the Assumption of Maria in Tblisi in the Caucasus. After the passing of the Polish and Lithuanian canons, the bishop's council became German. Two positions on it always remained filled by clergymen of another nationality so that the diocese of Tyraspol always kept equality.

15. The transfer of the episcopal see to Tyraspol

It had been agreed between the Holy See and Czar Nicholas that the state was to fund the construction of the necessary buildings for the diocesan bishop, for the diocesan court (consistory), for the seminary for priests with a preparatory school (seminary for boys) and finally also for the residences of the cathedral chapter. The schismatic clergy went into an uproar when the news of the establishment of a Catholic bishop, a diocesan administration, a cathedral chapter and seminary spread in Cherson. Not for anything in the world did one want to tolerate a Catholic bishop's see in Cherson. On the other hand,

Czar Nicholas I, autocratic as he was, could have commanded immediate acquiesence. But it seems that with such an intolerant opposition, Bishop Ferdinand Helanus himself did not desire to live among such a large number of enemies. In the same manner, the coadjutantof Mohilev, Bishop Holowinski, seems to have voted for a transfer of the bishop's see to the new diocese. How would the Holy See have otherwise so readily given up all claim to Cherson and transferred the residence of Bishop Kahn to the small, insignificant city of Tyraspol? It was namely foreseen that because of the religious fanaticism of the Russian clergy and people the founding of new Catholic institutions in the city would be the objects of jealousy and hatred by the population. These animosities could easily lead to huge problems and hinder the furthering of the Catholic cause. The Russian bishop sent a letter of complaint to the Holy Synod in St. Petersburg in which he emphatically pled for the synod to prevent the establishment of a Catholic bishop with a diocesan administration. Since a Catholic bishop could easily reside in the neighbouring, flourishing city of Odessa and could administer his diocese from there, nothing made more sense than to transfer the bishop's see from Cherson to this port city. No schismatic (Orthodox) bishop was residing there as yet. It was just that even Odessa was not to serve the new diocese as its center. Jealousy did not allow that. There were also political considerations which were used as excuses. Odessa is a border city and in case of war,

1. Canon 396 paragraph 1.

would immediately be prey to an enemy's attack. For this reason a state of siege would have to be placed on the city and this would all cause the regular pattern of religious life and the administration of the diocese to be inhibited. Since the government of the czar could not be convinced to propose a better city as a residence for the bishop of Cherson, for Archbishop Ignatius Holowinski had died in the meantime (1855) and his important patron, Czar Nicholas I, had also removed himself from the world stage (translator's note: the implication is that he poisoned himself), the Holy See gave in so that the question of the location of the bishop's see would not endanger the existence of the diocese which had just come into existence.

So the Holy See encouraged the diocesan bishop, Ferdinand Helanus, to go to his diocese. Since there was not even a Catholic church in Tyraspol and even no respectable building could be located for bishop's residence, the bishop himself did not even know where to settle. The circumstances forced him to remain in St. Petersburg until 1856. In the meantime he carried out visitations of all parishes in the gouvernement of Cherson and in Tauria, travelled in the Crimean Peninsula; administering the sacrament of confirmation in all of the places. In the year 1853 he consecrated the beautiful Church of the Assumption of Mary in Odessa. The outbreak of the Crimean War in the year 1854 caused the head pastor to return to St. Petersburg again. According to the decree of establishment, one of the two suffragan bishops who were to be assigned to the ordinary was to reside in Saratov on the Volga. The diocesan bishop, Ferdinand Helanus now set his sights on this place. This was decisive for the future place of residence for the diocesan bishops of Tyraspol. The Russian government seemed to also be in agreement with this temporary resolution of the question concerning the see. It rented the respectable two-story building next to the Catholic Church on German Street as the residence for the ordinary. Later the Apostolic See also gave its consent to the residence of the bishop in the city of Saratov on the Volga. At that time Saratov was the most prominent city upon the entire territory of the diocese of Tyraspol.

Since the parish for the Catholics was a very small one, it had only a single priest, Reverend Snarski, who was generally called Father Superior. Both dignitaries of the cathedral chapter and the four canons were, to be sure, appointed by the papal legate, but no one had arrived at his destination as yet. Since it was determined that the diocesan bishop would reside in Saratov, they waited for the right moment to begin their journey to Saratov. However, before this, one had to find a domicile for them. This factor was closely tied to the question of the establishment and opening of a seminary for priests for the members of the cathedral chapter could not live from their meager salary. All had to be active *as* professors in the seminary for priests. A spacious building had to be found for the seminary for boys and priests in which, besides the rooms of the pupils, the entire college of professors could take up residence. Because of this, the government rented a large complex of houses on Moscow Street, the main street in the city, in which the seminary and the professors could all comfortably accommodate themselves. But not all of the prelates and canons could be employed in Saratov. The new bishopric still lacked enough priests. Canon Maximilian Orlowski and Prelate Rasutowicz remained in their previous postings; the former as the clergyman in St. Peter and St. Paul Church in Tblisi, which he had built himself, the latter *as* the clergyman of the Church of the Assumption of St. Mary in Odessa. Not until the summer of 1857 were there five canons of the Tyraspol chapter residing in Saratov. For the first time the aged bishop, who had already attained his 70t11 year of life, could celebrate a pontifical mass in the small cathedral church with a full number of assistants.

16. Opening of the diocesan seminary

The greatest concern which lay upon the shoulders of the aged bishop was the establishment and the opening of a seminary as a place to educate priests like a greenhouse. Above all, the theological subjects had to be divided among the members of the cathedral chapter. In the absence of a proper salary, they had to take on the scholarly

lectures and education in both seminaries. In doing so, not every difficulty had, by far, been eliminated. It was very difficult to solve the question of the schools; that is for the boys and the seminary for priests, so that they were filled with good, morally-minded boys and candidates for the study of theology. These also had to be recruited in the first years after the establishment of the institution. Since hardly a few candidates with the proper educational prerequisites could be found in the German Catholic colonies for the study of theology, the ordinary sent a call to the seminaries for priests in Vilna, Kovno, Minsk and Zhitomir. Soon several candidates from these educational institutions applied for acceptance in the Tyraspol Seminary which was to be inaugurated and located in Saratov. Among them were: Baranowski, Baczewski, Turczynski, Barski, Gibulsz, Michalski and several others. The seminary for priests was opened on September 1, 1857.

The first lectures had to be held in front of a dozen students. From the diocese itself, a few with hardly sufficient preliminary education entered the school and among these were Krinicki and Prince Tumanov/Tumanoff, but he soon went to Rome and that ended the propaganda, as well as Arasov/Arasoff. All of the pupils needed special tutorials in Latin. Since the majority of the students spoke Polish, the Polish language was used as the medium of instruction when Latin textbooks were utilized. During the initial years of its existence, the seminary for priests had a Polish character. As there was no hope of getting large enough numbers of candidates from the German colonies for the seminary for priests because of the lack of Catholic high schools/secondary schools in them, the diocesan bishop, at the same time as the inauguration of the spiritual seminary, founded a seminary for boys according to Tridentine rite. More or less, the school had the same curriculum as a High School/Junior College. The German diocesan clergy aided the ordinary by providing stipends for 25 poorer boys. Thirteen of these free spots were reserved for the southern and twelve for the northern parts of the diocese. The scholarships for those from the south were determined by money which the farmers in the south had deposited with the Ministry of the Interior, that is, with the Catholic council in St. Petersburg. Those in the north were supported by a yearly tax. The prospects for a speedy filling of all of the free places in the preparatory school seemed to be very positive. It was just that one's hopes were just not fulfilled. Recruiting officers had to be sent out into the diocese for the school for boys. The rumour had spread that the entire governing bodies of both institutions were Poles and that for this reason, the boys and youth would not receive a German education. Many parents, whose sons eagerly wanted to be accepted into the preparatory school, were of the wrong opinion that their reception into the seminary for boys would already determine the question as to whether they, after graduation, would be accepted into the seminary for priests and would have to become priests. This wrong view was probably influenced by the situation that the pupils in the seminary for boys also wore a clerical robe. To be sure, the German diocesan clergy also wanted to have ministers who came from their ranks, but only a few parents could bring themselves to decide to let their sons choose the ministry. This happened because they were afraid they would be unsuitable as clergy. The faithful membership had experienced too many examples of unworthy clergy. Since the diocese of Tyraspol had belonged to the archdiocese of Mohilev, was too far away from the ordinary's see, and in most cases not the best, but the weaker clergy were sent to pastorally care for the German colonists, the people were fearful for their sons when they chose the ministry. One had to deal with all of these impediments. It only gradually happened that all of these prejudices were removed. Lastly, the bishopric lacked a geographic center where the diocesan see and the seminary for priests and the seminary for boys could be constructed. Since the bishop's residence with the diocesan court and the ministerial educational institutions were situated at the farthest end of the diocese, the seminary and its preparatory school was located too far from the southern members of the diocese. In order to enter the seminary for boys, the boys had to undertake a journey of about 1,500 versts (995 miles) and even more. This journey was very difficult and not without danger. The journey was mostly by water, upon the Black Sea and the Sea of Asov, on the Don River up to Kalatsch and from there about 60 versts (40 miles or 64 kilometers) with the mail coach to Tsaritsyn and then from this city ·on the Volga upstream on the Volga until Saratov. There was no possibility of visiting the parents during summer holidays. A boy from the south of the diocese had to bid farewell to his parents for many years if he went on a journey to Saratov to enroll at the seminary. In those cases where the educated young man graduated from the seminary for boys, entered the seminary for priests and, after four or more years studied philosophy and theology and became a priest and then journeyed to his distant homeland for the celebration of his first holy mass, the parents did not recognized their son again. After a long number of years the little boy had become a young man. The sending of boys from the extreme south into the north of the diocese, as everyone knew, cost the parents more than a small sacrifice without even considering the high cost of the journey. But the boys also had to make big sacrifices because they regularly had to spend their summer holidays with German colonists in the north until, at the beginning of the 1870s, rail connections were established with Odessa. Because of these reasons, the number of students from the south in the seminary for boys remained very limited right into the 1870s. The number in the seminary for priests was dependent on the number in the seminary for boys. For this reason, the percentage of clergy, which the seminary for priests produced during the first years of its existence, was also small, if one does not count those priests who originated in Poland and Lithuania Nevertheless, the aged Bishop Ferdinand had the fortune to ordain the first graduates of the seminary as priests. The first German priest, upon whom Bishop Kahn laid hands, was Johann von Nepomuk Schamne, a colonist's son from Graf. Soon several other colonists' sons from the north and from the south of the diocese followed in his footsteps.

The following priests belonged to the first group: Valentin Weber from Sulz, Balthasar Kraft from Kleinliebental, Rudolf Reichert from Landau, Father Leibham from Franzfeld, Alexander Boos from Obermonjou, Sicard from Katharinenstadt, Dorzweiler from the same colony, and Mitzig from Goebel among others. In the year 1860, Franz Xaverius Zottmann entered the seminary for priests. He was 33 years old and had completed his philosophical and theological studies in Munich, Wuerzburg and Eichstaett in Bavaria. After one year he was already ordained in Saratov as a priest. He was the first German who was ordained by Bishop Ferdinand Helanus Kahn. We will refer to him again later on.

17. Bishop Ferdinand's administration and his death

When the Dominican Ferdinand Kahn was elevated to the title of a diocesan bishop, he had already reached the age of 63. The years of his active manhood had long passed. It was just that the aged man was still very vigorous. The time was filled with rumors of war. It was to be feared that if war should break out with Russia, that the country would use the south of the new diocese as a battle ground. In fact, a war in the Crimean Peninsula with three European powers broke out in 1854. The outbreak of war-like hostile actions forced the diocesan bishop to discontinue his journey of visitation which he had begun and, because there was no set residence, to withdraw to St. Petersburg. There the question moving the bishop's see from Cherson was brought up, for that is where the permanent residence of the bishop was to be constructed. Because of these circumstances, the new head shepherd was forced to administer his faraway and widespread diocese from St. Petersburg. For the time being the administration had to be restricted to communication by mail. The noble goal which the Holy See pursued with the establishment of a new diocese seemed to be unattainable. As we have already read previously, in October 1856 the see of the bishop of Cherson was transferred to the insignificant little city of Tyraspol. In the same year the aged diocesan bishop Ferdinand Helanus received a suffragan bishop in the person of the inspector of the Catholic Spiritual Academy in St. Petersburg, Vinzenz Lipski. The first suffragan bishop for the new diocese was to live as a permanent resident in Saratov on the Volga. The new suffragan bishop did not go to Saratov, but to Odessa where he took up residence in a small house next to the Church of the Ascension. This house still stands today. This is what both bishops had agreed upon. The diocesan bishop himself chose his temporary residence as Saratov. In place of the suffragan bishop, the members of the Saratov parish and the Catholic residents of the Volga were able to greet their own diocesan bishop on

October 10, 1856.

We have mentioned above that the government had rented the respectable two-story house next to the Catholic parish church in Saratov as a residence for the shepherd of the diocese. This is where the aged bishop, who had already reached his 69th year of life, took up permanent residence.

Since the news of the coming arrival of the diocesan bishop had spread in the north of the diocese, a lot of issues had already been presented which awaited the decision of the bishop. During the first while, they consumed a lot of the bishop's time. The most difficult concerns for the elderly gentleman had to do with the establishment of the seminary and its preparatory school, and the recruitment of pupils from the seminaries of other Polish and Lithuanian dioceses as we have read previously. As long as the diocesan shepherd resided in St. Petersburg, it was rare and at large intervals to have complaints registered by entire congregations against their ministers. Now that the bishop was close, these grew on a daily basis. There was one complaint that the priest understood too little German, another congregation complained that the priest was shooting all their dogs! One priest was accused of having shot a rifle without warning and thereby having caused a young lady to become so frightened that she had become ill with debility. One congregation complained that its priest liked to drink a lot and that he treated the members of his flock very roughly and called them insulting names. The diocesan bishop treated the congregations politely. As he had spent a long time with the military, his military habits were evident when he had to deal with unjustified and unreasonable complaints. This was evident each time when he received individual complaints in an audience. Often he would have them kneel in repentance while he was occupied in his small room (office). So that those who were being punished did not get up for the set time from the floor, his little pet house dog had to sit in front of them and indicate by barking that they had gotten up. The dog was well-trained for this. He had some farmers with unwarranted complaints against their ministers locked up for several hours in a dark little room in the bishop's domicile. Some parishes petitioned the bishop, to immediately change their clergyman. They did not consider that the bishop, in light of the great lack of priests, did not have any priests at his beck and call in order to replace the priests who were to be transferred. With such strict disciplinary enforcement, it did not take long before unwarranted complaints soon become rare and finally almost completely ended.

Besides the Catholics in their diocese, the bishops of Tyraspol had to administer about 30,000 Catholic Armenians as Apostolic administrators. With few exceptions, these lived in Transcaucasia and in the Crimean Peninsula. Since these eastern people did not speak a European language and priests from their ranks could only rarely express themselves with difficulty in Russian, their administration was difficult for the head shepherd of Tyraspol. In order to make communication with them easier, an Armenian Catholic administration in Achalzych was formed which was within the jurisdiction of the bishops of Tyraspol. Generally an Armenian clergyman of rank headed it and he was supported by two advisors. The chairman and the advisors were appointed by the ordinary of Tyraspol. The office of a secretary could be given to a layman. The administration of this council was also difficult for the ordinary. On the one hand, among the clergymen of this small ethnic group who had received too little education and who were almost all married, and their priests and members on the other hand, there were often confusing situations which were mostly caused by Eastern plots. Since the Armenians, according to the way of the Eastern peoples, in their petitions and written complaints, always wanted "to state everything," their scribes were always very windy, unclear and confusing. It often happened that they contradicted themselves regarding important points. After Bishop Ferdinand had become better acquainted with this small ethnic group, every week he would place the correspondence which had arrived into a large envelope, seal it and write one word below the return address: "moltschaty," and sent it to the "Clerical Administration" in Achalzych. Of course, they had to try to peacefully settle all the complaints and misunderstandings. In those cases which it could not resolve, the issue had to be sent to the ordinary of the diocese of Tyraspol for a decision. This military way of dealing with things caused the complaints to become rarer, more reasonable and easier to untangle. Since the bishop realized that Europeans could never learn to properly understand people from Asia, he tried to get rid of the little group of Armenians. He was not successful in doing this. His successors also had to administer these mountain people until the year 1909. After the prerequisite conditions for this had been worked out between the Holy See and the Russian government by his immediate predecessor, the author of this history was the first person able to separate them from the diocese.

Despite his great age, Bishop Ferdinand Helanus still visited the diocese and administered the sacrament of confirmation to the faithful. 1. Nevertheless, he seems to have only entirely visited the area of Saratov and Samara. He sent suffragan bishop Vinzenz Lipski, who was eight years younger than he, to the south. After the death of the diocesan bishop, Bishop Lipski also visited the northern areas of the bishopric where he administered the holy Sacrament of Confirmation to all those who had not been confirmed. This included the small children. He dedicated the first houses of God in the diocese which were of stone such as in Odessa and in Astrachan.

To be sure, the Catholic people in the north called Bishop Ferdinand by his name and this was Bishop Kahn or the first bishop but his most popular name was "the long-toothed bishop," for he had several artificial teeth put in. He was not loved much by the rural

German Catholic population because of very strict discipline which bordered on militarism. He is supposed also have had a stern look which made it seem as if he wanted to look through everyone. As the shepherd of the diocese the late departed had worked as much as one could expect from an aged person between 70 and 80. He took leave of secular time in Saratov on October 6, 1864. His death happened suddenly at noon, as he prayed the "'Angel of the Lord" (angelus) aloud and the angelus bell was ringing in the hall of the bishop's residence. He was 77 years old and had led the flock of Tyraspol with his shepherd's staff for almost 15 years. He left about 3,500 rubles for the construction of the cathedral. His earthly remains rest in the vault of the Gothic chapel on the cemetery in Saratov.

1. Bishop Kahn had a very practical catechism published for the diocese. His immediate successor had it published in a revised edition. The most beloved prayer book for men was the "Geistliche Hauszierde" (Spiritual House Ornamentation) and for the women the "Grosse goldene Himmelschluessel" (Large Golden Keys to Heaven).

18. The consistory

The so-called consistory aided the ordinary in the administration of the diocese. Canon law describes this term only as a solemn gathering in which the Holy Father appoints the cardinals and the bishops of vacant dioceses. The consistories of the dioceses of Russia do a lot of the ordinary's work. In part, those issues pertaining to the diocesan curia which are not of a purely spiritual, or are of a mixed and civil nature, fall within its jurisdiction. It generally has three or four advisors who are, by Russian law, called assessors. All clergy members of the consistory were appointed by the ordinary but, according to the regulations of Russian governmental law had to be confirmed or approved by the minister. The consistory is, according to actual canon law, the last resort in regard to marital issues and in canonical court procedures against clergy who can only be removed by this court. As a rule the bishop, besides the contested matters brought forth by the clergy, also transfers the criminal cases concerning clergy to the consistory. Apart from the chairman, the vicar general or official, there are three or four assistant judges, the defender of the accused, the lawyer in contentious and criminal cases concerning priests, the promoter of justice, a secretary, an archivist, treasurer and several clerks. The consistory supervises the statistical records of the parishes. It publishes these books, numbers and counts the pages, binds them and stamps them with the seal of office and the signature of the official and the secretary. It also publishes financial books for all churches, oratories and chapels in the diocese and the books for the registration of those who were confirmed and of those converted. At the end of the year financial reports concerning income and expenses of the churches are audited by it; that is are examined.

At the beginning of each, year all curates of souls submit exact copies of all official acts which are confirmed by the imprint of the parish seal, so that they can be placed in storage in the consistory. The baptismal, marriage and death certificates which are issued by the clergy are valid according to Russian state law. The clergy of all confessions in Russia were recognized as state registrars in the empire of the czars. Nevertheless, in matters of great importance, state law required an attestation or confirmation of the above-mentioned certificates by the diocesan consistory. It had the right to issue documents which had not been entered into the church registers after previous research concerning the facts (baptismal, marriage and death certificates) and to have them entered into the respective church registers. Furthermore, part of its mandate was to correct mistakes which had crept into the church registers. The consistory supervised the discharge of wills in which church bequests had been made by the testator. It collected the sums which had been bequeathed and, if needed, did so in a court of law or by means of court police who specifically dealt with such issues and sent the funds to be deposited with the Catholic chancellery council in St. Petersburg. In these matters, several of the officials of the consistory were more bureaucratic than the Russian government in that they also regularly transmitted bequeathed mass monies, which according to their very nature were not part of a foundation, but to be used locally, to the chancellery council. However, this took place because of too great a fear of somehow breaking government laws. Large sums were lost because of anxiety.

The method of doing business which the consistory had, in so far as it was not regulated by canon law, was very ponderous. It had to present a preliminary inventory or resolution concerning all of its decisions. When it came to these decisions, the history of the entire course of events or process concerning the matter which had to be decided upon was recorded. These facts and decisions were then presented to the ordinary for his analysis or approval. Only after he gave written approval could the directive be implemented. This is what Russian laws required. Ibis ponderous method of doing business had been obsolete for a long time and was completely useless. It was just that according to Russian state law, one could not change it.

Until the year 1886, the diocesan consistory did not have its own edifice. Like the seminary, it was housed in a rented house until the late 1860s. When the seminary moved into its own building on Little Sergius Street, which had been purchased by the government, the consistory was also transferred to its main building. It took up the entire right wing until Rector Alexander Boos was able to transfer it to a wing in the seminary courtyard which stood apart from the main building so that the main seminary building could be completely dedicated to the religious institution. In 1886, a modest, two-story building for the consistory was built on the furthest right corner of the seminary garden. By doing so the seminary was given the chance to enlarge its sparse quarters.

For the support of the consistory the government had provided a set sum which at the time of its issuance was already very meager. Now, after almost 80 years, with the devaluation of the Russian ruble, the salaries to be paid are even less than the salaries for male servants and maids who carry out the most menial of tasks. The czar's government was convinced at the time of the determination of the salaries for lower officials that they were robbing them of two, three and five times the amount. For this reason the salaries were low and did not suffice for the lower officials even for the most modest standard of living. When the salaries for the officials of religious institutions were set, the state government should have been of a saner view. Repeated applications for the raising of the payments for the civil officials of the consistory did not lead to even a little success within the ministry office. The state was always very disinclined toward everything that was Catholic. In the year 1908 the bishop of Tyraspol vehemently pleaded for an increase in the salary of the secretary who only received a miserable four hundred rubles annually and had housing. The minister replied: "There is reason for such an increase!"

It must be emphatically noted here that the Russian state did not provide the Catholic Church and its institutions even one single penny from the state treasury. To be sure, all contributions which the bishops, their consistories, their seminaries, their chapters and the clergymen of various parishes received on an annual basis went through the hands of the state or the government, but originated from the interest of the fund that had millions which the state had deposited for confiscated ecclesiastical and monastic estates in Poland and in Lithuania. The Church in Russia and in Poland would have been in much better shape in respect to material matters if the state had only provided the entire interest from these estates. From these monies, the state purchased its own building in St. Petersburg for the Department of "Foreign Confessions" and paid its officials in this Subministry which had only been formed in order to suppress the Catholic Church and its interests. It was a purely governmental institution for the protection of state power and the rights of the Russian "Orthodox Church" vis-a-vis the "foreign confessions." The

Russian government made no effort to hide this fact in the years immediately prior to the World War. The meager salaries were paid by the state to the clergymen through the consistory.

19. The bishop's chancellery

The diocesan consistory dealt only with the mixed; that is, religious-civil and purely civil matters of the diocese. The purely religious matters were personally taken care of the ordinary. In order to do so, he made use of his personal chancellery which was located in

the bishop's residence. This chancellery was administered by the personal secretary of the diocesan bishop whom the bishop, independent of the civil authorities; that is the Ministry of the Interior, appointed. He did not even have to inform the ministry concerning the appointment or the name of the appointee. The bishop's secretary was, as the nature of the office demanded, always a clergyman who had to be a master of several languages. He received his salary from the bishop as the meager salary which the state had coughed up for him did not even equal the size of an average illegal worker before the World War. The secretary also had a helper who also was paid by the ordinary. By means of his personal chancellery which, including the ordinary, was called the actual curia, the diocesan bishop discharged the appointments and transfers of clergymen, the dispensations for marriage and other issues, the correspondence with the ministries, with the school administrators concerning the appointment of teachers of religion in the secondary schools, with the governors, with the boards of various educational institutions and with the church council members of Catholic congregations. Various admonishments were sent through his office to the entire list or part of the parishes concerning unseemly or unfair treatment of the priests or other curates of souls, the mailing of various decrees, the mailing of pastoral letters, the determination of salaries for the curates of souls, their vicars, their leaves of absence, the issuing of passports for the Ministry of the Interior of the empire, the preparation of "celebrets" (Translator's note: a celebret is a document which attests to a priest's good standing, in possession of his faculties and permission to be outside his own diocese) for clergy who journeyed to other dioceses or to foreign countries and letters of reference for clergymen etc. The daily routine in the chancellery was very simple, the style of writing correspondence of a religious as well as of a worldly nature was succinct and only that which was essential was clearly handled without any digressions and without any oriental propensity to detail.

Because of this, all questions were quickly settled. The diocesan correspondence with the Holy See and especially with Rome was outwardly difficult. According to paragraph

17, vol. XI, part I of the Russian state law, one could only correspond with the Holy See by means of the Ministry of the Interior. Since this correspondence was carried out in the Latin language, it had to always be prepared in two copies and correctly translated into Russian. In the ministry, the translation was compared with the Latin original to see if it was correct. Only after authorization had been given was the correspondence sent to the Russian ambassador at the Vatican. Just as everything in Russia was very slow, so this was especially the case here. One had to be very patient when one sent a request to the Holy See. As a rule, three months passed until a reply was received from the eternal city. It was not exceptional to have to wait for half a year! For this reason, very extensive powers were bestowed by the Holy See upon the bishops in Russia. On one occasion a bishop of Tyraspol asked the Holy See for the power to grant several dispensations. As a

reason, he referred to the difficulty of recourse to the Holy See, as the teachers of canon law quote them. That caused the ministry to become upset. Charusin, the head of the department, stuck to the bishop like a bur. He thought it referred to the ministry and contained a complaint against it. This was entirely unjustified. For the ordinary, this took a lot of effort, correspondence and explanations of canonical law which were found in all textbooks of canon law and these certainly could not have referred to the ministry. Only after a long delay, did the ministry send the petition to Rome. Perhaps one would not have sent it if the bishop had not refused to leave out the reason for the dispensation and to state another "less offensive" reason. With the situation being like this, no one will be surprised if, as a rule, the Catholic diocesan bishops carried on their correspondence with the Holy See by other means. Another time a bishop had petitioned the head vicar general of the Franciscan fathers (PP. Franciscans) for two of his ministers for a parish. He had forgotten to note that his letter had not been conveyed to the vicar general by means the Ministry of the Interior as was prescribed by paragraph 17 of Russian law. The vicar general, in a letter, petitioned the same Russian ministry of the interior for an entrance visa for the clergy by referring to the bishop's petition. Through this the ministry realized that the bishop had avoided paragraph 17 of the law. Without delay the ordinary was called to account for this. Without a doubt, it would have gone badly for him if he had not been well-acquainted with the Prime Minister at that time. Mr. Stolypin ordered that this unpopular issue be quelled.

20. Franz Xaverius Zottmann

If divine providence has elected a mortal for the implementation of its decisions then it often takes him under its special protection from his boyhood onward in order to enable and prepare him for his future calling. It seems as if providence did the same thing with

Franz Xaver Zottmann. As he was appointed to intervene in the history of the diocese of Tyraspol in a very special way, a special section must be dedicated to his life and his work in the history of this diocese.

He was born to respectable middle-class parents on June 27, 1826 in the little city of Ombau in Bavaria and Franz Xaverius displayed his special talents even as a little boy. His father, Joseph Anton, did not allow the talents of his son to be wasted. At first, he had him attend the parish school and then had him graduate from the High School/Junior College in Eichstaett and Neuburg on the Danube River. At a young age the active boy already showed a great inclination for the ministry. Nevertheless, divine providence had the growing student go on a long journey until it escorted him to the altar. Despite all that Franz Xaverius never lost his intention of becoming a servant at the altar of the Most High. For this reason he studied philology, philosophy and theology in Wuerzburg first,

then in Munich, and finally in Eichstaett. On the side he diligently carried out studies in order to learn many languages. He had a special gift for this. Besides the ancient languages of Greek and Latin he understood Hebrew, Modern Greek, French, Italian, English and Spanish so well that he could fluently explain things in almost all of them. If he had been able to predict that the Russian language would one day become very necessary for him, he would very certainly concentrated his entire energy on the study of that language.

In 1853 the Greek ambassador at the Russian Court journeyed via Munich to St. Petersburg. In the capital city of Bavaria, Mr. Zoraphos; that was the dignitary's name, looked for a tutor for his son. A professor at the University of Mtmich recommended the candidate of education Franz Xaverius Zottmann to the gentleman. Thus Zottmann, after he had taken his teacher's examination, went to St. Petersburg. There he became acquainted with the lives of the highest members of society. This life did not appeal to him whatsoever. Since he did not have much to do, he used his free time for various studies. Above all, he applied himself to the study of Russian. Franz Xaverius became a well-beloved guest among the Dominican fathers at St. Catherine Church. On Sundays and feast days he was never missing in church. By his pious life and his frequent reception of the holy sacrament, he provided an edifying example to the world of the educated, which even then had already become very liberal. Since the Greek ambassador had already resigned in 1854 from his posting because of old age and illness and Zottmann did not want to follow his invitation to travel along to Greece but wanted to get to know Russia better, Zottmann accepted the invitation of the banking firm of Jordan in Moscow. He then worked for two years as a teacher and tutor there. There he used the opportunity to take the state examination as a High School/College Teacher at the university. Although he had never given up his intention to become a priest, he wanted to be a member of a clerical order where he would function as a teacher for the public. Zottmann had already learned Russian quite well. When the German Jordan family liquidated its business in Moscow, Zottmann was supposed to return to Munich. When he was just about to say farewell to Russia, good friends pressured him with the suggestion that if he wanted to become a priest, he could also do this in Russia; recently a diocese for 200,000 German colonists had been established in South Russia. They told him that his activity as a priest would certainly be more beneficial here than in his homeland where one was not experiencing a shortage of priests. They also stated that he would certainly be eagerly received in the new diocese of Tyraspol, whose bishop resided in Saratov. Zottmann followed the advice of his acquaintances and decided to go to Saratov. A person such a he, who already had taken theological and philosophical studies, was received with open arms at the Tyraspol seminary for priests. That was in late summer 1859. Since he could provide the best of certificates of moral conduct he had already received lower orders in the same year. Following this, on December 19th, he became a sub-deacon, and on the Feast of St. Joseph in 1860 he became a deacon. On the following Feast of Pentecost, priestly orders were bestowed upon him. The newly ordained felt more than happy since he had now attained the station to which his whole yearning and striving had been directed and for which he had prepared for so long.

The aged head pastor of Tyraspol was very happy to have won such a laborer and such a well-educated worker for his diocese. For this reason it was very natural that the bishop esteemed him highly and came to cherish him. For this reason, he did not want to send Zottmann to a German village, as Zottmann wished. Moreover, he kept him in proximity. He was to become not just useful for one parish but for the entire· diocese. Perhaps the aged bishop, whose days were numbered, thought that he would have a dignified successor in Zottmann at some point in time. Zottmann received his first position as a vicar at the cathedral church. This position was a part of the ministry of the parish of Saratov. The first clergyman of the cathedral chapter, Vinzenz Snarski, a Pole, was given the duty of curate of souls. The appointment of a German cathedral cu.rate was eagerly welcomed by the German members of the parish. Everyone highly treasured him because of his beautiful German sermons and his learning. That which Franz Zottmann painfully regretted was a lack of knowledge of the Polish language. However, he was already at that age in which the learning of another language presents many difficulties. As well, his position at the cathedral church was temporary, as everyone could easily foresee. And in fact, after not quite eight months, his call away from his pastoral position already took place on February 14, 1861. This was after not quite eight months. He was appointed as inspector (vice-regent) and professor of the diocesan seminary. One could only congratulate the institution for its good fortune in getting such a prominent pedagogue and professor. Zottmann's entire course of development had made him especially qualified as an educator and pedagogue of useful members of human society. By nature, he also had received a fortunate gift. It was a natural need for him to be concerned for young people. He felt much at ease with them and was happy in their midst. At the seminary, he was completely consumed by the duties of his occupation. His studies were always carried out with great zeal. For this reason, his colleagues in office, the rector of the seminary Canon Szelwowicz, and especially the aged Bishop Ferdinand, entirely recognized his splendid achievements. Without a doubt, the head pastor of the diocese would have received Zottmann into the cathedral chapter if a position as canon had been vacant. At least, he appointed him as an honorary canon of the cathedral chapter of Tyraspol. This was on September 1, 1863. This letter of appointment, in which his good qualities and accomplishments were listed, deserves to be added here in its exact wording. It was written in the Latin language and, in German translation, reads in the following manner:

"In view of your excellent service in regard to our diocese of Tyraspol, specifically your intelligence and experience, your zeal in carrying out your duties, your learning and piety, as well as your corresponding way of life and morality, which give credence to your character as a priest and member of the ministry (spiritual estate), we appoint you as an honorary canon of our chapter with all the rights and privileges which are rightfully acknowledged to be a part of this honour.

Issued in Saratov on September 1, 1863

(Seal)+ Ferdinand Helanus, Bishop of Tyraspol

21. The reorganization of the Tyraspol seminary

The administration of the newly-founded bishopric of Tyraspol consisted of Polish and Lithuanian clergymen. The sole exception was the aged diocesan bishop who was a German. All of the other ministerial positions were filled with clergy of foreign origin. The foreign clergy did not understand the German language. They initially had to learn it from the members of the parish. This was, however, fraught with many problems. Only a few learned German well-enough so that they were able to preach the Word of God or give religious instruction. For this reason, the sermon was generally read from a book of sermons or from a hand-written manuscript. The pastoral care of the parishes, 80 % of which were German and the leadership of the diocese by clergy of other nationalities could obviously not affect a salutary development in regard to the religious cause. However, as long as the place where future clergy were trained was not entrusted into the hands of German spiritual leadership, one could hardly think of the education of German Catholic clergy. Pupils for the seminaries for boys and clergy needed to be recruited during the first decade, but these soon withdrew. During the first ten years of its existence, the seminary for priests only produced one single son of colonists. This was Johannes Schamne from the colony of Graf.

This unfortunate situation could not be kept hidden from the Russian government. It caused suspicion as to whether the conditions in the Tyraspol seminary were not at fault. Added to this was the Polish insurrection in the year 1863, which raised suspicions in the government. In so far as the Catholic Church was active among the Poles and Lithuanians, a great persecution broke out which affected Saratov. Aged Bishop Ferdinand had reason to fear for the dissolution of the bishopric. The government repeatedly asked him the question: "Since so many German sons of colonists withdrew after a short period of residence in the seminary; could there be any real hope in the near future as to the pastoral care of over 200,000 Germans by German priests? They also asked if the administration of the seminary and the consistory would get into German hands. At the time of the establishment of the diocese, the government had only been concerned for the Germans who, by far, were the great majority of the faithful and the government had certainly not intended to found a new Polish diocese in the middle of the empire."

At the time of the opening of the seminary, the bishop noted this abnormal situation. A German institution could only function in a progressive manner if it was governed by German directors. Three years later, he took the first steps in order to invite German professors from abroad for the seminary. It was only because of the influence of his Polish surroundings and because of his great age that he was not able to carry out his intentions.

The fear that the government would, after his death, suppress the diocese of Tyraspol again, caused the aged bishop's energies to slag. These energies were affected so badly by a negative reply from the government concerning his request for the construction of his own bishop's palace, that he stopped doing anything. The decision of the ministry had declared that one had to yet wait with its construction because it was still not certain that the bishop's residence would be fixed in Saratov. Also, "one could not as yet recognize whether the German part of the administration and pastoral ministry in the diocese would soon become more important and more influential." In this reply, there seemed to be a veiled implication that the state government was going to dissolve the diocese. If all of the signs were not false, then it seemed as if the worst was to come. The unfortunate Polish rebellion of 1863 actually did result in the dissolution of two Catholic dioceses. These were the ones in Kamenetz and Minsk, which were dissolved in 1868 (Translator's note: the diocese of Kamenetz was annexed by the diocese of Lutzk and Zhitomir on June 3, 1866 and the diocese of Minsk was administered by the archbishop of Mohilev after the death of its bishop in 1869). The diocesan bishops were sent into exile. The continuing existence of the bishopric of bishopric of Tyraspol was also questionable. It seemed as if a catastrophe was to be feared even more ever since three of the ordained professors at the seminary for priests did not appear, after the Polish rebellion of 1863, to be satisfactory in the view of the government officials. They were caught off guard at night by the secret police and taken away. They were set free again later on but it was just that they were never to return to their previous positions, nor to take over a similar position in another religious seminary.

In such an uncertain and dangerous time, the aged bishop sought a man, who by his mediation could save the seminary and the diocese. This man was already at hand. In 1869, the providence of God had led him from a great distance, from Bavaria, to Russia and to Saratov. This person was the then supervisor (vice-regent) of the seminary for priests, Professor Franz Xaverius Zottmann. Since 1861, he had been the only German professor at the seminary and had been a priest since 1860.

Supervisor Franz Xaverius Zottrnann advised the diocesan bishop that the if the existence of the bishopric and its religious institutions were to be saved and be secure, this could only be accomplished by an immediate reorganization of the diocesan administration and of the seminary for priests. He recognized the great difficulties which had to be overcome in doing this. Without considering these difficulties, he took over the mandate of his bishop to recruit German educators for the school in his old homeland: He himself was placed at the head of the institution by the bishop. Supervisor Franz Zottrnann was a man with strongly developed feelings of consideration for others and a sense of righteousness. He foresaw the kind of hard feelings the reorganization of the seminary would cause for the rector of the institution and for the rest of the professors. He continually blamed himself that he had accepted his ordinary's mandate without the condition of compensation for the Polish rector. Even in 1900, shortly before his death, he wrote a letter to a priest who was a friend in Bavaria concerning this. He wrote the following: "It was in and of itself nothing evil but, to the contrary, something good, advantageous and meritorious to obtain German priests and German teachers for the respective German parish schools for almost 200,000 German immigrants who found themselves in a foreign land in the greatest of pastoral need without regular sermons, without Christian instruction, without pastoral visitations of schools, with a lack of opportunities for confession etc. All will admit that this was the case. But one can only ponder why my position in society was affected so much in carrying out this task. I only want to implore the patience of your reverend sir to give a very short explanation of what took place. The destruction of my social position began with the removal of the Polish seminary rector (regent), whose position, I, according to the desire of the German diocesan bishop Ferdinand Kahn for the complete Germanization of the seminary in agreement with the government, was to replace. But the removal of the Polish rector did not cause any great irritation among the Poles. They also had to admit that the rector could benefit the seminary very little if only the removal was done in an honourable manner with full compensation. But this did not happen and unfortunately I was not without blame and to my great regret .... He was also elevated by a Polish bishop to become a prelate, but unfortunately only after half a year; which should have happened immediately and even before my induction as rector ... However, because I do not want to belong to that group of priests who only want to say "it is my fault" in the mass, I must

confess that at that time, when the Polish seminary rector was let go, a mistake was made that would be fatal for me. It did not suffice that I pointed this out to Bishop Kahn and the government. In all seriousness and frankness, it would have been necessary for me to explain to Bishop Kahn and the government that I only wanted to accept the task of reforming the seminary if the Polish rector would have been recompensed before with an equivalent position and would have received a gratification in currency of two thousand rubles and a medal of an order and not just a prelature after half of a year. Then the situation would have been regulated without offense and no one could have said anything against it."

These words give voice to a genuine sensitive ministerial feeling and love which spares one's fellow brother in the priesthood but also shows true humility which moved Zottmann to sacrifice a lot himself to his ordinary in the name of canonical obedience. His biographer, Alois Zottmann, gives this commentary to these words: "The existing conditions would have completely naturally and without anyone's fault developed into the direction which they now had reached. A change must have created bitter and painful feelings and perhaps strong counter-currents among many Polish priests who had left their home dioceses and who had sacrificed themselves and worn themselves out over and over again for the German colonists in order to learn their language. It is always hard to give up old privileges which one believed, were to be enjoyed with full authority even when they seemed to be so critical and for a good purpose. But Zottmann's entire personality and life had been such that he never avoided problems if he saw that the execution of a project was good and necessary."

If one did not, according to the wish of the supervisor Zottmann, deal with the removal of Rector Szelwowicz and hurt sensibilities or did not consider that which was right, then this was mostly to be blamed on the aged Bishop Ferdinand Helanus. His former occupation always seemed to pop up and envelop his actions. I.

1. Indeed, Bishop Helanus was not a soldier, but only an instructor of religion in a military college.

At the beginning of 1864, after long negotiations, the government's permission to invite professors from Germany crone into effect. Supervisor Franz Xaverius Zottmann was charged by his ordinary with the following power of authority:

"'Ferdinand Helanus Kahn, by the Mercy of God and by the Grace of the Apostolic See, Bishop of Tyraspol, Knight of High Orders:

As German priests are lacking for several positions in our diocese, we hereby commission, with the approval of the ministry of His Majesty, the Emperor of Russia, the honorary canon Franz Xaverius Zottmann, supervisor and professor of our seminary in Saratov, to take a trip to Germany and give him the authority to undertake steps to recruit German priests. The necessary instructions have been communicated to honourary canon Franz Xaverius Zottmann and we only note here that it is our most anxious desire that, with the help of God, he may be successful in winning pious men who are truly members of the priesthood. For this reason we allow ourselves to commend this issue in the interest of the Glory of God and of our Holy Catholic religion to the gracious cooperation of the respective reverend Lord Bishops."

Decreed in Saratov on June 7, 1864
(Seal)+ Ferdinand Helanus, bishop

Without delay, Professor Franz Zottmann started his journey to the beloved homeland which he had left eleven years ago. The trip was long and very difficult, especially through the wide Russian steppes because one still did not have many railroads in the czar's empire. After a joyful reunion with relatives in his parental home and a period of rest, he tackled the execution of his errand. Today Russia is less known in Western Europe than China. Only a few Western Europeans had the courage to penetrate further into this "barbaric" country. Because of this, apart from the lack of priests in Germany, there were only a few ministers who decided to go back to Saratov, to the east of Russia, with Professor Franz Zottmann. Nevertheless, his efforts were not without success. He won Dr. Michael Glossner and Willibald Zottmann for the seminary and Father Beda Sebald for ministry in the parish. As these three reverends ministered for a long time in their positions in the diocese and left important influences from their blessed activity behind, the history of the bishopric acknowledges them with some data so that they may be remembered.

Dr. Michael Glossner was born in 1837 in Neumarkt in the Upper Palatinate (Oberpfalz) in Germany. After he had graduated from the High School/Junior College in Eichstaett, he entered the seminary for clergy in the lycee which was located there and where he studied philosophy and theology. He was ordained as a priest in 1860, worked as a teacher of religion in the schools of his place of birth until the recruitment by supervisor Franz Xaverius Zottmann for the professorship at the seminary in Saratov. He taught philosophy and dogmatics there according to the Thomistic method (of St. Thomas Aquinas) and did so with great success. He wrote a dogmatics text consisting of two volumes and a little book on grace. In his dogmatics handbook, he used the lectures of his famous professor in Eichstaett, Dr. Ernst, as a foundation. When Pope Leo XIII celebrated his golden anniversary as a priest, Dr. Glossner wrote the splendid feastscript/ festschrift in the German language which made him known far outside the borders of Germany. Toward the end of his life he was a co-worker in producing the Yearbook for Philosophy and Speculative Theology (founded by Ernst Commer in 1886). Beyond this, he wrote various shorter philosophical treatises. He left Russia in 1877 after he had done very blessed work in the seminary from 1865 onward as the supervisor and professor and since 1872 as the rector and professor. In 1875, when Bishop Zottmann visited his homeland for the first time, Dr. Glossner administered the diocese. The Russian emperor bestowed the golden pectoral cross upon him and Order of St. Anne of the Third Class. After his return home, he continued to work for a while in his native diocese and then as vice-regent and professor at the seminary in Regensburg. His last move was to Munich. He died at an advanced age in Munich. Dr. Michael Glossner was a deep thinker, a diligent professor, a pious priest and a great admirer of St. Thomas Aquinas. His students never forgot him. All of them praised him a great deal.

Willibald Zottmann, a countryman of supervisor Franz Zottmann and namesake but not related to him, was the same age as Dr. Glossner. He was born in Stirn near Spalt in Bavaria. After concluded philosophical and theological studies in Eichstaett, where he translated various works in English and in French into German, he worked as a teacher of religion and teacher of the French language in Ingolstadt. From here he accompanied Glossner as a professor to Saratov. He taught moral theology, church law and church history very effectively and very aptly. He was especially respected because of his talent for oratory and his powerful voice. He returned back to Bavaria one year later than Dr. Glossner; that is in the summer of 1878. He also left his students with an indelible imprint of memories. In the year 1893, he died as a priest in his native diocese. After the departure of Dr. Glossner, he functioned for one year in the position of rector of the seminary. Both reverends were appointed by Bishop Franz Xaverius Zottmann as prebendaries/canons. When they withdrew from the diocese they gave up these honours.

The Capuchin Beda Sebald, who accompanied the above-named professors to Russia, stayed in the diocese the longest. He had received permission to remain outside of his order from bis superiors. He belonged to the religious house in Wemdingen. For many years he led the parish of Franzfeld in an exemplary manner. The people tell many peculiar stories about his life and work. In Kandel, where he led pastoral work for several years before his return home, Father Sebald built a large church which was one of the most beautiful in the bishopric of Tyraspol. A few years before his death and because of the call of the superiors of his order, he returned again to his Capucin monastery in Wern din gen in Bavaria. "How I thank my dear God," he wrote to his sister who had married in Russia, "that I can spend some time in my monastery before the end of my life in order to prepare for death."

Supervisor Zottmann had also recruited the longtime director of the High School/Junior College in Lohr on the Main River for the seminary. Because his father was not in agreement, nothing came of him going to Russia. In the same manner, many years later, the nephew and subsequent biographer of his uncle, Reverend Alois Zottmann could not decide if he should follow his uncle's invitation. Without question, this was caused by the fact that his uncle, who was already bishop of Tyraspol, continually expressed the desire to resign in order to withdraw to a monastery in a foreign country.

In October 1864, Supervisor Zottmann began the return journey to Russia together with the three aforementioned reverends. The trip went via St. Petersburg, which was the easiest way back then. Without a doubt, Zottmann intended to introduce the newly recruited professors to the ministry in order to quickly resolve various important issues in favour of the seminary. In St. Petersburg Zottmann and his companions for the first time learned of the sad news concerning the death of Bishop Kahn.

22. Suffragan Bishop Vinzenz Lipski, curate of the chapter

After the death of aged Bishop Ferdinand of Tyraspol, the cathedral chapter elected Suffragan Bishop Vinzenz Lipski as the curate of the chapter. The Tyraspol chapter had already informed the ministry and the archbishop of Mohilev, who resided in St. Petersburg, of this election. Because the Catholic bishops and administrators of the Catholic dioceses of Russia had to give an oath of allegiance before the minister before they began their period of service, the newly-elected cathedral curate had to appear in St. Petersburg for this purpose without regard to his advanced age. He was already 69 years old. The position of Zottmann and his companions became very awkward. With the death of the German shepherd of the diocese they had lost their main support. One could not hope for energetic support for the new issue of Germanizing the seminary by the new chapter curate because he was a Pole. Just as little, could one expect no support for this plan from the then archbishop of Mohilev. Only the Russian ministry was for the Gennanizing of the seminary. In view of this situation, Supervisor Zottmann, together with his three German clergy, had to await the arrival of the curate of the chapter for Tyraspol, Suffragan Bishop Lipski in St. Petersburg. The journey which Bishop Lipski made took place during an unfavourable time of the year. It was very long and difficult. Because of the advanced age of the bishop, they could only travel slowly. After the arrival of the new ordinary, the negotiations were initiated. It was just that the solution to various decisive questions hit upon big problems and became protracted. It was only in

February of 1865 that they came to a conclusion. Rector Szelwowicz was declared to be removed from his position as, by the way, had been decided by Bishop Ferdinand. However, this was without any compensation and must have been just as painful for him as it was damaging to Zottmann. J;3esides this, Zottmann's considerateness and sense of what was right and wrong could not be reconciled with this type of a removal from office. Supervisor Zottmann took his place as rector. Dr. Michael Glossner replaced Zottmann as the supervisor. Both were bestowed, at the same time together with Willibald Zottmann, with professorships at the seminary. Bishop Lipski resided in Odessa when the chapter in Saratov elected him as the administrator of the bishopric. After all the questions concerning the seminary were resolved, he returned to Saratov with both Zottmanns and Dr. Glossner. At the end of March all arrived safe and sound at the bishop's residence and were eagerly welcomed by all of the entire clergy and the faithful. Tyraspol rejoiced that it had a bishop once again. After the unfortunate Polish uprising, difficult years began for the Catholics of Russia. There were a considerable number of differences of opinion between the Apostolic See and the Russian government which were expanded even further by the suppression of the two Catholic bishoprics of Minsk and Kamenetz in the year 1868. Many bishops in Russia and in Poland had to go into exile. Tyraspol also remained orphaned for eight years. It was very fortunate that the chapter curate had received consecration as a bishop which empowered him to carry out all of the pontifical acts for the diocese.

Although the situation of the Catholic Church was one of oppression, one had still gone a step forward toward the extended goal of providing the German parishes with native German ministers. In the main, the seminary for priests was German. One could be secure in the fact that within a reasonable space in time, the German parishes would be supplied with German clergy. It was also the justifiable hope that with time, one would have a German diocesan curia.

Besides the German board directors and professors, the previous Polish and Lithuanian professors were also active; who as yet, had not been done away with by the Russian government. Somewhat later, that is under Bishop Franz Xaverius Zottmann, several Polish professors with a higher education were such as Klimaszewski and Szpakiewicz were added. These were fluent in German to the point where they could lecture in that language in various subjects. A friendly relationship soon developed between the Polish and the German professors. This is proven by a letter which was written by Supervisor Dr. Glossner. The genuine Catholic and clerical attitude was strong enough among the entire roster of professors that it superseded all national differences. The suffragan bishop and chapter curate, Vinzenz Lipski, soon understood the newly-created order. His good example certainly helped the most, in the amicable and peaceful relationship among the clergy at the bishop's see. If one had not recognized Suffragan Bishop Dr. Lipski as a Pole because of his accent, one could not have come to the conclusion that he was of Polish extraction by his relations with the German clergy and faithful of the diocese. He was fair to all of the nationalities in his far-flung diocese. When he started to administer the diocese of Tyraspol, he was already 70 years old. Despite his advanced age, he still travelled through the entire northern part of the bishopric, administered the Holy Sacrament of Confirmation to all, including the little children, since one could not, in light of the conditions in that era, know whether or not a bishop could soon again journey through the diocese. He even consecrated several churches such as the churches in Mariental and Katharinenstadt, which were the only churches in the colonies of the North which were built of stone. Bishop Lipski had shortly before travelled through the South of the diocese as the suffragan bishop in the name of the diocesan bishop. The faithful of the diocese continued to remember Bishop Lipski for a long time. Because of his short stature, he was called the "little bishop." As the time, during which his administration took place, was very stormy, he led the little ship of the diocese of Tyraspol with unusual intelligence and great skill through the raging waves of the era. He obtained the house in which the bishops lived as renters through buying it as his own property in which he now personally resided. In the year 1871 he sold it to the state as a permanent dwelling place for the bishops of Tyraspol. Governor Galkin-Vraskin had been engaged by the Ministry of the Interior for the closing of the agreement of purchase with Bishop Lipski; as can be seen by the bill of sale. The bill of sale, like many other important documents, together with the bishop's archive fell into the hands of the Bolsheviks, who probably destroyed it. The deal was closed with the lawyer Dybov of Saratov. The house cost 20,000 rubles. In the year 1865 it was enlarged more than the size of the original building and the state gave 20,000 rubles for this purpose, so that the entire lot together with the diocesan palace attained a value of 40,000 rubles. Today the same building has a value of at least 400,000 gold rubles. Since the funds for the purchase price were taken from the church fund in St. Petersburg, for this reason alone, the house together with the land lot are church possessions upon which the state cannot make any claims.

Suffragan Bishop Vizentius Lipski administered the diocese until August, 1872. After the appointment of the new bishop for the diocese, he moved to Odessa where to spend the rest of his days in a little house next to the Church of the Assumption which still stands today. He died there on December 11, 1875 and reached the age of 80. His earthly remains were interred in the vault of the Church of the Assumption of Mary in Odessa. The proceeds from his house were mostly used by the bishop for the support of priests who had been exiled after 1863 and for the poor. Over 6,000 rubles were bequeathed for the construction of the cathedral in Saratov. One prominent characteristic of the chapter curate was his generosity toward the poor and his concern for the

establishment of peace for which he made many, and not insignificant sacrifices.

23. The seminary for priests under German administration

By the appointment of German directors and professors, the seminary itself took on a German character. The seminary for boys moreover had only pupils from the German colonies. To be sure, the seminary for priests was attended almost completely by Polish and Lithuanian students (alumni), but there was a sure hope that from now on not all of the graduates of the seminary for boys (Translator's note: a High School/Junior College) would not turn their backs on the seminary for priests, but that some of them would enter the institution and dedicate themselves to the ministerial office. This hope was not false. Many prejudices against both of the institutions were taken away among the colonists by the seminary directors becoming German. The seminary began to have closer relationships with the German members of the diocese. During the first years, one already noted a certain growing number of pupils who wished to attend the preparatory school. Without question, the continuing expansion of the railway network helped this happen. Until then, it had been very limited in this big country. The German farmers in the south of the diocese could send their sons by train to Saratov via Moscow. Soon one noted a lack of space in the rented seminary building on Moscow Street. The diocesan administrator Lipski repeatedly applied to the ministry for the construction of a larger and more suitable building for both schools. Finally, ten years after the establishment of the seminary, on August 29, 1867, the institution, boarding school and teaching staff could move into the new, spacious building on the "Little Sergius Street" (Malo Sergejevskaya). Bishop Vinzentius Lipski had invited the most important officials of Saratov for the opening and dedication of the new school. With the governor at their head, they appeared in full strength for this celebration. On this occasion, the diocesan chapter curate held a nice speech in Russian which made a very good impression upon the civic officials who, until then, had considered the Poles to be the enemies of everything Russian and their language as well. This was even more so, as the Polish Head Shepherd spoke their language like a native-born Russian. Perhaps this public appearance in the Russian language was a contributing factor so that the seminary later never had to feel any pressure on the part of the state officials. This was even more tactful of the bishop, as he, with his superior Russian, to a certain degree, compensated for that which was lacking in the pronunciation of Rector Zottmann. The bishop personally held the act of consecration and, after the sacred ceremony, invited the officials, who had also attended with visible signs of devotion, to a good breakfast. The suffragan bishop, by his kind and friendly manner, had won the fondness of one of the offices with which one continually had contact and with which one desired and needed to live in love and in harmony.

The entire instruction in both institutions was given in the German language with the exception of Russian literature and history. These teachers were Russians and Poles. Instead of the Latin textbooks, German textbooks, with the exception of moral theology and liturgy, were used in the seminary for priests. This factor immeasurably promoted progress in regard to knowledge. Above all, Rector Zottmann had the vision of the seminary in Eichstaett to use as an example for his reforms and his directives. The latter institution served as an example for all religious institutions in Germany to emulate at the time when Zottmann studied there. During his visits to Saratov to his uncle the bishop, the biographer of the bishop who followed Lipski, his nephew, Father Alois Zottmann, would often frequent the Tyraspol seminary. He wrote of the impressions which the seminary made upon him. "During my visits to the seminary in Saratov and during the reading of various reports on it, I as a seminarian of Eichstaett who had risen up from the ranks, felt very much at home."

In his pastoral letter which the bishop directed to members of his diocese in the year 1882, the ordinary described how the institution had developed during his rectorship:

1. The diocesan seminary of Tyraspol consists of a seminary for clergy (a seminary for priests) and of a seminary for boys.
2. The subjects taught in the clerical seminary are the theological courses: dogmatics, moral theology, an introduction to the Bible, hermeneutics, Biblical exegesis, liturgics, homiletics, pastoral theology, canon law and church history. Apart from this, philosophy, Roman literature and Russian history, literature and the art of composition are taught.
3. In the seminary for boys the subjects being taught are: religion, Latin, Russian, German and French languages, mathematics, world history, the natural sciences (physics, geography and cosmography) (Translator's note: the science which deals with the whole order of nature), calligraphy and church hymnody. Also, there are always several pupils who in also in addition learn to play musical instruments. In addition to this, on Sundays and festivals, the students and pupils, as well as the choir, assist in the celebratory worship services in the cathedral church. The bestowal of lower orders to the students always takes place during the third year of the theological course of study. The bestowal of the higher orders takes place during the fourth year of the theological course.

    Our seminary also has two free places for students at the religious academy in St. Petersburg, in which distinguished students from all the Catholic bishoprics in Russia and in Poland, after the completion of their studies in diocesan seminaries, continue their studies for another four years, and are able to attain a higher theological education.

4. The seminary for clergy has 18, and the seminary for boys has 25 free places. There are a total of 43 free places. Besides the 43 free pupils/students, according to available rooms, another 30 pupils can be accepted who pay their own fees (self-payers/independent students).
5. The entire annual income of the religious seminary for the free pupils/students

who are being educated is 15,000 rubles (about 30,000 marks). In this sum, 1,875 rubles are included which the German colonists pay on an annual basis for the support of 25 pupils/students; 12 from the northern and 13 from the southern colonies.

6. Since an average of four free pupils/students finish the seminary every year and, besides this, once in a while free pupils/students from the seminary for boys withdraw, either because of a continuing state of poor health or because of lack of ability or because of a lack of inclination to enter into a religious profession, on average six free spots can be granted every year. In doing so, one is always very careful to make sure that there are12 incumbents of free spots in the seminary for boys from the northern and 13 from the southern colonies (highlanders and lowlanders or northerners and southerners).

Although poverty, in and of itself, is not yet a reason for getting a free place, poor boys are preferred, especially orphans, if they, in terms of spiritual gifts, diligence and progress, fit into the institution.

7. The school fees and fees for room and board come to 150 rubles for the whole year (about 300 marks).

8. The seminary administration is strictly concerned about the conscientious appropriation of the available means so that the pupils/students have sufficient and nutritious meals as well as clean beds and receive appropriate clothing. For the close supervision of the pupils, students from the upper classes are appointed, even though the seminary administration itself, according to its ability, strives to supervise everything personally so that propriety, order and cleanliness reign everywhere. The pupils have common daily morning and evening prayer in the seminary chapel where (God be praised!) the most Holy Sacrament of the Altar is kept. Every day they attend the Holy Mass in the seminary chapel and attend the celebratory worship services in the cathedral church on Sundays and on festival days. At the beginning of each school year, they have three full days of spiritual exercises in order to prepare for classes and so they can learn to concentrate more easily.

9. Because of the law concerning compulsory military service, a favourable rule has been set up for Roman Catholic seminarians so that those students who have reached the age of compulsory military service (21 years) can continue their studies at the seminary without any interruption until they have ended their 24th year of life and, if they have then already received holy orders as a sub-deacon, as is almost always the case, they are then completely freed from military service.

So far the religious seminary in Tyraspol has produced 49 priests of German heritage, 17 priests of Polish heritage and two of Georgian heritage, which makes a total of 68 priests.

The discipline which Rector Zottmann carried out was not too strict but also not too lax. As a longtime educator he had learned to appreciate the golden middle of the road method. He led his students on this road. Himself being of honest and upright character, he sought to raise upright and independent personalities. In this the seminary for boys was a fertile field of labour. In doing so he always attempted to be a shining example to the students in his genuine sacerdotal way of behaviour. He was a thorough teacher for his students and they always spoke of him with great esteem. Since he himself was a great admirer of the Mother of God and showed great loyalty toward the Holy Father, his students learned these virtues from him according to the Latin proverb: "'verba movent exempla trahunt/words move, examples draw." As a professor, Rector Zottmann had high expectations of his students. But all confessed unanimously that one learned a lot from him, that excellent order held sway in the institution and, at the same time, many were drawn to the priesthood. During Zottmann's rectorship, both schools were, without a doubt, at their highest level in terms of knowledge. It was their golden age.

Zottmann laid heavy emphasis on the ascetic education of those who were entrusted to his care. Modesty and mortification (Translator's note: of the flesh) were very prominent. His biographer reports the following about his later life: "When not too long ago, a request was directed to him that he might procure the acceptance into the seminary in Saratov for a Bavarian student, someone among his associates guessed that the applicant might be that student who shortly before had found fault with and had disparaged the conditions in his seminary in a liberal newspaper. He gave the reply to the request by saying that at his advanced age and his poor health he could not deal with the issue; however noted in a letter to an acquaintance concerning the issue that if this student was truly the fault-finder, then he could only wish that same person would come to Russia "for the mortification of his flesh and to learn modesty."

If a man of providence such as Franz Xaverius Zottmann is promoted to such an influential post, as that of the rector of a seminary for boys and a seminary for priests, then the institution receives direction, in a spirit which is closely related to his spirit. This was also the case with the school of Tyraspol. It inherited much from the spirit of its first German rector. His spirit did not only affect the schools at the time of his rectorship, but also long after his departure during 18 years as bishop. His spirit held sway for many years after he had laid down his shepherd's staff and had withdrawn into solitude. Zottmann's activity was of foundational and decisive importance for the school; for the education and training of the clergy of Tyraspol. Just as the seminary for the priests of a diocese can be called the heart of a diocese, the influence of the first German rector was the most important and reached out to the entire diocese under St. Clement its patron saint. This is rightly and nicely ascertained by Zottmanns biographer.

24. Franz Xaverius Zottmann, 1.

What would have become of the newly-established diocese of Tyraspol if Franz Xaverius Zottmann had not come to Russia and to Saratov and had not entered the priesthood there? This question must be asked by everyone who records the history of the diocese. It is only when this question is answered properly that Zottmann's significance for the religious life of the Catholics in South Russia can be viewed from the proper perspective. To be sure, providence has innumerable ways at hand in which to achieve its designs. God could have sent another German priest as a mighty man. None the less, God's providence tends not to hinder things developing naturally. Meanwhile God's providence connects with the natural pattern of life and undergirds it. However, in the history of the diocese of Tyraspol everyone sees very clearly how God's providence led Franz Zottmann during his early life so that providence would serve in the deliverance of the seminary of Tyraspol and of the diocese. Aided by wise providence, Zottmann's early life molded him in such a way that it formed the natural foundation upon which providence continued to work.

Not quite eight years passed before Tyraspol received a new Head Shepherd. The diocese was orphaned for about eight years. According to human judgment, this seemed to be a misfortune for the bishopric. Since God had selected Zottmann as the shepherd of the bishopric, this orphaned state of the bishop's see was anything but that for the diocese. Franz Zottmann had just been the head of the seminary for priests in Saratov since 1865. He had transformed it according to the model of the seminary in Eichstaett and had given it a German character. Thus everything in it was new novel and had

1. Great men often go their own way and it is not exceptional that they are poorly understood by their neighbours and considered to be odd people. Franz Zottmann was also referred to by many as being an odd person. To be sure, there was much that was

exceptional in his character from the time of his earliest youth. One noted the differences in the characteristics which he brought along during the time when he was bishop. His outward appearance and his long hair, according to the custom of the Volga farmers, were especially striking. He did not adopt this from the members of the diocese later on in life, but already wore his hair long as a student. His clothing was somewhat shabby and this was often noted. His way of walking was also notable. It may have been the result of his great nearsightedness. At first glance, he was a man who did not show enough concern for outward appearances. But he had not attempted to be outwardly careless concerning his clothing and his comportment. This was completely natural to him. For this reason, there was something original which flowed out of a nature which had formed him as an individual. He had a great preference for the colour red. As with the Russians, red and beautiful were words which had the same meaning.

not, as yet, made an impression that was deep enough in the lives of the clergy and of the people. Above all, everything had to be solidified. This needed a number of years to be effected. The most suitable man for this was the founder of the new order. Accordingly, Zottmann could not be separated so quickly from that which he had created. The seminary would have been freed from his direct influence if he had been the bishop of Tyraspol. In the meantime, the little ship of a diocese could be safely steered over the waves of these volatile times by the suffragan bishop and Cathedral Curate Lipski. Thus the year 1872 approached. Lipski had piloted the steering wheel of the bishopric for seven entire years and not without great skill. Nevertheless, he had become 77 years old and the weaknesses and frailties of old age were more and more evident. It was time for another worker to replace him at the rudder. For this purpose God had selected Franz Xaverius who, in the meantime, had gotten to know the colonists and their sons well. Zottmann was qualified for this job. He had a solid and extensive knowledge, was rich in experiences and the knowledge of human nature. Besides this, he was in his 46th year of life. To be sure, he sought to distance himself from the honour and the heavy burden of a position as bishop in that he even nominated Suffragan Bishop Lipski to the government. Meanwhile the Ministry of the Interior had nominated *only* Zottmann to the papal curia News of Zottmann's blessed work had also reached the Holy See. Even as a layman in St. Petersburg, he had attracted the special attention of the dignitaries of the clergy; of Archbishop Holowinsld and his successor. The deep piety, which the tutor of the Greek ambassador exemplified, had never been noted in St. Petersburg among adult and well-educated young men. Letters of recommendation from the religious leaders for the candidate for bishop nominated by the government were secretly received in the eternal city. Because of this and after short negotiations, Franz Xaverius Zottmann was already pre-consecrated as the bishop of Tyraspol on March 2nd.

As the Catholic bishops in Russia had to swear their oath of allegiance to the Czar before being installed in their offices they had to appear in St. Petersburg for this purpose. It was there where the festive consecration of the appointed chief pastor always took place. The government of the czar was itself interested in having the consecrations of bishops take place in the residential city of the czar and not, as canon law dictates, in the respective cathedral churches of the bishoprics. In this way the state government of Russia wanted to imitate the custom of the Eastern Latin/Roman Church according to which the bishops subject to the patriarchate of Constantinople (Istanbul) would always be consecrated in the "emperor's city." The practice was supposed to strengthen the people in the belief that they received the leaders of dioceses through the emperor's rule. As the Holy See tolerated this practice, the newly-appointed bishop of Tyraspol was also consecrated on June 11, 1872 in St. Petersburg in St. Catherine's Church. The festive consecration was carried out by the Bishop of Kamenetz, Antonius Fialkowski, who had, one year previously, been called from exile and elevated to the see of the archbishop of Mohilev. He was assisted by the bishop of Lublin, Baranowski, and the suffragan bishop of Saratov, Vinzentius Lipsld. The consecrator and now archbishop of Mohilev, to whose church province the bishopric of Tyraspol belonged, had been exiled from 1868 to 1871 to Simferopol, a city within the diocese of Tyraspol. In his will he had bequeathed the sizable sum of 7,000 rubles to the poor little church in his place of exile. When the Skopinski Bank crashed, the donation, apart from 2,000 rubles, was lost.

The journey to Saratov was begun soon after the consecration of the bishop. It could be done by train, as the railway system had already been extended to Saratov. The first Sunday after the arrival of the new pastor of the diocese, he celebrated his first pontifical mass. It was attended by members of the diocese who had assembled from near and far. The little wooden House of God could, by far, not hold them all. Many had to attend the worship service by standing on the street near the church. At this point in time, not having a large, more worthy House of God for the bishop's city became even more evident. The Polish members of the church in Saratov were also present in large numbers at the celebration. After transferring the administration of the bishopric from the aged episcopal chapter curate, the new diocesan bishop first held a shorter speech in beautiful Latin and after that a sermon in Russian to the faithful who were assembled. The bishop had obviously not counted on the fact that, until that point in time, no one had ever heard a sermon in the official language. Thus this was an unwelcome, unexpected novelty. This was especially true for the Poles who, because of political, national and other reasons rejected everything that was Russian. The Poles had also not forgotten the way in which the previous rector, Szelwowicz, had been removed from his position. Many considered his successor in the position, Franz Xaverius Zottmann, to be the cause of the removal. As a matter of fact, all of the conditions were unfavourable toward Zottmann.

Evil tongues attempted to throw suspicion on the German rector within the rank and file of Polish society. One did not understand Zottmann's noble concerns well enough. Zottmann had already suffered a lot because of this slander when he was the rector of the seminary for priests. He was not to be spared the fact that his elevation to the diocesan see of Tyraspol would give his enemies cause to make him even more unpopular in Polish social circles. There were many attempts to even make light of that which he said in his inaugural speech. His deficient pronunciation of Russian would have added to this. In Polish circles, one stated that the German bishop in Saratov, among other things, had said in his Russian inaugural speech: "We are apes." The fable was spread far beyond the borders of Russia proper. Every person who knows the Russian language knows that the bishop said: "We are all under an obligation." The final word in the sentence is "obyasany" in Russian, and the accent is laid on the first a. If you place the accent on the second a, then the stress is wrong and the word itself does not mean apes at all and this is what the leading pastor of the diocese is supposed to have stated. The speaker must have said "obyasany" instead of obesyany. Many clearheaded Poles and all of the German audience, who understood Russian perfectly, did not hear this in the speech. The testimony given by the Germans is even more unclear because the German members of the diocese were also unhappy because the speech was not held in the German language, as the bishop was not able to speak Polish. The dissension, which the first sermon given by the new diocesan bishop created among the faithful must have cause him heartache, and even more so because one made fun of it. The Head Shepherd comforted himself with the fact that the lot of the disciple is not better than that of his divine master. "The servant is not greater than his master. If they persecuted me, they will also ·persecute you." (John 15:20).

Bishop Franz Xaverius had too much trust in God, in order to let himself to be discouraged by trivial criticism and fault-finding. He began to lead with his shepherd's staff; using the same energy with which he, seven years previous, had begun and completed the reform of the seminary for priests. On July 2, 1872 already, he sent the first blessing with his pastoral letter to the flock which had been entrusted in his care. In this letter, he confesses his weakness and unworthiness for such a high office as that of a bishop; a duty which is too heavy even for the backs of angels. The office of bishop seemed to be especially burdensome and filled with responsibility during such a difficult time and because of disorderly and unregulated conditions such as held sway in the diocese of Tyraspol until that point in time. With the Apostle to the Gentiles

(Translator's note: literally: "to the nations or peoples"), he confesses that: "I am afraid." But he then comforts himself again together with the same apostle: "But I do not despair." (II Corinthians 4:18). He promises, with the help of God, to fulfill his episcopal duties toward those entrusted to his care conscientiously and according to his capabilities. The promise of the Lord encouraged him by that which Matthew wrote in chapter 28: "And know that I am with you always; yes, to the end of time." His period of service for 18 years proved that he remained faithful to his promise until he laid down his shepherd's staff because of illness and a lack of strength.

25. Bishop Zottmann's concern for a good ministerium

If the diocesan bishop is the head of the diocese, one can refer to the diocesan seminary as being its heart. Just as a human being must take care that his heart, this chief organ of the human body normally and continuously keeps beating, so also the diocesan bishop must direct his primary and chief concern toward his diocesan seminary. The head pastor of the bishopric obtains his helpers from the seminary and they are the workers in the vineyard of the Lord. What can even the smartest, most zealous missionary bishop do without a well-educated and pious, zealous and mission-minded clergy, all of whom need to be concerned for souls? He can only do a little; very little! If religious-moral unruliness holds sway in a bishopric, then one will, above all, have to look for the main fault among the clergy because they will not be setting the example in their high calling which they need to do. For this reason every intelligent and mission-minded bishop diocesan shepherd will seek to have his seminary for priests prominent in a way which corresponds to its noble purpose. He will keep a watchful eye that proper order rules in it, coupled with ecclesiastical-religious discipline which will keep going upon the golden middle of the road in regard to virtue and piety. He will keep watch so that the virtues 9f modesty, obedience, humility and self-control, of a willingness to make sacrifices and Christian mortification of the flesh, will be especially practiced. For this reason he will let himself be informed by the directors of the institution concerning the spirit which rules from his own point of view. However, he will also endeavour to get to know the seminary for priests to grow by his own observation. For this reason he will often, and especially on festive occasions look in on his seminary. Bishop Franz Xaverius was able to fulfill these requirements according to the best of his powers. If he was at home, he attended the opening of the new school year. Upon this occasion, he gave an impressive, very practical speech every time to the students. In the same manner, he ended the school year by taking part in the festive act, distributed allotted gifts to excellent students, praised the good students and reprimanded those who either did not behave properly or who allowed themselves to become lazy. He dealt with everyone according to what he deserved. He was often a guest at theatre performances at Christmastide and in May and went along on excursions as a guest of the institution. At the receptions at the festivals of Christmas, Easter and Saints' Days, Zottmann always delivered speeches to the students in a fatherly tone of voice. For most of the students, these talks were remembered for a long time and their salutary powers did not miss their mark. The diocesan festive days were always distinguished events and had an excellent noon meal with beer, for which the Head Shepherd had donated the money. His entire relationship with the students and pupils of the seminary was that of a good father to his children. For this reason, the latter always remained attached to their diocesan shepherd in child-like love and devotion.

Bishop Franz also took care of getting good instructors for the institution. Because of his appointment as the bishop of the bishopric, the institution had lost an able and thorough teacher. This position had to be filled anew. Supervisor Glossner, who had been in this position until that point in time, was appointed as the rector and he determined that Professor Willibald Zottmann, customarily referred to as "the little Zottmann," would be the supervisor. Both gentlemen were diligent professors. In terms of training the students, they continued to work according to Zottmann's spirit. In order to complete the staff of teachers at the school, Zottmann called two other reverends with a higher education. They were the subsequent private prelate of his Papal Holiness, Klimaszewski and a minister of the diocese of Kulm by the name of Glass. Both were fluent in the German language to the point where they could lecture in that language. I. These gentlemen taught at the seminary for such a long time and until the seminary itself produced solid educated teachers. One of these was Father Wolf who, immediately after finishing his studies, was employed as a professor at the seminary.

The seminary progressed more and more under the rectorship of Dr. Glossner. He accomplished first-rate work in terms of scholarship. It is sufficient that we remember Father Matery, Professor Wolf, Anton Zerr; the subsequent bishop of Tyraspol, the diligent pulpit speaker Father Mitzig and Father Altmeier. Dr Michael Glossner was a man prone to risks and his profound lectures on dogmatics filled his audience not only with amazement, but everyone looked up to this tall, lean, ascetic figure. His appearance was always reflective and the first time one met him, it betrayed the profound scholar. He followed the scholastic method of lecturing. He was one of the first German pioneers who used the methods of St. Thomas. His dogmatic and philosophical lectures were very much like those of Aquinas. He also won his students as advocates of this great master of high scholastic philosophy. Many a famous university in Europe would have been proud to have such a superior professor. He remained unforgettable to all of his students. He is the author of a dogmatics text in two volumes which was actually adapted to his audience. It was only a fine reference book in the hands of its author. Because of the all too great distance of the author from the place where it was printed, it suffers as a result

    1. Robert Glass was a German.

of too many corrections of printing errors and was published in a second edition. A second little work from the pen of Dr. Glossner is the teaching concerning grace which can be counted among the best short treatises concerning this subject.

Dr. Glossner was a very talented professor but on the other hand, he was also little-suited for practical things, as is the rule with well-educated minds. Because of this, during his rectorship many larger financial deficits cropped up in the seminary. As a conscientious priest, he was too inexperienced in the affairs of this world. He could not believe that people show the good side of their character in order to hide their inner craftiness and deceit. Thus, he could not believe that the German business manager of the seminary would practice deceit in the management of its affairs. This infamous seminary business manager slipped a significant part of the funds, especially those which had been set for the meals served in the institution into his own pockets. In doing so, the cunning administrator was always careful that the income and expenses noted in the financial record books always harmonized with each other. His eleventh and most important "commandment" seemed to be the one that was called: "Do not allow yourself to be caught." Because of the theft and deceit which the German Russian business manager of the institution practiced, the seminary got into trouble. The meals became so bad that the students became very weak and many had to leave the institution with the initial symptoms of tuberculosis or another illness. There was also a lack of proper hygiene in the institution. Above all things, there was no attempt to provide for good air in the rooms. As the institution did not even have a water closet (restroom) and it would have been easy to install, as the city had excellent water works installed at the beginning of the 1870s, all of the rooms in the seminary had the smell of defiled air coming from the lavatories which had been poorly placed and had to undermine the health of the boys and also of the adults. The dissatisfaction which the students had concerning the food and with the household conditions essential for life steadily grew. In the meantime, the thievery of the manager, whose name was Steinberg, became so brazen that even the rector could no longer ignore them. One undertook steps in order to send the man packing.1.

    1. For this, one had to have the assent of the government because he had been hired by it.

Meanwhile, the economic situation of the institution had been completely ruined because of the long-term indulgence of the administrator, so that the diocesan bishop had to repeatedly turn to the members of the diocese for benevolence for the seminary_. The economic mistakes and awkwardness of Rector Dr. Glossner was one of the main reasons that in the summer of 1877, he made an attempt to apply for a release from his position. At the same time he also gave up his position as canon as he intended to return to his homeland in Bavaria. With a heavy heart, Bishop Franz Xaverius dismissed him, as one foresaw that the Russian government would, in the near future, require German professors to become Russian subjects. But he did not want to become a Russian citizen. In light of the great services which he rendered to the diocese of Tyraspol and to the seminary, the diocesan bishop bestowed upon him the office of honourary canon. Besides this, the Russian government, upon the occasion of the presentation given to him by the bishop, had brought about the bestowal of the Golden Pectoral Cross to him from the czar and bestowed the Order of St. Anne of the Third Class upon him.

After Dr. Michael Glossner's departure, the diocesan bishop promoted Professor Willibald Zottmann, called "little Zottmann,"1. to be the rector of the seminary. He was also an excellent, scholarly teacher, although he was less gifted than Dr. Glossner. However, the students profited a lot from his lectures. He taught moral theology and Canon Law, and gave instruction in mathematics in the higher grades of the seminary for boys. He had the unusual gift of making his lectures very appealing and of keeping his audience alert. If Dr. Glossner seemed to be almost only intellectual, then God granted this priest a deeply sensitive heart. Wherever he appeared in a parish at a special festival as a preacher he simply captivated his entire audience. He combined deep emotion in his sermons with a powerful voice that was the voice of a native-born pulpit orator. The people could never become tired of that which he preached. Even today the old colonists who heard this little, and yet great man recount parts of his sermons filled with the Spirit of God and remember him with awe and love.

It was just that the rectorship of Willibald Zottmann only lasted for one year. After the departure of Dr. Glossner, he was strongly inclined to return to his homeland. For the same reasons as Dr. Glossner, he resigned from his position and from his standing as a canon which had been bestowed upon him several years previously by Bishop Zottmann. With him, the last German professor at the seminary bad withdrawn. In the summer of 1878 the little man, left Saratov and Russia forever. This was mournfully regretted by all and he left grateful memories behind with the students and the people of the north where he was known. While Dr. Glossner was active scholastically in his homeland, Willibald Zottmann took over a parish in his home diocese of Eichstaett.

1. In comparison to Bishop Zottmann who was a big man.

26. The Tyraspol seminary under Rector Boos

Without a doubt, the departure of both clerical compatriots, of Dr. Glossner and Willibald Zottmann, must have caused the diocesan bishop to be saddened. On the one hand, he had lost both of his strongest supporters at the seminary and on the other hand he lost his brethren of the clergy from his homeland. The old Capuchin, Father Sebald, was the only one who continued to persevere with hint He was far away from the bishop's see, in the colony of Franzfeld in Odess and active in pastoral ministry there. For about one year, the vacant position of supervisor at the seminary waited to be filled. Bishop Zottmann's choice fell upon the minister of Mariental, Johannes Burgardt, who had worked during almost the entire duration of his previous ministry in the colony of Landau. Unfortunately, this appointment proved to be less than fortunate. To be sure, Burgardt was a good pastor, but not a good pedagogue, Among other things, he did teach to the satisfaction of his students and had a knack for this as he came from the school of the three foreigners: Franz and Willibald Zottmann and Dr. Glossner. In educating and in disciplining he followed great strictness and administered strong corporal punishment for boyish pranks done without any evil intentions. Thus he often took away the main meal which was served at noon and even had some whipped by rough and ignorant servants with birch rods. The entire seminary suffered under the tyranny of this man. Some students publicly cited the words of Schiller (Translator's note: a German poet): "Wherever barbarous powers rule senselessly, no educated person can be formed," and they demonstrated in front of the supervisor. That it did not come to an open revolt among the pupils against such an uncivilized and inconsiderate rule of the supervisor is only thanks to the pacifying influence of the rector, Willibald Zottmann. Nevertheless, after his departure, during the second year of Burghardt's supervision, the general dissatisfaction of the students for the ministry and pupils in the seminary for boys exploded. In a show of this, many students and pupils withdrew from the institution. · Unfortunately, no one had the courage to bring the situation before the bishop and to request relief. One also did not want to complain to the new rector as he had just been newly appointed and one knew him too little in order to establish greater trust in him. And yet, one hoped that Burghardt would soon come to a stop with his tyrannical method of education. One was not wrong in this hope, as the sequel to the story shows.

After the departure of the Rector Willibald Zottmann in the summer of 1878, the seminary received a new head director in the person of Canon Alexander Boos who had just been elected one year previously as the representative of the diocese to be a member of the Catholic Religious Committee in St. Petersburg. He was born in the year 1842 in the colony of Obermonjou on the Volga. In the year 1854, when the dean of Katharinenstadt (Translator's note: today this is the city of Marx), Andrescheykovitch inspected the schools in his deanery, a boy in the school in Obermonjou made an especially good impression upon him by his responses, his development and his modest character. I.

> 1. The information concerning the boy, A. Boos, originates from a letter of the aged Father Andrescheykovitch addressed to the author of this history.

Back then, that is since the establishment of the seminary, the boys among the German colonists had to be recruited for the seminary. The dean took care of the bright boy and sent him to the central school in Katharinenstadt. In the meantime, the seminary in Saratov was opened. The lad, Alexander Boos, who in the meantime had made good progress in the county school, was one of the first colonist's sons who were accepted into the diocesan institution. There he also showed special talent, great diligence and good, moral behaviour. Having been ordained a priest by Bishop Vizentius Lipski in 1865, thereupon he was then soon appointed to be the administrator of the Church of the Assumption in Tblisi in the Caucasus. Back then, Saratov, Odessa and Tblisi were already the most important cities in the diocese. Unfortunately, there were only very few German-speaking Catholics in the capital city of the Caucasus. The new administrator had a parish there which was composed of Poles and Georgians. Despite that, he soon won the love and devotion of the members of his parish. For this reason, the members of the parish could, after 12 years of exemplary work, only separate themselves from their pastor with great difficulty. It hardly needs to be mentioned that leaving his beloved congregation was difficult for the curate of souls of the parish, who was then 35 years of age. However, it was the diocesan shepherd who called him to a new posting. His desires and natural feelings had to be sacrificed. But his position in the college in St. Petersburg was of short duration. After only a year, the head of the Department for "Foreign Confessions" declared that his diocesan bishop had appointed him to be the rector of the seminary for priests in Saratov. For him, this was an unexpected bolt of lightning from above as he had counted on the idea of remaining in St. Petersburg for a longer period of time.

The position of a rector at the seminary for priests was not a position which was to be envied. This was because the great lack of teachers for seminarians meant that a professorship, as well as a rectorship awaited him. To be sure, he always endeavoured to improve and perfect his knowledge. He always strove to remain up-to-date in the scholarly subjects which he had once studied at the seminary. It was just that the demands of the seminary students after a professor such as Dr. Michael Glossner would have been extreme and he would have not felt that he could not live up to them. What especially caused him to anxiously hesitate in taking over the rectorship were the pale faces of the students and pupils of the seminary. He had found out with what kind of economic woe the institution had to deal with. This was especially the case during the most recent years. He knew several students who had to end their studies because of ill health. He had also made the acquaintance of young graduates who, because of the insufficient meals and poor quality of life withdrew from the school because of being in the early stages of pulmonary tuberculosis. With frankness he declared before the head of the department that: "I cannot decide to take over such a position of responsibility before more tolerable economic and sanitary conditions for the school and its boarders have been satisfactorily provided for." As the seminary for priests was endowed and funded by the Russian state, it was clear that it was a governmental duty to take care of the improvement of the economic situation of the institution. The state had to remove the reasons which Canon Boos gave for not taking over the position for which he was intended. He told the representative of the government that he wanted to ask the reverend bishop to abandon his plan of appointing him as the director of the seminary. Since the department head saw that he was dealing with a man who so very much advocated for the welfare of the seminary for priests and the youth that were studying, he was even more convinced that Canon Boos should just accept the position. He now tried to personally convince him. When that did not help, he promised that he himself would very soon come to Saratov and examine the economic situation and poor standard of living in the seminary for priests and if need be make it his business to raises the standards of the conditions essential for life in the institution by means of a considerable cash grant. This worked. Canon Boos agreed to take over the rectorship. He was also immediately confirmed in the position by the minister of the interior. To be sure, according to Russian law, the diocesan bishop could appoint the directors of the seminary, but the appointment had to be ratified and confirmed by the minister of the interior. This type of appointment for the professors of religion of the seminary for priests also had to be kept by the bishop. As a rule, in the latter case, the bishops of Tyraspol did not subject themselves to the respective paragraph of the law. Fortunately, the ministry was also not narrow-minded in regard to this matter and did not demand that this paragraph in the law be kept by the bishops of Tyraspol. The bishops of Poland and Lithuania, in a similar situation, would not have been able to ignore state law without being punished.

In fact, the head of the Department for "Foreign Confessions," Massolov/Massoloff, visited the seminary during the first year of Canon Alexander Boos' rectorship, became convinced of its economic plight and raised the cash grant for the institution by several thousand rubles annually. Since the second position of suffragan in the bishopric presumably would never be filled, the ministry allowed that salary in the sum of 2,000 rubles annually to be granted to the seminary for priests. Above all, thanks to the energetic efforts of the seminary rector, Alexander Boos, the huge economic plight of the institution was solved.

In other words, the new rector of the seminary had already been meritorious even before he took over its leadership. At the start of the work in his position, one realized that this was a man, who managed the school, who was very familiar with conditions in Russia. One year ago already, that business manager of the seminary of whom we wrote above, had been replaced by an honest and conscientious man. Under the head leadership of the rector, the economic situation began to ameliorate. It is not something great to do something with many resources but he is great who accomplishes a great thing with few resources. That must be stated concerning Rector Alexander Boos. If one made a comparison between the economic achievements of Catholic religious institutions as; for example, the boarding schools with the same institutions which are led by average citizens or by state authorities, everyone would be amazed about the fact that the former accomplish the same goals with half of the funds if not more than those who receive generous grants. The Russian middle schools such as the High School/Junior College or the secondary school for modern subjects, sciences and Latin etc. receive a yearly subsidy of 20 to 30 thousand gold rubles, collect about 100 to 120 gold rubles as a fee from their pupils, had no boarding facilities in which 100 to 200 students received complete care, room and board and yet did not have any savings which could be seen at the end of the school year. During the first years of Canon Boos' rectorship, our Catholic institution in Saratov had one hundred students. It received annual funding of about 15,000 rubles from the state and from the colonists. The students, in so far as they did not receive stipends, at the beginning only paid 120 and in the later years 150 rubles for room and board and school fees. However, there were 43 students who received stipends who did not pay one single kopeck. Accordingly, the income of the institution was quite modest, especially when one compared it to those of state institutions. And yet, with these small funds, the seminary accomplished much more than the state schools with their generous sources of income. A comparison of the resources of both institutions will clarify the differences. The Tyraspol seminary received a subsidy of 15,000 plus 6,840 = 21,840 rubles from the state and from the Catholic members of the diocese; that is the German colonists. A Russian government High School/College received a subsidy of 20,000 rubles annually. Annually, it also received 20,000 rubles from 200 students which brought the total to 40,000 rubles. Altogether, the seminary spent 21,840 rubles, just 1,840 rubles more than half of the annual expenses of a High School/College. Besides this; and this is what especially needs to be emphasized, the institution provided care for 100 students and fed them which by itself was more expensive than the education. And everyone could be convinced of the fact that the meals and care given to the 100 students in the institution was good during the rectorship of Alexander Boos.

Since the taking in hand of the rectorship by Canon Alexander Boos (1878) the students were provided with very nourishing meals. In the morning they received tea and half a breakfast roll such as one purchased in Russian bakeries. The students could eat as much bread as they desired. Bread in Saratov is baked with rye and wheat flour, is very nutritious, and tastes good. Even in Russia, one does not come across this first-rate baking in many cities. Every student got two pieces of sugar with his tea, which was also served about four o'clock in the afternoon. The noonday meal consisted of two courses. There was a nourishing meat soup, except for the days of abstinence and three days of Lent during the week and two during Advent, with a large piece of meat and a roast with potathes which were very often fried in fat, or noodles, Italian macaroni, carrots, beans, cabbage and mashed potathes etc. In the evening the students had another roast and this was usually beef with some kind of trimmings as was the case at noon. The meals were always served in large portions. As the Volga is filled with good fish, the major fast days did not cause any special problems in the diet of the students. Many especially were partial to eating the good, Russian buckwheat, and also yellow millet which provided grits when it was well prepared. During the summer there was also desert, the water melons or so-called arbusen, which actually originate in the lower course of the Volga and grow especially well were eaten. In terms of taste, they surpass all kinds of fruit and produce and are truly refreshlng on hot days when one is very thirsty. Naturally, on Sundays and holidays, beer had to *be* served; otherwise one could have thought that the students were not Germans! The German national drink caused the young to people to be especially glad.

The new seminary rector was not as happy in the position of being a professor of dogmatics to which the bishop had appointed him as compared to his work re: the economic situation at the seminary. Dogmatics had been a subject which had been well-taught by Dr. Glossner. Because of his own gifts Glossner was born to lecture on speculative subjects. Glossner's students would have immediately noted deficiencies in a good lecture on dogmatics even given by a better professor of dogmatics. The students of the seminary for priests soon expressed their dissatisfaction. They requested a different professor for this subject. If Boos had followed the Thomistic method in his lectures, which Dr. Glossner had strictly employed, one would not have found the difference between the two professors being too great. A former student of Dr. Glossner's would have more easily satisfied the grumblers. Since the bishop became aware of this unpleasant issue, the diocesan shepherd had the students in the two highest classes appear before him. Among other things, during this meeting there was mention made of the dean of Katharinenstadt who had been Glossner's student and had already, at the time of his studies, shown great talents and love for this so important subject. Professor Boos resigned from this professor's position and Dean Anton Zerr was called to become the professor of dogmatics at the seminary. This already happened during the first half of the school year under Boos' rectorship. The young, imposing, newly-appointed professor even arrived in Saratov before Christmas. With his friendly character, he soon won the hearts of his students. After the holidays, Professor Zerr, who up to this point had steadily given evidence of his scholastic achievements, held his first lectures. Very intelligently, he strictly stuck to the scholastic method of teaching. Since a professor or tutor or someone in authority gets the mind to become receptive most easily through a detour via the human heart rather than in a direct way, the good lectures of the new professor were soon appreciated by his audience. These lectures were, by the way, well-presented.

There were many who called Professor Anton Zerr a second Dr. Glossner in the way he presented his lectures. However, this was much exaggerated, but meanwhile so much was certain, that the diocesan bishop had not fooled himself and that a gifted successor for the teaching chair had been found for Glossner. Zerr's lectures were of benefit for the institution. Rector Boos restricted himself to the introductory subjects concerning the Holy Scriptures and he accomplished great things. His lectures in exegesis were not as good. By the way, exegesis was a minor subject at the seminary. Professor Zerr also displayed solid scholarship in regard to physics, which he taught in the seminary for boys. His students hardly enjoyed any other subjects more than this one. Because of this, they also made great strides in this subject. With the exception of the first semester of teaching, during the rectorship of Canon Alexander Boos, contentment ruled among the students of the institution. Just the severe discipline, the strictness of the supervisor, was like a mountainous burden upon the feelings of the young people. Several boys could not take his discipline, declared that they were sick and entered the hospital near the institution. Old Mr. Sigrist was the family physician at the hospital. As a rule, he prescribed a strong mustard-poultice for this "patients" and its burning soon made them ambulatory again, so that they returned to school. "Happily," the old physician soon died and the new one, Mr. Bonvetsch, treated the patients more "humanely." He soon determined the cause of their illness.

1. However, there was a lack of thorough grounding in his lectures, as the author himself was persuaded, as he personally attended Prof Zerr's classes.

Supervisor Burghardt had little aptitude as a teacher. The drills which he held before the start of the new school year were also similar to his strict nature. Once, the sun was shining very strongly during religious meditations. The air in the closed rooms of the seminary was stifling. Without considering this, he did not even allow the little boys, who also had to participate in all the contemplations, of which they yet understood nothing, outside into the garden or the yard in order to catch a bit of fresh air. They could have broken the silence which he had fanatically urged! With such an attitude, such lack of consideration and such a lack of wisdom, it could not fail that right from the beginning the newly-registered students began to hate seminary life. Some could not endure the three days of contemplation. For this reason, they fled home. But Mr. Burghardt did not learn anything from this for his own personal growth, and above all, for the benefit of the youthful students. Meanwhile, the heavy yoke placed upon them by this strict teacher was born by the pupjls of the seminary for boys, which was a special burden for them because they had to -do endure it for three entire years. When the boys, while on their return trip from summer holidays, initially received the news concerning Burghardt's removal from office, they intoned "'Holy God, We Praise Your Name." Professor Anton Zerr was appointed to fill his position. This appointment was welcomed by all of the students in the institution. The new supervisor soon won over the love and devotion of his students by his friendly character and his liberal (less restrictive) application of discipline in the seminary. For this reason, his work in teaching was very successful. The seminary became much more popular among the German population of the bishopric. The number of students grew from year to year. Soon the space could once again not hold all who asked to be accepted into the institution. Apart from the rector and the supervisor the following were also active as professors at the seminary:
Raphael Fleck, secretary of the diocesan curia and who had also been a student of Dr. Glossner and Willibald Zottmann; Canon Robert Glass from the diocese of Kulm in West Prussia; Canon Baczewski, and finally the custodian, Kaspar Ruscheinsky, a son of German colonists from Bessarabia.

After his dismissal, Father Johannes Burghardt was appointed as the priest in his place of birth. But he could not control his strict way of thinking in pastoral ministry there either. When people made confession to him, it was pure torture. The situations in which an individual received absolution from him when he confessed for the first time were probably not more numerous than those in which the father confessor did. not give absolution. Penance was given to many at first and after a period of time, they had to appear in order to finish the confession and to receive absolution. For this reason, Easter confessions dragged out in this parish throughout almost the whole year. For this reason, there was a general inharmonious atmosphere concerning the too strict priest. In the end he moved from the parish residence to his orchard which he had acquired in close proximity to the village and administered his parish from there. This increased the bad feelings toward this curate of souls. A wise person states: (Sirach 3:27) "A stubborn heart will have evil happen in the end." That proved to be true with Rev. Johannes Burghardt. Our dear Lord let him fall (Translator's note: the implication is "fall into sin"). The scandal which he caused had to be atoned for and the sinner had to be severely punished and reformed. For this reason the bishop sent him to the monastery for reform near Aglona in the archdiocese of Mohilev for repentance and recovery. After his return, the ordinary did, in fact, give his former parish back to him again. He spent his last years of life there and was a fine example to all. Shortly before the outbreak of the World War, he suddenly died.

27. Supervisor Antonius Zerr, suffragan bishop of Tyraspol

The supervisory position which Professor Anton Zerr had was of short duration. He had been appointed to this post shortly after his call to become the cathedral canon. As is the case in new bishoprics, in which the bishop continually has to deal with a lack of priests and the church positions are subjects to quick changes, thus it was also the case in Tyraspol. After ten years of administering the diocese, a distinct decline in physical health became noticeable with Bishop Franz Xaverius. According to the report of the physicians, he had a bad heart condition which was visible outwardly in that he had a peculiar red colour in his face. The bishop had taken over a diocese which was in its beginning stages. Firstly, he had to create the conditions in order to even somewhat work effectively. Nothing was regulated. The great majority of the parish clergy were not fluent enough in the language of the colonists in order to freely proclaim the Word of God and to give religious instruction in the school and during Christian teaching (Translator's note: this was a time when children, youth and adults were instructed and was usually held Sunday afternoon). The result of these shortcomings was a lack of knowledge of religion and the degeneration of morals among the colonists. It was very fortunate that public faith views had not been affected by this and still remained genuinely Christian Catholic. Continual complaints of entire parishes against their pastoral curates required quick redress and change which the Head Shepherd could not tackle because of the great lack of priests. To be sure, the greenhouse for priests to alleviate the situation had effectively developed. It was just that there were still too few vocations for the priesthood among the youth studying in the seminary. All of these things caused great concern and worry for the diocesan shepherd. In his trouble, the bishop complained: "Hardly had the seminary prepared a half dozen young people to the point where they had been prepared in the subjects so that they could be ordained as priests," when I received the sad news that half of them withdrew." "They all wanted to marry," he lamented one other time. In conclusion, there were, among the few clergy within his pontifical office, always some who were prone to drink. For this reason one saw one or another cleric who bad become prone to drink do penance for his mistakes under the supervision of his chaplain. Bishop Zottmann felt he could no longer bear the burden of work. For this reason J;ie petitioned the government to contact the Holy See, so that a suffragan bishop could be appointed; for two had been envisioned for the diocese.

At the same time, in a roundabout way, he nominated several candidates to the ministry and to the Holy See. More than all the other candidates, he recommended Anton Zerr, the supervisor and professor at the seminary for priests, who was especially favoured by the diocesan bishop. The rector of the institution, Canon Alexander Boos, would have not been any less suitable in taking on this position. Besides this, he was older and more experienced than Anton Zerr, spoke Polish well, and had worked successfully in various positions. Nevertheless, he was less popular with the diocesan bishop than Professor Anton Zerr. His somewhat rough character could not compete with the mild personality of the supervisor. The Russian government also interceded with the Holy See for the appointment of Zerr by means of the head of the Department for "Foreign Confessions (Translator's note: Denominations)," Mr. Massolov who had become acquainted with Professor Zerr during his visit to the seminary in the year 1879. The dignified appearance of the young cleric was especially liked by the high official. For this reason, Professor Anton Zerr was preferred over all the other candidates for bishop and pre-consecrated as a suffragan bishop (Translator's note: literally and in Latin, a minor bishop) on March 3, 1883 for Diocletianopolis (Translator's note: this is a city in Bulgaria named after the Roman Emperor Diocletian which at one time must have had a Roman Catholic diocese) and consecrated in St. Petersburg on May 22nd in the same year. Thus the diocesan bishop now had a youthful bishop's helper who became a first-rate in the governance of the diocese. He also often made use of his suffragan bishop's aid. From this time forth he relaxed again and determined to restore his affected health in health spas abroad. During these times he always made an extended visit to his homeland Bavaria. The relationship between both bishops generally remained one which was friendly and good. It was only strained once because the diocesan bishop did not permit his suffragan bishop to celebrate the Pontifical Mass from his cathedra. At that time, this was within the power of the diocesan bishop. According to new canonical law, the diocesan bishop can allow any other diocesan bishop to officiate from his cathedra (Translator's note: bishop's throne) under a baldachin (Translator's note: a canopy of state over an altar or throne) but not a suffragan bishop.

After Bishop Zottmann had received a suffragan bishop, the desire to completely retire came to him again and, if possible, to a monastery for he thought about ending his life in solitude. His motto (in Latin) was: "Inter mortem et officium/Between death and the office (work post) there should be an interval."

Since supervisor Anton Zerr had been elevated to the rank of a suffragan bishop by passing over Rector Boos who was older and more deserving, this fact must have affected Canon Alexander Boos in a somewhat unpleasant way. Every passing over or demotion which has not been caused because of special reasons causes the person who was passed over to deny himself and to practice Christian humility. For this reason it is a great test of the person who was set back. This is even more difficult when the person ranked higher in authority suddenly becomes the subordinate. This was the situation of Rector Alexander Boos as often as the suffragan bishop administered the bishopric in the absence of the diocesan bishop as his vicar general. The inner battle which the Christian and priest must fight with the old Adam, was, to be sure, not visible to the human eye, but the omniscient eye of God saw the struggles which it cost Canon and Rector Alexander Boos. The irreproachable, good priest won the battle. He honoured his former subordinate and appeared in the presence of the suffragan bishop at festivities leading the students and pupils of the seminary. This also happened when he was not representing the office of the diocesan bishop and was not his senior in order to congratulate him. When he did so, he kissed the suffragan bishop on his hand or on his ring before all the others and in this manner gave an illustration of submission, humility and his obedience. Because of his many deeds of service to the seminary, his irreproachable, priestly behaviour and his piety, all of the students in the seminary liked him a lot.

28. Johannes Antonov, supervisor and professor of the seminary

As a result of the elevation of supervisor Anton Zerr as suffragan bishop, the supervisory position, which was very much connected to the supervision of discipline for the students, and their education, was vacant. With the dearth of suitable priests for such a powerful position, this time months passed before a new supervisor was appointed. The appointment of this person caused the diocesan bishop Franz Xaverius many worries. In vain did one look for a long time among the German diocesan clergy for someone who would be inclined to fill the position. This was because with the departure of Supervisor

Anton Zerr, the professorship for dogmatics became vacant. No one considered himself capable of successfully lecturing on this subject and to the satisfaction of the students. In light of this situation, Rector Boos suggested the nomination of the priest of the parish in Kutais, Johannes Antonov, as the supervisor and professor of dogmatics. Boos had already gotten to know this gentleman in Tblisi and had learned to highly esteem him. Without a doubt, Antonov surpassed all of the clergy in the diocese in regard to a solid education. He only had one deficiency: he was not able to speak the German language, the mother tongue of the students. Nevertheless, one comforted oneself with the idea that Antonov would soon learn the German language in being with the students and in the meantime he could make himself understood with them in the official Russian language. On the other hand, Antonov spoke Latin as easily, fluently and correctly as his mother tongue. These factors were determinative. For this reason Reverend Johannes Antonov was called to the seminary by Diocesan Bishop Zottmann in the fall of 1883.

During the first half of September, the newly-appointed supervisor arrived. More than anything else, the rector longed for him to arrive, for he had to carry the whole burden of both positions of rector and supervisor. He was supported in his work of overseeing order in the institution by the young cleric Georg Bayer. However, he entered the Catholic Religious Academy in St. Petersburg at the beginning of the school year. Shortly before, upon the urging of Rector Alexander Boos, the Tyraspol seminary had gotten two complete scholarships for study at this school of higher education and the first spot was filled for the first time now. The students of both seminaries also yearned for the quick arrival of the supervisor, since the rector could not deal with their various affairs. Finally the word came: The new supervisor has arrived! All of the students were struck by this news. Everyone wanted to see him; one wanted to welcome him. This was proof of how the students knew how to treasure the teacher who would be closest to them and what kind of a close relationship there would be between him and the students.

After the new supervisor had rested somewhat from the long trip, the rector also wanted the students to be introduced as a group to their educator and welcome him. Nevertheless, the lively Caucasian wanted to see the students and become acquainted with them, without allowing rest for a little while beforehand. After the greeting with a beautiful rendition of the song "May he live and flourish for many years," given by the seminary choir, Antonov, a tall, dignified figure, held a nice long speech in such fluent Latin that one would have believed that an old Roman from the time of the first church fathers had returned from the dead and was speaking to the students and this not in a dead but in a mother tongue which was still alive. The words were not forced; but were completely natural. They rolled off his tongue with such ease as one can only hear when a person is speaking his mother tongue. This was the first, fluent Latin speech which the students had heard. No wonder that it also made a deep impression upon the students who understood ~t so that this would never disappear. After the return of the students to their dormitory rooms the speech became the topic of conversation for the day. All congratulated each other for the good fortune of having received such a solidly educated supervisor and professor. After the first lectures in dogmatics, which the new professor held in the Latin language just as fluently as his speech, the students of the seminary for clergy could no longer keep back their emotions of thanks toward the old rector. They sent the oldest students of the most advanced class to thank him that he had seen to it that such a superb professor had been appointed.

And in fact, Johannes Antonov achieved excellent results through his lectures. His solid education and excellent gifts had made him especially qualified for the teaching profession. After the completion of the High School/Junior College in Kutais in the Caucasus, Rev. Glachov/Glachoff sent the talented youth to the Urban College in Rome (Translator's note: this college was founded by Pope Urban VIII). There, over a period of eight years, he graduated in philosophy, canon law and theology. As a result of his progress he received various awards and was called upon during student debates to give presentations before cardinals and before the Holy Father, Pius IX of blessed memory and he, as the defender of various theses and by his excellent achievements already attained general esteem and respect. The priests of the Society of Jesus sought to win such a talented graduate for their order. It was just in this case that he would have had to never see his homeland Russia nor his elderly parents ever again since Russian state law did not allow Jesuits to enter Russia. For this reason Johannes Antonov, after the attempt to win him for the Jesuits, decided to return to Russia. But a former student who studied religion in Rome was forbidden to take charge of even a very low-ranked ecclesiastical position. In order to get out of the way of all of these obstacles, he did not receive one single consecration in Rome. Rather, with the permission of the then prefect of propaganda, of Cardinal Simeoni, he had all of the consecrations bestowed upon him by the Latin archbishop of Smyrna, Spaca Piedra. After the death of his benefactor and parish priest in Kutais, he was appointed to be his successor by Bishop Zottmann. Since a parish does not eagerly like to lose such a likeable curate of souls who had become beloved such as Johannes Antonov, one can imagine what kind of sadness the news of the calling away of their minister brought forth. Many petitions to have him remain in the parish were sent to the bishop's court. However, they could not be taken into account. Finally, the members of the Kutaiser parish were convinced of the fact that Antonov could do much more for the church, for religion, and for the spiritual care of the Georgians in general and for the Georgian parish in Kutais in particular, by being in close proximity to the diocesan shepherd. These considerations quieted and comforted the mourning members of the parish even more when they realized that their dear and former curate of souls had received a promotion in his office.

Soon after the arrival, several young students of the third year class were to receive consecration as sub-deacons. The new supervisor had not even unpacked all of his things and set up his home. Nevertheless, he desired, as he stated, to also do something for the candidates for consecration. Therefore he held a very impressive,lecture about the sub-diaconate which the ordinands would never forget as long as they lived. This lecture, held in Latin as well, was the most beautiful one which they had heard concerning this consecration until that point in time.

Without a doubt, Antonov was the most prominent teacher which the Tyraspol seminary ever had. He was on the same level as Dr. Glossner in terms of scholarship, but he outdid him by his vivacity and the clarity of bis lectures. He dealt with the most difficult questions of dogmatics with such skill that even the least intelligent student understood him. What should especially be emphasized is that he had so mastered the Latin language that he could deal with even the most difficult questions with such facility and ease and with such fluency of speech that it was as if he was speaking in his mother tongue in regard to the most familiar of things. How hard it is for a theologian to explain abstract questions with examples or to explain them. This seems to be unthinkable for a European professor; if not outright impossible. The gentleman from the Caucasus, who had received a solid education in Western Europe, always found points of contact in the comparisons of both worlds; of the supernatural with the natural, in a very easy way. This was the result of a vivacious and versatile imagination. His limitless imaginative powers discovered new examples and new ways of doing things over and over again. These seemed to envelop him from all sides. By means of these, he would bring the abstract concept to be explained so near the senses and to the mind, that he could view it up close and had to comprehend it. If Dr. Glossner's lectures were profound, thorough and full of awe in regard to the eminence of the questions, which this scholar explained, then the lecture which Antonov gave was clear, lively and descriptive and also easily accessible to the less intelligent mind. The former primarily occupied the mind upon which he made great demands and only in a secondary sense did this affect the emotions of the heart. The latter took hold. of the divine truths with great adroitness. He took them out of their mysterious depths, clothed them in attractive attire, drew them in bright pictures and brought them close to the audience in a tangible way. In doing so, he understood how to make the divine truths so alluring and often to describe them in such a fascinating way that they took ahold of all of their mental and emotional capabilities. Dr.

Glossner was more of a philosopher and dogmatician for an intellectual, well-educated audience. He would have been the right professor for the Catholic Religious Academy in St. Petersburg which required four years of philosophy and theology as prerequisites. Antonov was the right professor for a religious seminary. Through this comparison of both of the great educators which the Tyraspol seminary ever had, everyone can deduce the kind of great advantages which the student body of the religious educational institution of Tyraspol received from the philosophical and dogmatic lectures given by Antonov.

Latin was an impediment for the students but not for the professor. But the former also soon began to express themselves fairly easily in Latin so that the students from Tyraspol who continued their studies at the Gregorian University (Translator's note: a university in which most professors are of the Jesuit order and located in Rome, which was founded by St. Ignatius Loyola) were more proficient in their ease of expressing Latin than all others. Antonoff's students handled the language of the church better than the earlier alumni of the seminary for priests.

Antonov was also a superior pedagogue. How many educators of youth must first acquire their special ability by studying diligently for many years? And if they have learned how to teach, then this is still not something which belongs to them; that is it remains a theoretical science. With Antonov this skill was not something which he acquired by means of his studies. With him it was a natural gift. He was a born pedagogue. How much did this tireless man accomplish in the seminary for boys without understanding the mother tongue which the boys had? Among the young boys he was young like they are without losing any kind of respect from them. He was well able to give advice against mistakes. No little mistake and no improper steps escaped his observation. And still no one considered his watchfulness over everything as anything burdensome. This was all just self-understood, necessary and natural. How hatefully he could describe evil and reprehensible things and how loathsome the depravity! With what fire he inspired his audience! His power of persuasion was just marvelous. One day, he discovered that an upright student was about to leave the seminary because of a lack of vocational calling. Wearing his surplice and stola and crucifix in hand he received him in his residence and spoke with him with such effect that all at once the student lost all of the doubts in regard to his calling into the priesthood so that he became a good and pious priest. This was the one who was the later author of the History of the Volga Colonies whom the Bolsheviks shot in the year 1921. Every two weeks he taught the pupils of the seminary for boys about every question of life which one could think of. This instruction was given in the form of a conversation which he was able to very nicely give with a lot of humour. In his conversation and his comments he was at times very intellectual. As much as he recommended and favoured piety, the right amount of piety needed to be kept. It happened that a boy overdid it with praying. He began to always and during his free time kneel and pray in the chapel. He asked him about the excess and the over-exaggeration and right away he wanted to complain against this to St. Anthony. For this reason he stated this piece of humour which could not be copied. "But that is already too much St. Anthony!" He carried out discipline with strictness but without being rigoristic. In the most difficult and most confusing situations in life he always found an easy way out. Not even the most difficult times of testing could make him perplexed or cause him to lose heart. He was quickly able to deal with the most difficult cases. If he was perplexed or made mistakes sometimes then he would very gladly humbly retract them. He never used the rod with anyone. Even the most depraved people were not considered to be incorrigible by him. He only saw to it that such people were removed from the institution so that the good ones would not become depraved. During the entire period when summer holidays took place, he was almost always at the seminary and left the institution very seldom. One seldom finds a person and not even a clergyman who was so consumed by his occupation as Supervisor Johannes Antonov was. If a normal mortal person has a lot to do, he becomes tired and sleepy. With Antonov this did not seem possible for the more he did and the more his duties piled up, the more life and therefore the more activity he developed.

He had a truly child-like attachment to the Holy Father and great devotion and love toward the dear Mother of God. With him the latter was often very moving. He knew how to implant love toward the Apostolic See, toward the Holy Father and to the dear Mother of God in his students as well. He was especially in a good mood when their feast days took place. Right after he was appointed, he introduced the rosary which he prayed together each evening with the pupils. He also introduced the May devotions. So that the latter did not take up too much time, he searched for· a May booklet which had been shortened a lot. As such a booklet was no longer available in German he had the out of print translation of an Italian author printed and given out using his own funds. Through him the love and devotion to the dear Mother of God was carried forth into the entire diocese. This was however done by his former students and because of his influence. The rosary prayer was also spread among the people by the clergy who had been his students. The festival of the immaculate conception of Mary was celebrated especially well at the seminary. He saw to this. In the large seminary hall an altar was erected and richly decorated with tropical plants and flowers upon which a nice statue from Lourdes surrounded by electric candles with different colours stood resplendent. A large plate was placed in front of the statue at the feet of the Mother of God. With a deep bow, he first and then all of the students and pupils placed their letters into the plate. These letters were directed to the immaculate one. In these letters the students presented their concerns and petitions to the immaculate Mother of God. When all of the letters had been placed at the feet of the Mother of God statue, then a cleric took the plate with its contents to a fireplace which was situated in the hall where alcohol was poured over it. Then it was burned with everyone watching. Then the 12 students of the seminary for clerics went before the altar and recited the most beautiful Latin words of praise to the immaculate. They did this in the way in which it stood in the prayer book for the evening prayers according to the high note of the festival. At the conclusion a deacon held a speech in the German language praising the dear Mother of God. During the pauses the seminary choir presented beautiful pieces of music which were accompanied by the harmonium and often with stringed instruments. This beautiful celebration made a very special and good impression upon the boys; but also upon the older students of the seminary for clerics and the guests present with whom the diocesan bishop had fellowship. This made a very solemn and religious impression.

Since during the last school year, that is during the last class of the seminary for boys, the immaculate was the patron saint of the class the octavo was held at the end with the class singing it at the festival in a celebatory manner. Lourdes and its environs were presented artistically so that one had an exact idea of this famous place of pilgrimage. The Ave Maria Stella was recited in front of the statue of the Mother of God in the ten languages which the boys individually could understand; that is the languages which each of them knew. As a rule one could hear German, Russian, Polish, Georgian (Grusinian), Annenian, Italian, French, Czech, Latin and the language of the Tartars. The moving celebration ended with a procession accompanied by the singing of the choir and which moved through all the rooms in the institution. Supervisor Antonov, in his conversations with the students usually talked about the octavo of this festival in Lourdes to which he had previously made a pilgrimage. Since he was studying in Rome at the time of the Vatican Council, this was often the subject of his conversation.

Soon after beginning his position he recognized the bad situation of having two institutions existing in the same building. He tried to separate both schools from each other as far as this was possible. Since this was not possible because of the lack of space he added to the rules in the institution whereby the pupils/students in both schools were not to have contact with each other. Before and after walks, which every teacher had to have with his class, a short little prayer was spoken by all. The rules and the and spiritual exercises which had already been introduced by Rector Franz Zottmann and his successor were considered highly by him and he did not change them whatsoever. Antonov was very concerned about the exact holding of the liturgical ceremonies. That is why he himself took over the lecture about the liturgy. During free hours the students then had to practice the liturgy exactly. If someone was sloppy in holding the liturgical ceremony, then he had to allow himself to be reprimanded. When the next conversation (lecture) took place, which he held every two weeks with the students, he described the mistakes made with Caucasian liveliness and by imitating their worthlessness and offensiveness and called such inaccurate and incorrect liturgical ceremonies orientalism, yes orientalism! Then he held the liturgical ceremony himself and let it be repeated by several students until it was held in a right and proper manner. The effect of his constant teaching was that the worship service in the cathedral and in the seminary chapel were held in a very exact and uplifting manner. "Don't think," he used to say: "That the ceremonies only have a meaning which is less important. The exact handling of church ceremonies gave Cardinal Manning (whom he personally knew) the first impetus toward his conversion."

The students of the seminary soon found out how much Supervisor Antonov loved the most Blessed Virgin Mary and how highly he honoured her. In the first year of his work a boy in the preparatory school made the mistake of allowing himself a very coarse infringement of the seminary rules. He feared that he would be seriously punished for this. Then a little wise guy recommended: "Go quickly to the supervisor and tell him that you are sorry for your mistake but because of love toward the Mother of God you will promise that you will be better." He will forgive you if he hears that your promise comes from love toward the Mother of God."

One can ascertain that the diocesan bishop was happy with such a pedagogue and professor and was exceedingly glad to have found such a person among his clergy. If a position for a canon had been vacant, he would have soon received this apostolic man into the cathedral chapter. In the meantime he received him into the minor cathedral chapter by giving him a sacristan's position.

It was just the great men of whom this story reports were often unknown for a long time. This is what also happened to Professor Johannes Antonov. 1. While some considered him highly, he was underestimated by others. Yes, some of the clergy in the diocese who did not even know him personally had a really bad view of him. Some even demanded his removal from the seminary. It was just in later years when he, because of his age and his offensive and tireless activity was not able to do very much work, that his excellent work was completely honoured. Diocesan Bishop Eduard von Ropp got him a papal

1. Johannes Antonov had three doctorates in philosophy, canon law and in theology. One would never have gotten to know that from him. It was only after his death that the diplomas were taken from his papers.

house prelature at first and when Antonov, because of his age and lack of German language ability was passed by at the time of an election for a new bishop for Tyraspol he got him the position of papal pronotary ad instar with the right to wear a mitre and staff when High Masses were celebrated. 1. Pronotary Antonov made use of this privilege only once and this only upon the urging of his diocesan bishop. For 25 years the apostolic man wore the surplice of a sacristan of the cathedral chapter of Tyraspol! Four times he had to experience that his former students, having gotten positions as a canon and a prelature, were seated before him in the chancel. To accept such humiliations in an even-tempered way and to bear them is hard for a Catholic priest. Only love toward God can bestow the necessary strength upon him for him to bear this. And yet Supervisor Antonov stayed in his position. What had those done in his situation who underestimated him so much? Certainly their humility would not have been enough to bear similar demotions if not to say disdain in an even-tempered way. All intelligent knowledgeable people who knew this situation will agree with this judgement. Antonov's humility however lasted through all of these hard testings which God's inexplicable decree sent him. This was the humility of a child of whom the divine Saviour says: "Whoever humbles himself like this child is the greatest in the Kingdom of Heaven." (Matthew 18:4).

1. Antonov's greatest deficit was that he did not understand the German language and it was a mistake on his part that he never learned the language of his students. However he deserved to still be somewhat excused for this. Firstly, he was burdened so much with the duties of his calling that the learning of a language which was completely foreign to him would have cost him heroic effort. Secondly, all of the students and pupils understood Russian well enough and the students in the seminary for clerics understood Latin in order to communicate with their pedagogue and professor.

29. Bishop Franz Xaverius Zottmann's work

When Bishop Franz Xaverius Zottmann took over the administration of the bishopric, it numbered about 200,000 Catholics of German nationality. With very few exceptions these all lived in villages with just Germans which were called colonies. There were about 35,000 Poles and Lithuanians in the cities and in Transcaucasia there were 6,000 Grusinians or Georgians residing who professed the Catholic religion. Thus the German diocesans formed the vast majority of believers of Tyraspol. Because the bishopric had been primarily formed for the benefit of the latter the diocesan bishops had to direct their pastoral care toward them because their pastoral situation was in a bad way. Despite this, the faithful of other nationalities or minorities as one expresses oneself at present could not fall short. A placing of them in the background was far away from the thoughts of the pious and very conscientious diocesan shepherd. His German character would also have protested against something like this. For it is a known fact that no nation on earth can easily separate itself from its feelings of nationality, like the German can. For this reason it happens that the German colonist, with the single exception of the Russian, assimiliates out of his own initiative into the nations to which he has immigrated.

If Bishop Franz Xaverius was still not of this sort then he was still concerned in the most careful way to satisfy all of the nationalities present in his bishopric. Neither could gross national fanaticism make him angry, as he was striving above all else to bring to life a growing presence of pastoral care among the neglected German colonists of Southern Russia. That could however only be achieved by the education of s German pastoral clergy and the filling of the German-language parishes with German-speaking, better said German pastors who originated among the colonists. In this so very important matter, Zottmann decided to follow the use, the practice of the Catholic Church which sees to it that everywhere a native clergy is established which knows the language, the customs of the people and the situation in the country where they reside and can accustom themselves to this. If despite this fact one brought the accusation to Bishop Zottmann that he was not favourable toward the Poles then this accusation is not justified by anything. Many facts even reveal the opposite. Although the cathedral chapter under his pontificate still counted two Polish prelates and one canon: Jotkiewicz, Orlowski and Onoszko, he still appointed Mr. Kaspar Baczewski to be a canon. This gentleman was, to be sure, a Lithuanian but he always considered himself to be a Pole. At that time there was no differentiation made between the Polish and the Lithuanian nation. All Lithuanians in the diocese were viewed as being Poles. Canon Baczewski, since he knew the German language quite well, was later employed as a professor in the seminary for clerics.

Because of a lack of suitable teachers, Bishop Zottmann asked the archbishop for a young professor who was a Pole and who had just ended his studies at the Spiritual Academy in St. Petersburg. Pupils from Polish parents were always accepted into the seminary for boys and also into the seminary for clerics even though German colonists' boys were often rejected because of a lack of space. The bishop also took the Polish priests under his wing who had been exiled to Siberia. He was able to make happen that 18 clergymen, who were not allowed to return to their homeland, received permission to take over a postion in his diocese. He gave several of them a place to stay and eat for years on end and took care of them like a father did for his sons.

Bishop Franz Xaverius was a man who knew how to honour the good characteristics of every nation. How often he praised the inner religiosity of the Polish people, their great attachment to the church and to the clergy when these congratulated him during festivities directed toward him. He praised them in front of the pupils in the seminary. In opposition to this he did not agree with the actions which the Poles took against the Russian government. One needed to, he said in the interest of the Catholic cause, avoid more now than before everything in which the Russian state could see an effort toward the political separation of Poland from Russia. The Catholic Poles were to follow the principle: "First we are Catholics and then we are Poles and not the other way around." His views are interesting and he wrote about this issue in a letter. He said: "Much was already destroyed by the revolution of 1831, then by the rebellion of 1846 and especially by the revolution of 1863 in regard to church matters so that there would only need to be one more single failed revolution in order to get rid of the entire church organization (tabula rasa = clean the table or a clean table in Latin). But still I do think that now the Poles still have a better view of Russia and could attain great advantages for the Catholic Church. They should, as it might seem to me, be able to hold a meeting of their notable clergy and secular men with the people's deputies and after coming to an agreement among themselves send a petition to the czar with the following contents: They want to give up the restoration of Poland and give up all efforts toward that goal and without reservation honestly want to join their Russian brethren people and the common great Fatherland if the czar signs a new concordat with Rome in which he, among other things, also guarantees the following: 1. The obligation to raise children as schismatics in mixed marriages is removed. 2. The bishops are free to appoint priests, free in the administration of their dioceses and in the establishment and development of their seminaries but they are not able to, without special permission, either appoint priests from other places neither are they free to accept foreign students who want to study for the ministry into their seminaries. 3. The communication with Rome is open. 4. For the establishment of monasteries and nunneries the permission of the government is necessary and those that have been built by foreigners may not be accepted without special permission from the government. Of course one must make a few important concessions as the Department for Foreign Denominations knows the concordates and religious situation in other countries quite well. In this regard one can hear many a pointed comment. I am of the view that Russia would accept the proposal of the Poles and least attempt this for at present it is very important to them that all Slavic nations among themselves and with Russia be politically united. This is my opinion and perhaps it is false but it at least rests upon my inner convictions which have been acquired by observation.

From the great strength of faith of the Polish people and from the indestructible attachment to the Holy Father and the Catholic Church he comes to the conclusion: "For these reasons I am very inclined to accept that a people with such a powerful faith may just still be called to play an independent role (Translator's note: in the world)." These words sound, after they have shown to be true after the restoration of Poland, like a prophetic prediction in the mouth of such a pious prince of the church. They were spoken at the end of the previous century. However they also prove how unjustified some Polish hyper-patriots were in judging the bishop.

Above all the bishop is a teacher of the lambs entrusted to him. For he is a successor to the Apostles and the Divine Founder of the Church told them: "Go and teach all peoples." Matthew 28:19. Bishop Zottmann practiced the teaching office of the bishop in three different ways: by means of pastoral letters, in shorter lectures in his house chapel during daily Holy Mass and in his sermons during his confirmation and visitation trips. During the time of his pontificate, in any hurdles especially were placed in the way of this ministry of teaching by the Russian government. However Bishop Franz Xaverius was able to cause people to remember in a very lively way the statement of the Apostle to the Gentiles: "The Word of God is not bound."(2. Timothy 2:9) From time to time he sent pastoral letters to the members of the diocese in which he, as a rule, tried to have improper customs, which were a part of their life, come to an end. For this reason, the pastoral letters had to do with present-day problems for which an admonition seemed to be necessary. The pastoral letters were, for the most part and so that they would not have to be placed under Russian censorship, sent in written form to the deans who then had them copied by the pastors who were placed under their authority. However this was a difficult way in which the Word of God had to be sent in order to reach the faithful. The bishop's pastoral letters could only be read to the people from the pulpit but not spread around in many copies among the people as this was the case later on in the diocese. One pastoral letter had the matter of the inadmissibility of self-established holidays as a subject. On a second occasion it was the teaching in regard to an invalid marriage which had been performed with hindrances to the marriage which were a cause for separation. A third time it was the depravity of addiction to drinking alcohol and then there was a letter in regard to the situation in the schools etc.

In almost every Holy Mass Bishop Zottmann held a very short speech of five minutes duration to those present. This was his private mass which was attended on a daily basis by many Catholics in his house chapel which was available to all. In these lectures he spoke about and encouraged the holding of the commandments of God and of the Church and the exercise of various Christian virtues or he explained in a very popular manner the various teachings of the holy Catholic faith. His natural talent for catechization was especially evident during these lectures.

The diocese of Traspol consists of an area of not less than about 14,000 square miles. To be sure, the Catholics do not live as spread out as this is the case in some disapora dioceses. The German immigrants had settled in larger groups of villages. Thus the northern part of the bishopric consisted of four large groups of villages. These groups were only separated from each other at smaller intervals. The southern part of the diocese had six such groups but they were separated from each other by a greater distance. Here one had to travel hundreds of kilometers from one group to another. However, the great distances made it hard for the visiting Head Shepherd to visit them, especially since these distances often had to be covered by wagon. At that time the railroad system in Russia was not as extensive as in the 20th century. One great hindrance which was problematic for the bishop's confirmation and visitation trips was the prohibition of the government and not that of the law. This was often made illusory by the ministerial circulars as in this case. Meanwhile, several times the government still allowed the confirmation journey. Naturally, upon this occasion, many thousands upon thousands had to be confirmed. In those regions which would probably not see the Head Shepherd in the future, the bishop also gave the Holy Sacrament to little children. During this hard activity the bishop often still directed words of admonition to the people. If there was a festival day, then he often held a pontifical mass with a festive sermon wearing his bishop's robes. As a rule, these sermons of the Head Shepherd made a powerful and indelible impression upon the audience. This was also something from which the people who opposed the Church could not exclude themselves.

30. The construction of the cathedral in Saratov

To be sure, the little wooden chapel which had been built by Father Landes S.J. (Translator's note: S.J. means the Society of Jesus - the Jesuits) was later extended by means of a new addition, but was still not a dignified cathedral church. Outside of mission countries, there was probably no cathedral as pitiful as the one in the bishopric of Tyraspol. To be sure, the Russian government had, in the agreement with the Holy See, agreed to the new construction of a cathedral church for Tyraspol, but until then had not fulfilled its promise. Here as in the case in other countries, it was a matter of fulfilling set responsibilities which had been determined by concordats with the Holy See. To a large degree these promises, whose fulfillment are tied to expenditures of money, do not come to fruition and are forgotten. This was also the case with the promises given by the czarist government. Of course no one should be surprised concerning this when the government is non-Catholic if those who want to be Catholics provide a poor example. Bishop Franz noted that he would only get a worthy cathedral unless he built it himself with freewill donations, which would be collected in the diocese during the years 1878 and 1879. Besides this, 3,346 rubles had been deeded in his will for the building by diocesan bishop Ferdinand Kahn. Suffragan Bishop Lipski had willed 6,389 rubles. The collection in the diocese amounted to 46,000 rubles. During the construction further donations were received. The construction was taken over by architect Konstantine Nevski and built in a quick tempo in the renaissance style. A committee headed by Cathedral Canon Kaspar Baczewski supervised it. One could have been of the opinion that the czarist government would not create any difficulties for this project as it was released from the responsibility of building this House of God on its own. It was just that it was customary for the system of government then in use to hinder things when it came to ecclesiastical affairs. It probably rejected the first grand proposal which had been drawn up in beautiful Gothic style because the high Gothic steeple would stand higher than all the schismatic churches of the city. There was no by-law in state law which forbade this, but the will or even more the arbitrary action of the imperial officials was often its own law. Proof of this fact was provided by the steeple of the Lutheran Church in Saratov, which had been completed one year before the completion of the Catholic cathedral. This church is very close to the same height as the highest tower of the Russian churches in the city; namely that of the Russian cathedral church and is higher than all other steeples in the city! Thus a more modest plan had to be drafted. This draft had two steeples and is significantly lower and simpler than it was in the first architectural drawing. This is also the reason that the House of God is too small for its eminent future usage. Nevertheless, the church, which is located on the nicest street in the city; "German" Street; is very dignified and also beautiful. The interior is richly and colourfully painted and decorated with gold carvings in the manner which the Russian people and the colonists in the diocese prefer. Since the cathedral is very bright, the gold set upon a white background is very easily recognized and makes a solemn impression upon the visitor. Among other things, the church has three very beautiful statues which were done by an artist in Paris. There is a very beautiful statue of the Virgin mother of God in the nave of the church which rests upon a special throne, one of St. Pius V with a tiara and threefold papal cross held in his left hand and giving the blessing in his right, and of St. Philomena, Virgin and Martyress, holding the palm branch of victory in her right hand. Both are co-patrons of the diocese and are located in two niches near the high altar on both sides of the patron saint of the diocese, the painting of the St. Clement I, the pope and martyr who suffered a martyr's death in the Crimea under Emperor Trajan. (Translator's note: His name was Marcus Ulpius Nerva Traianus). Since 1896, a beautiful Walker organ is situated on the balcony. It probably belongs to the best examples of this world-famous organ factory. The building consists of two naves. The second one extends out to a round apse. It is not much smaller than the main nave because it needed to be roomy for seating for canons, for the alumni of the seminary for clergy, and boys and for the dignified carrying out of pontifical services. The beautiful pontifical ceremonies were also held there for many years in a beautiful and dignified way; and strictly according to Latin rites. To the praise of the faithfi.tl of the bishop's city, it is to be mentioned here that the House of God was very well attended on Sundays and especially on holidays. Bishop Zottmann consecrated the church in a very festive manner on May 20, 1881. The faithful from far and near attended this festival. It was actually the festival of the whole diocese. The House of God could not hold the number of attendees. Upon this occasion the consecrator held a nice speech in the German language and from which certain sections are to be repeated here. "Brothers in the Lord! You have gathered here today in such great numbers from near and far in order to participate in the consecration of this temple. That which you yearned for so long, of which much was spoken, hoped for and been anxious about; this has now been accomplished by the gracious help of God. The new cathedral church of Tyraspol, which at the same time is the parish church of the Roman Catholic congregation in Saratov, stands completed before our eyes. Even if it is of modest construction and modest size, it is still sufficient for the required needs. For this reason this day is a day of joy and praise for this local congregation as well as for the entire diocese of Tyraspol and we rightly implore the words of scripture during this day from Psalm 113 "This is the day that the Lord has made, let us rejoice and be glad in it."

When the diocesan consecrator had given a short review of the collections, the expenses, and about the building, he thanked the donors and all who had helped in the construction of the building, and did so in a heartfelt way. After a short directive in regard to the significance of the items for the furnishing of the church, he closes with these words: "You now note, beloved in the Lord, how everything that is found in and that which happens in a church is beautiful, noble and meaningful. And for this reason your church is truly a rich spring from which divine grace and favours flow for you and from which heavenly comfort and support also flows and is brought to those who are ill and dying.

For this reason you should, beloved in the Lord, love and treasure your House of God; eagerly and regularly attend it and always piously and devotedly take part in the worship service and the proclamation of the Word of God. In the Holy Scriptures we read in: Ecclesiastes 23 and 10: "It is a great honour to serve God. The glory of the rich, of the noble, of the poor is the fear of God. Great judges and powerful men are held in honour, but no one is greater than he who fears the Lord." Every Christian heart is to be a temple of God, for St. Paul, the great apostle to the Gentiles states: "Do you not know that your bodies are the temple of the Holy Ghost who dwells within you?" You are pleased that your House of God is so friendly, bright and richly decorated with gold and with paintings, but regular and piously-faithful attendees decorate a church even more beautifully. Certainly, the most beautiful adornment in a church is that which is living and breathing. The living adornment of the church is a deeply religious, pious and virtuous congregation which understands how to honour its church as the house of God, to treasure it and to use it for its salvation. Amen."

Under Bishop Franz Zottmann, 25 new parishes were established. Until then, vicarage positions always had to be neglected because of the great lack of priests. The revival of religious life, which mainly came from the Head Shepherd of the Roman Church, caused a ripple effect, without regard to the great obstacles, into the ranks of the bishopric of Tyraspol and made this rich field of God flourish; bringing forth great blessings. Above all, this was caused by the introduction of the Third Order of St Francis of Assisi and various other brotherhoods, which caused the heart of the diocesan shepherd to rejoice greatly.

31. Bishop Franz Xav. Zottmann's resignation and words of farewell

The exhausting activity of a bishop in a diocese such as Tyraspol, which he had taken over in order to administer, which was just in its beginning stages and in which almost nothing was regulated but much was in a state of disarray, above all, had to strongly affect his heart and his nerves. The activity of building up the seminary had already weakened Zottmann's health. Without question, the climate in Saratov, in which there is only a Siberian winter and an African summer without fall and spring, added to this condition because of the crass changes in weather. Meanwhile, the noble bishop had to work at various problems with which he had to battle. The statute of Russian Law 17, Volume XI, I. T. alone caused such problems for the diocesan bishop. According to this statute, no correspondence could .be carried on with the Holy See except via the Ministry of the Interior. To do so was punished severely. For this reason, the bishop had to use such care that correspondence, which according to divine right, had to be kept secret was sent without being intercepted by the vigilant Russian police. What headaches this caused while he was awaiting a successful reply from the Eternal City! How distressing was the situation of the diocesan shepherd when, without ado, the absolute authority of the state commanded that he administer that territory which Russia-had annexed to its territory by its victories in the south of the empire! Whether the Catholic bishop had the right to do so was not even questioned by the state, which held to the damaging logo: "Might makes for right." And this came from a government which does not recognize any authority which comes into conflict with its presumed absolutism. All of these things damaged his health before he got old. Sometimes, during the night he experienced suspicious attacks which, to be sure, quickly passed by, but caused the bishop to think that soon his life would come to an end. Before his death (this had been his heart's desire for many years), he wanted to be alone with God, his creator, in a lonely monastic cell and prepare to meet him in a worthy manner. "Mortem inter et officium, praestat esse interstitium" (Between life and death there should be an interval.)

Already in the year 1882, when he was able to fulfill his long-desired wish to travel to where everything started (the Latin phrase is: ad lirnina) in order to pray at the graves of the holy apostolic princes and to speak with the Holy Father, he urgently requested the Holy Father to relieve him of the office of a bishop of Tyraspol. The pope, who received him with open arms on the top of the stairs, as the first bishop from Russia who had travelled in centuries to where it all began and who recognized in Zottmann such a worthy disciple of the apostles, did not however grant him his request. The great, world-experienced-successor of St. Peter had considered himself fortunate to have such a coworker in that so closed and absolutistic country. Bishop Zottmann had also travelled to visit the successor to St. Peter against the will of his government and was in danger of

being discovered by Russian spies during his journey to Rome. The pope, with sincere words, encouraged Zottmann to continue to lead the little ship called the diocese of Tyraspol through the storms of that era as he had done in such a blessed way under the protection of God up to that point. Bishop Zottmann used his lengthy stay in his homeland as a time in order to have his health restored and in order to secretly travel to the Eternal City and to give a report to the Holy Father regarding the religions and ecclesiastical conditions in the diocese which had been entrusted to his care. He undertook this journey without the permission of the Russian government, which had strictly forbidden Catholic bishops to travel (Translator's note: the implication is travel to the Vatican in Rome). In Saratov one feared that the government would inflict disciplinary punishment upon the bishop after his return because of the breaking of such an important law. It was just that the ministry preferred not to pay attention to the "unauthorized" journey to Rome by the bishop, just as it had also often closed its eyes in regard to other improper things of which Zottmann was culpable. The government understood Zottmann's thinking and good intentions. In situations where his conscience allowed him to do so, he sought to avoid any conflict with state laws. The government valued this accordingly. Six years later, the bishop again made a request to be relieved of the administration of the diocese. As he, in the meantime, had received a suffragan bishop in the person of the youthful Professor Anton Zerr, he firmly hoped that he would receive his dismissal. But this time his petition was turned down again. But the Holy See gave him permission, which the government also gave him the right to carry out, to restore his health abroad for half of a year. From the start, his vacation was extended.

While he was temporarily living in Ornau, the sick bishop asked anew for the acceptance of his resignation. Finally, the prelates in the office of the papal nunctio/ambassador in Munich received the advisement that the issue should be resolved. For this reason, the prelates of the papal embassy in Munich undertook a visit to Omau. After lengthy negotiations, his wish was fulfilled. Thus, all at once all of the burdensome concerns were removed from the heart of the aged and ill head shepherd of Tyraspol. He had one more important duty to deal with. He still had to direct a word of farewell to his former flock. He did this on December 20, 1889 in moving words which are printed below:

Franz Zottmann
By the Mercy of God and of the Apostolic See; grace unto you. The Bishop of Tyraspol to the Honourable Clergy of the Diocese: I greet you and bless you.

"Honoured brethren! An old proverb states: "mortem inter et officium praestat esse interstitium/Between life and death there should be an interval." Already during the time which I spent as a boy in the Junior/SeniorHigh School/College and which I spent as a young man at university, I had the intention, whenever it was possible, to spend the last phase of my life in the peace and quiet of a monastery. This is a desire which followed me throughout my entire life and remained in my heart after I had become a priest, and even then, when I, also not because of any merit, was elevated to the honour of bishop. As is probably known to you, the governance of the diocese of Tyraspol presents one with a horrendous amount of work and the greatest of difficulties and vexations because of its special situation. Nevertheless, despite being of a weak disposition, I did bear this burden for sixteen years. It is even more difficult because the bishop has to make do without the aid needed for the governance of the diocese as several canons of the cathedral chapter do not have their residence in Saratov and because of poor salaries and of a lack of space cannot even live there. As my poor health, with the passage of time and as a result of the strenuous work, has been weakened and my powers of perception have declined more and more, and because I therefore could no longer remain in the office of bishop for much longer in order to govern the diocese and could only fulfill a few necessary tasks, thus I respectfully implored the Head of the Church, that he would, in his grace, end the tie which bound me to the diocese of Tyraspol and allow me to resign from the administration of the diocese and, with the beneficent aid of God, without being diverted by anything else, to be able to use the remaining part of my life for prayer, L reading and meditation in order to prepare for a good death. The Holy Father, may God keep him healthy and safe for a very long time, after repeated petitions, finally deemed that this desire be fulfilled. In order to inform you of this, honourable brethren, we directed this pastoral epistle to you.

For the respect and obedience which you, honoured brethren, showed to me, your bishop, I would like to thank you from the bottom of my heart. I especially thank the honourable cathedral chapter which supported me in the administration of the diocese and served in an excellent manner leading and administering the seminary. I would also like to thank the very honourable deans, who fulfilled the duties of their office in such a praiseworthy manner and did not let an opportunity pass by without showing their obedience and respect both themselves and on behalf of their faithful parishoners.

Honourable Priests! If l leave a new and more worthy cathedral church behind, then that is more to your credit than to my own. If I, by means of a collection of contributions over a period of two years, was able to solve~ dangerous crisis in the seminary for clergy, then this could only have taken place by means of your cooperation and rich generosity. And again, it was you, who during the last Eastern War and later, when the members of the diocese of the gouvernement of Saratov and Samara were afflicted with famine who gave much support when I asked for it and collected donations from the faithful. Having often admonished you by means of pastoral letters, you were determined to carry out the sacred functions of your office in the spirit of the holy religion (Translator's note: a reference to the Christian Church and specifically to the Holy Catholic Church), to proclaim the Word of God zealously, to do whatever was possible to take care of the catechesis of the children and of the parish schools. You also tried to introduce order and honour in the Houses of God and and you have also entirely shown that you did this in a praiseworthy manner. In that I recognize all of this with great joy and confirm I very much wish that you continue to work in a praiseworthy manner; for as the Holy Scriptures state: "Only whoever stays faithful to the end, will be saved." (Matthew 24;13)

Through the division of the large parishes, with very few exceptions, about 25 new parishes were formed and many new churches and chapels were built so that a more regular and normal type of pastoral care was possible almost everywhere. The diocesan seminary, which is presently attended very well, is making good progress and the hope is justified that within a short time not only that all of the parishes will be filled but that there will also be a surplus of priests who can be appointed as vicars among the pastors of the widespread parishes.

However, in Christ dearly beloved brethren, I can not leave you without even having given a short and admonishing word from a shepherd in this last letter which I have given to you. In the centre of all pastoral instruction we may rightly be considered to have the given us the beautiful words of St. Peter, the Prince of the Apostles and the first visible head of the Church: "Feed the herd of God who have been entrusted to you and take care of them not with force, but of your own free will according to God's will and not in order to have shameful gain but out of love; not as such who reign over the inheritance of God but as examples to the flock who have become this from their heart. And if the Head Shepherd should appear then you will receive the crown of glory which does not fade." (1. Peter 5:2-4). This brethren, is what you are to always have in front of your eyes and that should be your intention. The present century in which we live is corrupted by naturalism and pantheism and the Christian religion almost went under because of this and it has been infected by many political and social fallacies and it shows every authority; to the ecclesiastical as well as the worldly that it holds animosity and is hateful toward the Christian religion. Therefore take care most beloved in the Lord that you carefully encourage the souls in their faith; those placed under your care and those of the faithful without which it is according to the Scriptures impossible to please God. This also encourages child-like obedience to the Holy Mother, the Church. Never be lacking in thoroughly teaching those placed in your care the Catholic Religion and to thoroughly admonish them that they in every life situation and in all kinds of times remain true to the Roman Catholic Church and that they be ready to suffer even the most trying times rather than to fall away from the faith. Keep and further in yourselves and extend to your flocks the spirit of unity with the Holy Father, the Roman pope who is the infallible teacher and the highest shepherd of flocks and pastors as well as also your bishop the shepherd and_ father of the entire diocese; for priests which have not been led by this spirit are no shepherds but hirelings who do not act as shepherds but disperse the flock. The holy Church of God is comparable to a huge tree which overshadows the entire circumference of the earth and its roots, even if they are visible support and nourish the entire tree and Christ is the Lord of this tree. The trunk of the tree is the Pope in Rome who is the visible head of the Church and the branches are the bishops; the twigs are the priests and the leaves and fruit are the faithful.

Beyond this also incalculate worldly obedience to those faithful who have been entrusted into your care so that they are honourably obedient to the laws and officials without whom there can be no empire and community. For you know well with which power and authority the apostles sent by God showed obedience toward worldly power and wanted this taught. (l.Peter 13-14; Romans 13:12)

Consider then, dear brethren in the Lord, that you be true shepherds of the church and eager proclaimers of the Word of God; conscientious grantors of the mysteries of God and experienced physicians of souls and fill all of your responsibilites with zealous care in that you try to be everything to everyone. With care in regard to our times, join great pastoral wisdom to your praiseworthy zeal without which even excellent knowledge and first-class priestly morals can never bear respective fruit. Wisdom is always counted among the four cardinal virtues and blind zeal does not build up but destroys. Carry out the callings which have been entrusted to you without mutual disunity and jealousy for every parish someone has stated has the same heavy burden and can either bring heaven or hell to earth according to how the parish is served.

Do not forget that what you owe as a debt to God, the Holy Mother Church, and what you owe those souls entrusted to you, what you owe to your own salvation, and what kind of a strict judgement from God awaits you so that you do not open the springs of salvation to others but prepare yourselves for eternal perdition. For this reason seek to preach as much by your good way of life as through your words for a good example is the best sermon. Oh, my brethren how we must greatly tremble that the close relationship with the mysteries which we have attained in an awesome manner and the daily contact with the most holy things not bring us to perdition! 0 how terrible that the most pious and most experienced authors declare that which experience confirms in regard to that terrible hardening of the heart of a priest who has been burdened with countless sacrileges. This makes the conversion of a cleric much more difficult than that of a layperson.

Finally, as I leave dear beloved brethren in Christ, not without deep pains in the soul, I implore that God the highest and best Lord grant you every good thing and every good fortune and I entrust myself to your memory and to your devout prayers. For the last time and from a heart full of love I grant you and your flocks the bishop's blessing in the Name of the Father and of the Son and of the Holy Ghost. Amen."

These beautiful words of farewell given to the cathedral chapter of Tyraspol and to the deans and the clergymen and women of the parishes were without doubt taken note of in Saratov but according to what seemed to be did not get to the hearts of the spiritual leaders. Otherwise, the author of these sentences who had a position in Saratov at that time would have heard something. Somehow and for some reason someone must have "hidden" (Translator's note: literally: placed it under the green sheet) this bishop's letter and not allowed it to reach the public.

32. Suffragan Bishop Antonius Zerr, bishop of Tyraspol

Bishop Antonius Zerr was born on March 10, 1849 in the German colony of Franzfeld near Odessa and was one of the most gifted graduates of the Tyraspol seminary, from which he graduated in the year 1971. Because of a lack of priests he administered the position of a procurator at the seminary. This was because he was young and could not, after ending bis studies, be ordained as a priest right away. Ordained as a priest, he was appointed as the administrator of the parish of Preuss not far from Saratov. The chapter vicar, Suffragan Bishop Lipski who ordained him as well as Bishop Franz Xaverius Zottmann who followed Bishop Lipski thought highly of the young, imposing and very talented priest. After about four years of praiseworthy work, the ordinary sent him to be the administrator in Katharinenstadt where until that point in time Father Adrescheykovitz, a Dominican, had served in great blessing and who according to his own wish had received the parish of Astrachan. The parish of Katharinenstadt is the only village parish in the diocese in which Catholics lived mixed with a much larger and wealthier Lutheran majority. Actually this colony is more of a city than a village. Because of its choice location on the huge Volga River and in the middle of many German colonies there was continual and lively trade with most of the German and Russian villages in two counties; those of Nikolayev and Novouzenchen. Here the diocesan bishop needed a talented and more worthy representative of the Catholic Church since as a rule the deanery was yoked to the parish position. At the same time, Administrator Anton Zerr was appointed the dean of the northern region of the Meadow Side. This is how the left shore of the Volga is called. The young priest administered both of his positions in an exemplary manner and for the Christian growth of all concerned. But God's providence had chosen him for more important positions. Because of his zeal in his studies and because of his talents he got the attention of the diocesan leadership.

In the winter of 1878 Bishop Zottmann called him to be the professor of apologetics, of dogmatics and philosophy at the seminary for priests in Saratov. By means of his lectures and his friendly character the new young professor soon won the high respect and love of his students and all of the pupils in the institution. All wished him well in his position as supervisor of the seminary. The yearning and proper wish of the pupils was not fulfilled for a period of three years: Supervisor Johannes Burghardt was relieved of his position and Professor Anton Zerr took his place. It is superfluous to note that Supervisor Zerr led a mild rule of the institution. This he did without the discipline or the piety of the students having to suffer. To the contrary, there was a lot of progress noted within a short period of time. The saying of St. Francis de Sales also showed itself to be true: "With a drop of honey you can catch more flies than with a pail of vinegar." With great sadness the students bid the very beloved supervisor adieu when he left the institution in 1883, as he had been appointed to the position of suffragan bishop of Tyraspol.

Suffragan Bishop Antonius Zerr was just 34 years old when he was elevated to this important office. He was at the pinnacle of his manhood and so he could provide many great services to the weak diocesan bishop whose health was suffering. This was in the administration of the bishopric.

Bishop Franz Zottmann had, since his earliest youth the hidden desire to spend several years in a quiet cell in a monastery at the end of his life in order to prepare himself well for death which he, because of weak health and his heart problems always considered to be just around the corner. Now after he got a suffragan bishop he thought even more than before about his complete withdrawal from the turbulence of the world. Time and time again he had petitioned the Holy Father Leo XIII, but it was only at the end of 1889 that he had received his wish granted. This was mentioned previously. This time the diocese of Tyraspol was not to remain orphaned. On December 18th on the day in which Zottmanns resignation was accepted, the Holy See appointed Antonius Johannes Zerr as the consecratory diocesan bishop of Tyraspol. This was, however, done after previous discussions with the Russian government. Thus for the first time the bishopric had as its head a bishop who had come from the German colonies and as a son of colonists was familiar with all of the conditions in the diocese, its customs and traditions in a most thorough way. And yet as a Russian citizen, he was also faithful toward his homeland and had feelings for the fatherland.
The administration of the bishopric did not need to be bestowed on him in a festive way as this was common during the festivities during inthronization as he was at the time of his pre-consecration a vicar general and administrator of the diocese. As the appointment had taken place during the winter, the celebration for the inthronization was held in the next spring. Priests and members of the diocesan leadership came from all of the parts of the widespread diocese in order to partake in the moving celebration. The entire diocese congratulated him. They were glad to see a son of their own people in the bishop's see.

Especially moving and most solemn was the moment in that celebration when the members of the cathedral chapter, the deans, the priests and other priests among who were honoured elderly men stepped up to the cathedral and either bowing deeply or kneeling before the new Head Shepherd gave him as a sign of obedience and respect the gift of humbly kissing his ring and thus showing their worship to him as God's representative. During this high moment in time all of the people present certainly cherished in their hearts the desire that the new shepherd of the diocese would use his shepherd's staff peacefully for the wellbeing of the little flock which had been entrusted to him. Many of the clergymen feared that there would be changes and more changes in the highest offices of the diocese as this happens at times in similar situations and through which peace in the diocese would be disturbed. The seminary was concerned about certain issues. The future showed that these were justified. The seminary for priests was according to means taken care of by teachers. Among other things Rector Alexander Boos, Supervisor Johannes Antonov, his brother who had for several years attended the propaganda (Urban College in Rome) and who was older, Kaspar Ruscheinski, Raphael Fleck and Joseph Kessler who was active simultaneously As the parish vicar. In the seminary for priests, life quietly continued. Then late summer 1891 came. Everything seemed to be in the best of order when suddenly the young professor Joseph Kessler, who was also the vicar at the cathedral church, was relieved of the positions which he had filled since 1889 and was appointed as the administrator of the Catholic parish in Simferopol in the Crimea. This appointment was a promotion for him rather than a demotion as some seemed to think. For the young priest had been specially trained as a professor after finishing a course in philosophy and theology which lasted eight years and he spent four of these years at the Spiritual Academy in St. Petersburg where he had attained the degree of Master of Theology as the first of any of the colonists' sons. He had received special education and so his simulateous position in Saratov was in no way something which made one jealous. As the priest in the parish was often busy as an instructor in religion during the morning hours in the Middle Schools, the largest part of the work in the parish lay upon the shoulders of the vicar. The result was that the parish office duties very often collided with each other. How often he sat in the confessional, which he could not leave, while the students at the seminary were waiting for him to teach. For this reason the newly-appointed administrator gladly went to the place to which he had been appointed, especially since there was no hope of just being employed as a professor at the seminary.

Several months later Rector Alexander Boos, who had been so vital for the seminary for priests and had done so much for it, received his demission and appointment as the priest of the parish of Kishinev in Bessarabia. This call was the same thing as ripping the unity and the peace of the diocese apart. The largest number of clergy, and one could state the healthier part looked upon an order such as this as unjustifiable in the highest if not an act of revenge. lb.is move estranged the hearts of most of the clergymen of the diocese from the diocesan shepherd. If Bishop Zerr had clearly seen the undermining results of this removal from office, he would not have carried it out. The diocesan bishop who had evidenced his noble views so often as a professor, supervisor of the seminary and as suffragan bishop to so many people could not possibly have made this mistake. How often is someone in authority kept back by good advisors in his midst, so that he does not make thoughtless and damaging moves? The bishop's environment and his advisors did not attempt to give him their views in regard to certain ordinances which had to be given but advised him according to their own special interests. History teaches that Rehoboam's fate has been repeated countless times without the respective person having thereby turned it to his advantage. Such decisive changes such as the removal from office of Rector Alexander Boos were made in the most extreme of cases. This is similar to a situation which took place during the World War when one made sure of the aid of other priests in order to have them support his illegal actions against the ordinary. Following this the seminary took the active help of the Ministry opposing the rules of the diocesan bishop which were carried out successfully using a telegram which was sent under a pseudonym. And this took place during a difficult time when that which was German in Russia was despised. this was, as a highly-honoured Nuncio expressed, Bolshevism in the church. So the contaminated seminary had to be completely disinfected if there was even something that was still to be saved.

In general, the administration under Bishop Antonius Zerr did not justify the good hopes which one had fixed. A large number of priests in the diocese were not sympathetic toward the administration of the bishop. Some of them used this situation by not distinguishing themselves from others to win the special favour of the Head Shepherd. They did this without knowledge and godliness. For this reason these priests were favoured more than all of the others. They were glad to have the special favour of the bishop and they got the richest parishes in the diocese. However, Bishop Antonius considered his friends as the most important priests in the diocese. This was, however, not the opinion of the large majority of the clergy and the public opinion of the people. - Whoever got a deeper insight into the records of the diocesan chancellery had to convinced of the fact that it did not fail to come to uncouth treatment in terms of respect and obedience by many a priest and layman toward the diocesan bishop. Every successor to the Apostles had this question directed to him by the divine Redeemer when he took

over the flock: "Can you drink the cup which I will drink?" And if the weak human being states with the Apostles: "I can do it." that is if he has taken over the leadership of a part of the Christian flock, then the cross and suffering are bestowed upon him in rich measure. He has to drink the cup of suffering right down to the sediment. "For the shepherd is not above the master." Matthew 10 :24 - thus intense suffering was not spared for Bishop Zerr. He had found a helper in the administration and he developed into a great worker. This was the old canon and later prelate, Kaspar Baczewski, who was a Lithuanian. He had already been appointed by his predecessor as an official in the consistory and he bore the burden of the consistory entirely upon his shoulders. The secretary of the consistory, a Catholic layman, and especially the three assesors helped him very little, as they had many things to do in other areas. Kaspar Baczewski was always a friend of Bishop Zerr and during the first years of his appointment by the pontiff, the bishop made him his vicar general and secretary. The great strength given to Baczewski who was already very old as vicar general and secretary caused that Baczewski's spirit trickled into the entire administration and finally came to fruition, especially when Bishop Zerr purchased an estate near Saratov with an orchard, residence and steam mill. The many disappointments and vexations which the administration of a bishopric of such a great size brought with it and with its particular situation and with its many cares made the bishop tired: Because of the impossible heat in the city, at first he just spent the summer months on his estate. Later on he spent the greatest part of the year there; until a few years before resigning he moved his residence completely to his estate in the countryside. He only rarely went to the city. He did so only when his presence was absolutely necessary for instance when his presence was absolutely necessary; when he had to ordain and carry out other holy acts or during the highest festivals of the year. The bishop gave the administration almost completely to his vicar general, Prelate Baczewski, upon whom he could depend completely. Prelate Baczewski was also a true servant of his Lord.

The ordinary was not very available to priests who wanted to speak with him; especially those who were not in favour with the bishop. If a priest of the last order announced an audience with the ordinary then the vicar general always tried to convince him to have him take care of his concerns via the vicar general as he had all powers given to him for such purposes. The way to the bishop was associated with expenses and finally one could not always also make the ordinary upset. The bishop's palace was a ruin and neglected. One saw neither a servant nor a house chaplain and seldom a servant who took care of the property. Bishop Zerr never got a house chaplain. For the most part the youthful professor of the seminary, Kaspar Ruscheinski, had contact with him. As a rule one had to get an old lady from the kitchen in the lower kitchen in order to find out where the honourable Lord Bishop was to be found, when he would be coming to the city, and where one would be able to speak with him. One could break one's bones on the steps down to the lower kitchen. The outward ruination of the bishop's palace and the residence were symptomatic of the situation in the church leadership. With this situation no one will be surprised that the diocesan bishop only visited a locality if the priest invited him for the consecration of a new church. Thus he visited the parish of Koehler as the suffragan bishop and consecrated its church. As the ordinary of the diocese he consecrated seven Houses of God in the deanery of Nikolayev and several in the deanery of Odessa and upon this occasion confirmed several thousand young teenagers. He also consecrated the churches in Marienberg, Neukolonie and Ober-Monjou and here he also confirmed several thousands of the faithful. Bishop Antonius did not undertake a visitation journey to the north and to the other parts of the diocese excepting the two deaneries which have been noted. That which especially impressed the faithful people was that the bishop did not hold just a single sermon or speech in the churches or prayer chapel (oratories) during his trips for confirmations. And yet the people yearned so much for these sermons and talks. What deep and unforgettable impressions that a sermon by a bishop with a mitre and a shepherd's staff had upon the faithful people, is demonstrated by the pontifical sermon which Bishop Zottmann held from the pulpit in Mariental. The people gathered in such great numbers in the large church that one was in danger of being smothered. It was a moving show when one saw with what kind of attention one listened to the Shepherd. One digested every word spoken by the episcopal preacher; oh the amazing inner emotions which were brought forth by his words! A special blessing rested upon the sermon of the Head Shepherd of the diocese who is actually the real teacher of the diocese whom God himself sent. Because Bishop Zerr had never held a speech or a sermon when he was on his visitation and confirmation trips, he did not have personal contact with his flock. This always left a disquieting emptiness in the minds of the faithful.

What happened was that the city parishes were visited less frequently under the pontifical reign of Bishop Antonius. Outside of Odessa and Nikolayev he visited no other city parishes. The reason for this is that he could not speak the Polish language so well in order to hold a speech to parishoners who spoke the Polish language. For in all of the city parishes he would have had to actually hold a talk or a sermon. Under the leadership of Bishop Antonius Zerr the biweekly periodical "Klemens" (1. named after St. Clement I who was the patron saint of the diocese of Tyraspol) was founded by Professor and Canon Joseph Kruschinsky. This important fact which was a strong element for education in the Catholic life of the people and also educated them in terms of religion and the church must also be considered a result of the influence of the ordinary. The diocesan bishop earned special honours through the introduction of religious excercises for priests which have since then been held on an annual basis and which again always revived the spirit of priesthood among the clergy. During the year in which this was introduced the bishop himself held the conferences and took part in the exercises. This was a support to the clergy. Under the administration of Bishop Antonius a religious book and devotional store was opened in Saratov by the publishing house "Schellhorn and C-nie." This store obtained all of the books which were needed from Germany and Austria. This bookstore fulfilled an important need among the faithful. From now on the poorly made crucifixes which were made by local "carvers of the Lord God" disc1ppeared. They had aroused disdain, rather than being suitable for times of devotion. Immediately after taking over the bishopric, the bishop had exact rules set for the visitation of the parishes by the deans.

Finally, the ordinary sent two pastoral letters to the clergy and the faithful, of which the first one was also in the Polish language. The introduction of the mass book was of great importance. It was produced with an introduction by the bishop and stamped with his seal. Every priest in the diocese had to order this mass book of intentions. During the annual audit of the records and treasurer's books the book of stipends had to be reviewed by the dean and audited. All of the rules which have been mentioned were wise and created good. Since the ordinary did not urge that they were to be introduced, they were often not taken seriously. Unfortunately, the visitations were undertaken by one or another of the deans or the result of the visitations was very seldom sent to the episcopal leadership. For this reason even the best and most useful instructions and rules of the diocesan bishop remained without effect. Various mistakes in the administration of the bishopric made the ordinary lethargic and tired to such a degree that he did not want to have anything to do with the administration. For this reason he gave the leadership of the bishopric to his vicar general Prelate Kaspar Baczewski as has been mentioned aforehand. In the end the bishop asked the Holy See for his demission from the position. He was not especially beloved in Rome. He was sometimes not in favour especially after the Russian government wanted to have him elevated as the archbishop of Mohilev. Rome had heard that Bishop Antonius Zerr had occupied himself too little with the administration of his diocese, that he did not visit his diocese and that he did not keep the rule of staying in residence; also that he only seldom read a mass and that his vicar general, whom he had appointed as a prelate, had not held a single mass since 1881. These complaints were added to by others as well. That which made Bishop Antonius unbeloved among the Poles and the Lithuanians was his delicate mission which he carried out upon the wishes of Emperor Alexander III. In Kroze, in the diocese of Kovno, the governor of Kovno had wanted to take away the parish church from the Catholics. Since the Catholic population opposed this, pure force was used against it and there were even deaths. The head of the department, Prince Katakusen, had to investigate the situation upon the emperor's orders and report the facts to the czar. The prince let himself be bribed by the governor and lied to the emperor in that he indicated that the governor

was innocent and the poor Catholic people in Kroze were rebellious. Later the emperor found out about the real situation in a roundabout way and felt very ashamed. He felt that he had been shamed in front of "the most honoured of all sovereigns, Leo XIII." He sent the bishop of Tyraspol, Antonius Zerr, to defend the reputation and the honour of the czar and his government during an audience with Leo XIII. After the audience with the bishop the daily newspapers reported that the Bishop of Tyraspol had assured the Holy Father that the Catholic Church is not being persecuted in Russia and in Congress Poland. However, if some officials in the huge empire used their positions to the detriment of the Catholic Church this was not according to the interests of government. These facts were used by the Austrian Polish press to indicate that the Catholic Church was being persecuted by the Russian government.

As the correspondence with the Holy See according to Paragraph Nr. 17, Volume XI of the Russian state law had to be sent to the Ministry of the Interior in order to be reviewed, Bishop Antonius Zerr sent in his petition to the Holy See to be relieved of his office by the same Ministry of the Interior office. As the reason for his demission to the bishop's see of Tyraspol, he stated that he was in poor health. As he was considered a good person (persona grata) the government did not want him to leave his posting. It was suggested to him that he should remain in his office and a suffragan or consecrating bishop would be given to him who would aid him in his work. As a result of this letter the bishop no longer insisted that he be relieved of his office but at the same time he relinquished his right to appoint a consecrating bishop as he, in a certain sense, already had more help by the prelate than a suffragan bishop. 1. Baczewski - He could carry out the pontifical duties without extra effort as had previously been the case. The diocesan newspaper, which a short time previous had published the application of the bishop for his resignation, now proclaimed to the diocese that because of a great improvement in his state of health he would remain in his position. Thus almost an entire year passed by and no one thought about a change in the position of diocesan bishop. Then some Poles who were antagonistic toward the bishop spread the rumour that Bishop Antonius Zerr had been removed from his position by the Holy Father. A Catholic teacher brought this news to the villages. Like a prairie fire this troubling news spread around. The German clergy received the news with their own questions as they knew that the Poles were disinclined toward the bishop because of his mission in regard to the situation in Kroze. One priest who was a special favorite of the diocesan bishop wanted to hear the exact and specific facts regarding the situation from the ordinary himself. For this reason he secretly travelled to Saratov and asked the bishop, and was informed by him that there was no truth in the matter. Bishop Antonius himself was not up-to-date in regard to this his own affairs. He made the mistake that he did not contradict his application for his resignation which he had sent to the government so that it would be sent to the Holy Father.

Accordingly one could read into the situation that the petitioner still had kept his desire to resign unless the bishop would have had to retract. This did not happen. This is what, among other things, was declared by the then Archbishop Boleslaus Klopotowski. In the meantime this archbishop had been elevated to the see of Mohilev. For this reason the archbishop told the Ministry that the petition of the Bishop of Tyraspol should be allowed to be sent to Rome and this happened soon afterward. In a relatively short time the Holy Father fulfilled the petition. This news was spread chiefly among the Poles and Lithuanians, but Bishop Antonius Zerr was only informed at a later date. This was the reason for a contradictory reply to the priests whom he had befriended. But even the last fact was spread around among the members of the diocese in the south and was done so causing harm. That is, the rumour regarding the resignation or the removal of the ordinary was either fabricated or lied about. The reason that this took place was because of the priest who was his friend. He had thought that he was doing something good in regard to the affair. When he returned from Saratov he told the gathered congregation about the resignation on the first Sunday which followed; or as one had slanderously stated in regard to the removal of the highly honoured Mr. Antonius Zerr that it was an infamous lie which had been invented by the enemies of the ordinary. "After this rumour had been spread I myself undertook the effort and travelled to the highly honoured bishop in Saratov. He himself explained to me that he knew nothing about a resignation and did not think about it anymore. A year ago he had himself requested to be relieved of his position but now he was going to remain in his calling. The rumour in regard to his removal from his position was an evil-minded invention." Despite this, as the rumour regarding the removal from the position was confirmed soon afterward, many had the

1. Baczewski

suspicion that the bishop had in fact been removed from his office. The vexation which was caused by this was great. It was the cause of much damage to the way in which the bishop was regarded and that could have certainly been avoided. Soon afterward the "Klemens" published the news that the bishop had resigned. In the interest of the good cause and in order to minimize the vexation among the priests and laymen, the diocesan newspaper should have explained the resignation in a wise and apt way. Unfortunately, this did not take place because at that time only very few and especially few of the clergy had been informed about the real situation.

33. **Rector Boos' removal from office and farewell**

Under the rectorship of cathedral dean Alexander Boos, who was the first son of a colonist who had attained such a place of honour, the crisis in regard to the economic woes which had become a part of the scenario during the leadership of Dr. Michael Glossner was overcome thanks to Boos' prudence, efforts and experience. Already in the second month after the seminary had changed hands, the students got tea with two pieces of sugar and half a Russian bread dumpling instead of watery Riebel soup and rye bread. The midday meal was more nutritious and given out in greater portions. Since the excellent watermelons are native to Saratov and are fabulously cheap (one single large one only cost the ridiculous sum of five kopecks) and in terms of wholesale cost were only three kopecks each, the students received watermelon as desert after the midday meal. In the evening there was also a meat soup with a piece of meat included. The students were overjoyed when the meals turned to the better. Even though the previous manager had been replaced by an honest Catholic colonist, the rector was often seen looking into the supply chamber, into the basement and especially into the kitchen. He watched everything so that the servants always felt that the watchful eyes of the highly honoured rector were looking at them. Rector Boos was simply acquainted with the situation which was prevalent in Russia. Instead of allowing the manager of the seminary to make deals with the bakers, merchants and with the laundry at the beginning of each school year in regard to fixing the prices for their deliveries, he took this work upon himself. He had the business people come to him and made written contracts with them in which all of the conditions were set so that any kind of possible cheating could be avoided. He was even concerned about the heating of the rooms and no one was to be cold during the winter, but at the same time firewood was not to be burned unnecessarily. During the first year there were already big savings in terms of fuel. If one considers that Rector Boos took all of these cares and all of this work upon himself so that those placed under his care would be well taken care of, then one must give this man a lot of credit. Rector Boos earned this credit entirely since he also had to take over a professorship. He had not just arrived from a university so that all theological knowledge was still fresh in his mind. For this reason he had to prepare his lectures very thoroughly in order to achieve something, especially after such diligent professors as Dr. Glossner, Franz Xaverius and Willibald Zottmann. Despite this he found the time in order to take over all of the economic issues and to watch over them carefully. He did what every other rector would have passed on to an aid. His pupils and students have kept 'thankful and loving memories of Rector Boos. This was because of the many and great efforts which he took upon himself for their sake. Some people and unfortunately his superiors could not evaluate this man properly. One main reason for the misinformation and for the nonrecognition of this priest was that he entirely immersed himself in a conscientious fulfillment of the duties of his office and accomplished much more than even his adversaries could expect of him. He did these things because of love for the heart of the diocese, the seminary for priests and for the students of religion who were being educated. Without question other reasons for the misinformation had to do with the fact that he was a straightout man and that he had a somewhat rough temper. Unfortunately human beings generally dismiss the great achievements and even the heroic virtues of such a man. Rector Boos also saw to it that the school grew in terms of teaching knowledge and this occurred above all through the recommendation of the priest Johannes Antonov as a professor for the seminary. However the time of blossoming which had taken place in knowledge at the seminary during the time of the foreign professors did not return for "one swallow does not mean that summer is here." One always felt that there was a lack of diligent instructors. For this reason Rector Boos saw to it that there were two free places to study at the Catholic Academy in St. Petersburg. As the government did not want to create any more free places for students to study using state funds because this would have meant about 2,000 rubles per year, but was still favourably inclined toward the request of request of the rector, and Bishop Franz Xaverius Zottmann and the archbishop also approved of the application, two free places for students were taken from two other dioceses and given to the diocese of Tyraspol. The Spiritual Seminary/University in St. Petersburg was the only one in all of the Catholic bishoprics in Russiand and Congress Poland. It took the place of the former academies in Vilna and in Warsaw. Its main task was the education of professors for the seminaries for priests in the 14 Catholic bishoprics. For this reason acceptance in this school was determined by graduating from a seminary for priests and a four-year study of philosophy and theology. During the time when Rector Boos was at the seminary for priests in Tyraspol, its first graduates were also sent to university in St. Petersburg. In doing so Rector Boos did what was possible for the intellectual furtherance of the seminary. The service which he did for the greenhouse for priests was many-sided. His exegetical lectures were somewhat lacking but his lectures concerning moral theology were on a level which was reflective of the times. He had taken over these lectures after Burghardt had been removed from his position. Without a doubt the pastoral care in the diocese was greatly benefitted by this course. However the relationship between the former supervisor of the institution, who had been elevated as the successor to Zottmann on the bishop's see of Tyraspol and who had previously been the rector of the seminary as well, was not the best. One feared that after Bishop Zerr's elevation to the position of diocesan bishop there would be a change in the leadership of the seminary for priests. That which was surmised actually took place two years after the bishopric had been taken over by Bishop Anton Johannes Zerr. Canon Alexander Boos was removed from his positions at the seminary in the fall of 1891 and sent to be the priest in Kishinev in Bessarabia. However this was a hard blow for Rector Boos. Without consideration for his nervous state, which was not good, he humbly accepted the order of his former subordinate who was now his superior. Since life in Saratov and especially at the seminary was quiet and everything was progressing in the best of order, fairness as well as even more Christian wisdom would have advised that such decisive changes not be made. One must forgive men such as Boos with his power to act and his great achievements of their smaller mistakes and human weaknesses and in no case should they become the victims of one's special interests.

The day of the rector's departure from the institution, which he had led for twelve years in a praiseworthy manner, came. It was a day of sadness for all. He did not direct a long speech to the boarding students and the pupils in the institution of learning. With the spirit which prevailed at that time one could have misinterpreted one or another word. The pious priest wanted to avoid that. However the person who was leaving could not completely master his own heart. For this reason he ended his short speech with words in which he warmly recommended that the students practice obedience and respect toward their superiors. He also recommended that the students study and pray diligently. He also admonished them to pray for him and closed with the words: "My tears say more than my words."

The newly appointed rector of the seminary, the priest of the parish of Saratov and canon of the cathedral chapter Raphael Fleck was a priest of pure morals and great zeal for souls but was less gifted. In taking over the rectorship he also took over the lectures on moral theology and other affairs which the departing Rector Boos had done. Canon Raphael Fleck was capable of doing everything except teaching in an institution of learning for priests. He saw this inability himself. However, because of obedience he did not dare to contradict the will of his ordinary. The conscientious priest studied day and night. Because of too much effort he jangled his nerves so that he became mentally ill and had to be removed from his position after eight years of work. He was followed in that office by Canon Joseph Kruschinsky, who had been the docent for church history and canon law at the seminary for several years already. He was a skilled teacher.

The removal of the very deserving Rector Alexander Boos from his position hurt the good cause in two ways. Firstly, many of the best and most important clergy of the bishopric became estranged from the diocesan bishop and secondly the seminary for priests had lost the person who had placed its economic affairs upon a solid footing. The regression in terms of knowledge in the school was also a result of his removal. Under the rectorship of Canon Raphael Fleck the seminary had economic problems again. The replacement of the business manager by a young clergyman could not hinder the looming economic crisis. The meals were reduced so much that the pupils in fact remained hungry. The younger pupils in the seminary for boys called out for bread! The new business manager who was a priest, wanted, so it seemed, as he alone actually administered the finances of the seminary, to set the finances aright by radically saving. No pleas from the rector nor from the supervisor could teach the young inexperienced and self-glorifying clergyman a better way. It came to open demonstrations at the seminary and the boarding school students and pupils demanded the removal of the business manager who was a priest. He however was a special favorite of the diocesan bishop. One saying states: "Needs cause iron to break." The students of the seminary for clergy went en masse to the diocesan bishop in order to present their plea for the removal of the cheap manager. The spokesman, a deacon, spoke in an excited manner and completely forgot before whom he was speaking. The words were hard and very hurtful toward the diocesan shepherd. They must have vexed him a great deal. The diocesan shepherd quietly listened to the rough words. But suddenly the colour of his face changed. One could see the inner battle which it cost him to listen to this coarse language. He would have collapsed at that moment had not a more understanding student (1. Nikolaus Maier, who is at present the rector of the Monastery of the Good Shepherd in Berlin-Marienfelde and who accompanied Bishop Kessler to America) seen the bishop falling over and supported him with his strong arms. This student then spoke words of explanation and excuse for what had transpired. After the bishop had fought and won over the inner conflict, he promised to implement the necessary rules for the betterment of the economic situation at the seminary. The self-glorifying business manager was removed after the youthful rector, Canon Ruscheinsky who in the meantime had relieved Canon Fleck from his position, had himself told the Head Shepherd about the bad economic situation in the school. Soon a meaningful amelioration of the situation took place under the prudent leadership of the seminary and its management. This took place under the new rector.

In terms of its studies the school had not progressed under the rectorsbip of Canon Raphael Fleck. A talented and young professor by the name of Kaspar Ruscheinsky, a German, had died. To be sure he found a successor in another talented young gentleman. (2. - Canon Xavier Klimaszewski, a Pole with an academic education and a doctorate) However in order to become a diligent teacher the talented gentleman had to give to practice lectures aloud. To be sure Professor Joseph Kruscbinsky with his exceptional diligence and excellent talents attained a great deal of knowledge and this within a short period of time, but there were not enough teachers in the institution. The students: (3. The Germans) who had in the meantime finished their studies at the Religious Academy in St. Petersburg were not wanted for placement as professors at the diocesan seminary. This was done because of special interests on the part of some and as one stated because of principle! As they were fluent in Polish and other languages they could be used in urban parishes and this did in fact take place as time passed. In this situation one had to be glad for the good fortune of still having the elderly Supervisor Sacristan Johannes Antonov at the seminary as professor of apologetics, dogmatics and philosophy. At the same time he bore the institution; that is the seminary for clergy upon his shoulders. As a former

student of the Collegium Urbanicum in Rome he had received the directive not to leave the seminary. This was to take place only if the ordinary himself wanted to transfer him and in this case the ordinary was to let the Society for the Propogation of the Faith know about this. If the ordinary knew about this directive and did count on it cannot be determined. So much alone is certain. Antonov remained at his post without wavering during all of the troublesome times which affected the Seminary of Tyraspol from 1882 to 1910.

34. Eduard Baron von Ropp, bishop of Tyraspol

Bishop Antonius Johannes Zerr held the shepherd's staff over the diocese of Tyraspol for twelve years less five months. He was gifted by nature and was led by a desire for knowledge during his years as a priest. He had really increased in terms of his secular and theological knowledge and thus he was able to take good care of the duties attendant to his occupation. Besides the German and Russian language he had a sufficient knowledge of French and that which was very important for the leadership in a Catholic diocese in Russia was the fact that he was someone whom the government considered to be a positive person. Not long after taking over the administration of the bishopric Emperor Alexander III bestowed the Order of St. Vladimir of the Third Class upon him and thereby he became a part of the nobility and could pass on his title. One sign that he was able to understand how to remain within the good graces of the emperor was the fact that within a short time he was bestowed the title of St. Stanislaus of the First Class and St. Anne of the First Class as well as St.Vladimir of the Second Class. No bishop of Tyraspol had ever enjoyed such fondness and goodwill as Bishop Antonius von Zerr. Thereby all of the outward prerequisites of a very blessed time of activity were present. Despite this, the administration of the bishopric suffered. Love this living bond which bound the shepherd and his flock but especially the priests with their spiritual father the diocesan bishop was lacking. The most important reason was that mutual animosity had been caused by the removal of Rector Alexander Boos from his position and he had carried out his duties very well. A second reason which was just as important was the almost complete isolation of the bishop from his priests. By the fact that Bishop Zerr had himself represented in almost everything by his vicar general, Prelate Baczewski caused that the clergy rarely or never had an audience with him especially after he began to reside in his villa.

The separation which was caused by this was even greater because some clergy who were not special compared to others received the special favours of the bishop and had easy access to the diocesan shepherd. They also received easier parishes from him. A final reason was that the bishop because of always being represented by Prelate

Baczewski did not seem to know what was always going on. If there were questions among the church leadership from gatherings of priests in the individual deaneries which were hard to decide upon then Prelate Baczewski gave a report to the diocesan bishop. In many cases these issues were put in a bad light as the head shepherd loved peace but had had his nerves hurt by rough insults. This caused the bishop to get into a state of irritability. Instead of a peaceful answer or even a fatherly admonishment as was necessary the clergy who had gathered, for example, for a time of prayer which was to last 40 hours for the celebration of a church dedication or for spiritual exercises got a very irritated rebuke. From this came the fact that the bishop who had been led astray by false convictions thought that loveless criticism was being addressed toward him during the gatherings in regard to his administration etc. However the head shepherd had not just imagined the fact that he had a false view of the priests and the gatherings of priests. The favourites of the bishop of whom there was one or the other in every deanery, had put the actions and words of their colleagues in ministry into a bad light because they had special interests. They did this to the bishop. One of the mistakes of the bishop was that he considered such slanderous reports as being true and after that often undertook thoughtless steps which did no one any good but which harmed love, peace and mutual respect. These and similar situations between the bishop and the clergy would have become known in Rome because the Holy See had fulfilled the first attempt of the bishop for removal from his office: Without a doubt there were several candidates for elevation to the See of Tyraspol who had been designated such as the highly-honoured priest in Libau and canon of the cathedral chapter in Kovno, Eduard Baron von Ropp, the prelate of the cathedral chapter in Tyraspol Joseph Kruschinsky, the Papal House Prelate Klimaszewski etc. According to this there was not a lack of candidates for filling a bishop's see such as the one in Tyraspol. Above all the bishop needed to speak the German language well as the diocese still consisted of German colonists to the tune of 75%.

Since the flourishing growth of industry within the borders of this bishopric had caused many Polish workers to become residents in the diocese and in the south in the region of the Black Sea people in some villages had emigrated from Volhynia and these people used the Polish language, the Bishop of Tyraspol also had to speak the Polish language fluently. Besides these two languages Canon Eduard von Ropp also spoke the

French and the national languages fluently. Besides this he not only had studied philosophy and theology both abroad and at home but had also studied jurisprudence before his ordination and served in the Ministry for a long period of time. He was also a man of very broad learning which, given the circumstances in Russia, was also especially useful. He was also a man who had seen a good part of the world and had gotten to know Russia and its people. In the church he used his experience and his knowledge for the good of the Catholic Church. Under difficult circumstances he had built a glorious church while he was the priest in Libau and the members of that congregation will remember his name for a long time in the future. If there was money lacking for the construction of the House of God then he took it out of his own pocket. He is supposed to have taken many thousands of rubles from what he owned and spent it for this building. But the spiritual and individual growth of his parishoners lay more upon his heart than anything else. For this reason one often saw him not only in the confessional among the poor and destitute in his parish. He would comfort them as well as give as alms. Tireless in the proclamation of God's Word, wise and thorough in the administration of his parish, he was according to the Word of the Apostle, "Worthy of double honour." (1. Timothy 5:17) Because of these reasons the Holy Father Pius X appointed him as the Bishop of Tyraspol in the consistory of May 27, 1902. This See had been vacant since August 1, 1901.

After the celebration for the consecration had ended in St. Petersburg in which Prelate Kruschinsky and Canon Klimaszewski were present as the representatives of the cathedral chapter of Tyraspol, the journey to the diocese began with Chaplain Joseph Lasowski and both members of the cathedral chapter accompanying him. The Russian Railroad had specified a wagon without charge for the use of the new Head Shepherd and this is a sign that the higher state officials among the Russians were not mundane but generous gentlemen. In Western Europe one would not have been treated the same way. It was the middle of November and it was cold. Despite this the entire parish in Saratov and many diocesans from the colonies had assembled at the railroad station in order to receive and to welcome their new episcopal Head Shepherd. The welcome took place in two languages: Polish and German. There were also many clergy from the southern part of the bishopric who had come for the celebrations for the enthronization. The highly honoured Head Shepherd responded to the words of welcome with a short speech in Polish and in German. One immediately noted that the new bishop could speak both languages equally well. The first impression which the Head Shepherd gave was a favourable one. Everyone was glad to have a bishop who would satisfy both nationalities.

As the bishop wanted to hold his festive entrance into the cathedral and the celebrations for his enthronization on the following Sunday his first visit was designated to one in which he visited the diocesan seminary. After the adoration of the Host in the seminary chapel he held two long speeches in German and in Polish given to the pupils in the large auditorium. The students had not seen a bishop within the walls of the institution for a long time nor had they heard any words from the bishop. Thus their joy was even greater, as the newly arrived Head Shepherd, still recovering from the long journey, immediately spoke to them with warm and fatherly words. The next day the bells of St. Clement called together the diocesans from near and from far in the cathedral in order to welcome the new Head Shepherd and to take part in his enthronization. After taking over the diocese from vicar general and Prelate Kaspar Baczewski, Bishop von Ropp went to the pulpit and held two sermons to those gathered together. This was in Polish and in German. The faithful were very uplifted by the deeply moving words given by their new Head Shepherd. How wise is the rule of the Church that one of the most important duties of a diocesan bishop is to preach the Word of God. There is a special blessing which rests upon the sermon of the Head Shepherd because above all the admonishment of the divine Redeemer is given to him to: "Go and teach" (1. Matthew 28:19)-Through the proclamation of God's Word the shepherd really comes into living contact with his flock. Through this contact the bond of friendship and of spiritual relationships which God himself binds between the shepherd and flock is made stronger and endures as well as being made a stronger bond. ·

Moving and solemn at the same time was the oath of allegiance on the part of the cathedral chapter and the clergy. They either bowed or knelt and kissed the right side of the bishop in a humble manner. Whoever participates in this very moving and meaningful ceremony or sees it will certainly be moved by inner emotion. One noted how one or another of the elderly priests had tears come to their eyes during this ceremony. If only all would never forget their relationship to the diocesan shepherd, and that which they promised God and the bishop during this celebrative hour. The good relationship between the bishop and his spiritual sons would never be damaged and would not even be disturbed.

As the time of year in which Bishop Ropp began the administration of the bishopric did not allow a visitation of the congregations the new shepherd was moved to still journey south in the month of February of the following year to Odessa In the many parishes and heated churches there he could confirm, proclaim the Word of God and get to 'know the Catholic life there. However, this time the villages could not be visited because of the muddy roads. At the first possible opportunity Bishop Ropp visited many parishes in the north and confirmed everywhere, preached and investigated the affairs of the parishes. Like a rushing windstorm he went from village to village. Wind and weather, bad roads and neither heat nor cold bothered him. He felt an irresistible urge to visit all and to get to know all of the parishes as quickly as possible as if he expected that his activity in Tyraspol would not be of long duration. During the summer when all of the others retreated to the spas and to their villas in order to find peace and quiet and when in the southeast an African heat is prevalent, he visited several parishes in the Caucasus and had confirmation services. In Batum he consecrated a new church, preached everywhere in various languages and even heard the confessions of those to be confirmed together with the clergy. He sometimes did this for hours on end during the daylight. It is amazing that such a slender and weak figure could work at such a pace without getting tired. He was also the first Catholic bishop who visited the Armenian parishes on the other side of the mountains and encouraged them to remain faithful to the Holy Catholic religion and Church and gave the blessing to them as well. From the Deep South he travelled to the High North to the homeland with which he was more acquainted and where he sometimes had issues to resolve. From there he went to St. Petersburg in order to "force" various questions as he himself stated for which a solution had not been forthcoming from the government as the church had come upon great difficulties in regard to these. Above all, it was the seminary for priests which caused him the greatest of worry. There were too few teachers active there. Because they were over-worked they were not able to teach as they should have been able to do. This troublesome situation had to be changed. Above all the supervisor had to be relieved from his position because of the infirmities of age. There was also not a lack of well-educated knowledgeable men. The Catholic Academy in St. Petersburg had already educated some young priests from the diocese of Tyraspol. In Rome several more talented students studied at the Gregoriana. One of them had already finished his academic studies. Thus there was not a lack of suitable teachers in Tyraspol, despite the fact that there was a great lack of priests which was still a factor in the bishopric. One only needed to call these knowledgeable men and evaluate them. Until now only one single graduate of the Catholic Spiritual Academy had been appointed as a professor at the seminary and that person was Franz Xaver Klimaszewski. He was Polish. He was appointed after three miserable attempts with former students from the seminary for priests·. These were the clergymen Mizkiewicz (Mizkus), a Lithuanian and two Germans by the name of Scherger and Fix. One was simply more favourable toward the Polish teachers than toward the German. But the diocesan leadership should have been one which was friendly toward the Germans. Thus one appointed a German graduate of the University in St. Petersburg as the canon and priest of the cathedral church but not as a professor at the seminary.

35. Johannes Antonov, rector of the seminary for priests in Tyraspol

For twenty years Johannes Antonov was the supervisor of the spiritual institution in Tyraspol. As is evident from the previous description, he bore in order to speak with the Scriptures: "the burden and the heat of day." (1. Matthew 20:12) Not the rector but he was in the middle of raising and educating the students and everything naturally gathered around him because he was superior to his colleagues and all of his surroundings in terms of talent, education and energetic activity. His students were; loving, respectful and thankful toward him. His youth nature had shown a kind of intuition, which others, whose reason was troubled by special interests, could not fathom nor honour. The new and most worthy Diocesan Bishop Eduard von Ropp soon after starting his position learned about Antonov's activity and his blessed work and valued it highly. Antonov's students, whom he had prepared from boyhood until they were ordained, and whom he had led were chosen by him and elevated to cathedral chapter leaders and prelates while he the old pedagogue and teacher always remained a sacristan. As the new Head Shepherd did not have a canon to aid him he gave the supervisor the honour of being a prelate. Because of the resignation of the official of the consistory Prelate Kaspar Baczewski, this office became vacant. Bishop Eduard von Ropp elevated the youthful seminary rector Prelate Joseph Kruschinsky to the office in that he removed him from the rectorship at the seminary for priests and appointed Supervisor Johannes Antonov in his place. As the appointment of Prelate Kruschinsky to the highest position in the diocese was not at all a demotion but much more so a promotion, no one could protest against this. The office of supervisor with its professorship was given to the former priest in Kishinev, Joseph Aloisius Kessler. He was called to Saratov in 1903. Since the Ministry of the Interior did not want to allow the newly-elected supervisor to take such an important position, the highly-honoured bishop journeyed to St. Petersburg by making a special trip in order to as he said "force" this election and in the end he was successful in doing so. If it had been dependent upon Sacristan and Professor Antonov he would have never chosen the rectorship at the seminary for priests, for the responsibilites of a supervisor at the institution were really his primary focus in life. Among the boys and the youth the elderly priest became livelier all the time. The rectorship was less important according to this nature and it caused some of his talents to languish. Beyond this his physical strength was already broken because of the burden of years of work and by his restless activity. He had not allowed himself to have any longer period of respite. It is a general phenomenon that great minds do not break down under the weight of occupational responsibilities but only then when they are not allowed to carry them out anymore or they are removed from them. By continuing to carry out their occupation they seem not to lose their physical strength but seem to strengthen it. They revive when they are in the flow of things. They draw strength from the fulfillment of their occupational duties that physical strength which they must have in order to carry out those duties.

Examples of this are found in the lives of many great souls and saints of the Catholic Church. this is how it also was with Johannes Antonov. As long as he had the supervisory position which laid great claims upon the incumbent he was strong and he never lacked strength and was never tired. As soon as he took over the rectorship his physical strength also began to wane. The rector of the seminary lives in a house next to the main school building and because of his occupation he has less contact with the pupils. The steadfast and lively contact with the youth had become the reason for living for Professor Johannes Antonov. "I feel as if l have no relationship with the seminary over there anymore" he often stated. For this reason the new supervisor took over the position of the administrator of the school treasury. When this happened he was about to have closer contact with the pupils. Besides this, the supervisor asked him to choose a part of the work of raising the pupils. He chose the mass for the students which had been held until then by the supervisor. Despite this he always felt not *quite* right as the most important member of the seminary. His health seemed to suffer. He noted that his very good eyesight was worse. He had to wear strong eyeglasses. For this reason he already discontinued giving his lecture in philosophy in the year 1903. A diligent and young professor, Dr. Anton Fleck, a former student of the Germanicum in Rome, continued these lectures in a worthy fashion. In the year 1909 he also ended his lectures in dogmatics and they were also taken over by a former student of the Germani cum in Rome, Dr. Markus Glaser, whom Bishop Kessler had called to the seminary. He also did this work well. Soon the preconditions of a coming evil showed up, and because of this he stopped working entirely. He then occupied himself more intensively with. the management of the business in the institution. There was a special blessing which rested upon the institution during his rectorship. Despite the fact that he was constantly concerned about good food and care for the pupils he still saved the considerable sum of 35,000 rubles during a period of seven years. With these savings he expanded the rooms of the seminary and he built a two-story hospital which was absolutely necessary. He paid for 100 beds in the large bedroom which had been built by Bishop Eduard von Ropp. He set up the bedroom next to these. Finally he purchased a lot with 145 dessiatines on the Hilly Side of the Volga, upon which he built a farm for the seminary. He wanted to have a summer villa for the seminary for clergy and for the teachers of religion constructed on this property later on. It was just that he was not able to carry out these important plans. Divine providence had dictated that the apostolic man had to completely bid adieu from his beloved seminary for which he lived and for which he had sacrificed. To be sure, Rector Antonov who by nature had excellent health should have gotten to be 100 years old, but his constant and many-sided work and his lack of sleep at night consumed his powers before their time. In the fall of 1911 he had a stroke. He had extreme unction administered. A stay in a spa in the Caucasus brought no amelioration and indeed his health suffered even more. At that time he lived with the then Bishop Joseph Aloisius Kessler of Tyraspol who had followed Bishop Baron von Ropp in this office in 1904 and with his secretary in Essentuki in a villa which the bishop had rented.

From here he wanted to visit his friend Prince Tumanov who lived in the neighbouring spa city of Pyatigorsk. It was a hot and humid day. The diocesan bishop gave him strong advice not to go and visit. But as he still insisted, then the bishop's secretary was to at least accompany him. His modesty caused him to refuse this. After two hours he returned in a shocking state. His face looked like that of an epileptic. His tongue was lame and he could not speak at all. The bishop immediately recognized that the rector had had another stroke. After he had recuperated somewhat because of a doctor's aid he recounted that he had gotten the stroke in Pyatigorsk when he had climbed up onto a rise. He sat down on the ground beside the Catholic Church until he had recuperated somewhat. Finally he could get up with his own strength and get into the streetcar and ride to the railroad station. While he was on the return trip the railroad conductor asked for his ticket which he had purchased in Essentuki as a preventative measure. But because of his infirmity he could not find it right away. The railroad servant figured that he had someone before him who was drunk, shook his head in disgust, and left. While getting out of the train compartment; and it was only a distance of eleven kilometers back home, he lost his coat in Essenkuti. A Russian officer picked it up and put it on his shoulders. The friendly gentleman also accompanied him to the Railroad Station. The good man also figured that he was dealing with a drunkard, as a person who has had a stroke looks the same in the face as someone who is drunk. His sad fate was that the soul zealous and sober priest was considered to be a drunkard. This hurt him a lot and he bore his pain in submission to God's will.

Since there was no hope of recovery for the rector, he wanted to spend the last days of his life in his homeland the Caucasus. The bishop sent him, after he had somewhat regained his strength, to Tblisi to his brother Michael Antonov who was the priest at the St. Peter and St. Paul Church and the visitor in the Caucasus. In the fall of the same year, Canon Johannes Antonov journeyed to Saratov one more time in order to say goodbye to his beloved seminary for the last time. Meanwhile the bishop had already found a new replacement for the ill rector in the person of Professor Dr. Frison, one of the former students of the Germanicum, and he was appointed in the place of Johannes Antonov. A few weeks earlier the bishop had obtained an annual pension for the departing ill man from Prime Minister Stolypin who had then just made a visit to Saratov. The Prime Minister who knew the rector and his superior qualities felt badly about the poor ill man.

The rector, who had been removed from his office, remained in Saratov for only one week. One saw how difficult the separation from the seminary was for him. An ill person by nature desires peace and quiet. Travelling and saying goodbye always bring excitement with them. He left the city in the company of Father Mgebrov who was Antonov's very good friend. The bishop, his good friend, took the ill man to the steamboat himself. The seminary together with all of the professors also accompanied their former rector and professor to the river. After successive periods of rest in Astrachan, Petrovsk and Baku, the journey continued to Tblisi where he arrived together with Father Mgebrov without anything happening along the way. There he lived the life of a hermit. The then teacher of religion in the Middle Schools in the city asked the ill man one day if he feared death. He replied: "If I consider God's strict judgement I am fearful of something but if I on the other hand consider that I will see the dear and divine Redeemer Jesus Christ and the dear Mother of God after death I am ready to die immediately." Three days before bis death he became unconscious. After he had had his seventh stroke, the faithful and pious servant of God went to the better place which was on the other side. It was on Christmas 1912 on that great festival day in which he had enraptured his pupils so much for the love of God and the Redeemer. On this festival, on which the Son of God was born for humankind, Johannes Antonov was born for eternity in heaven. Three days later his mortal remains were buried next to St. Peter and Paul Church in Tblisi.

With the pronotary, prelate and canon Johannes Antonov a man descended to the grave as one appears only once over a period of centuries. He was the greatest of those which the small Catholic group of Georgians (Grusinians) can justifiably be proud of.

36. The religious life of the colonists under the clergy who were members of orders
Whoever had travelled through the German settlements on the Volga and the Black Sea regions will have noted that all of them are divided into groups and separated from each other in terms of their confession. This denominational separation took place because of a strict directive of the Russian government. "Because of the various religious denominations and in order to minimize every type of hatred and enmity people of one or the other religion are to be settled in certain counties." This is how the directive had been given. Only three settlements are mixed in terms of denomination. They are Katharinenstadt, Beauregard ontbe Volga, and Kronental in the Crimea. There was also a fourth little village in the Crimea where the Catholics lived together with the Lutherans. The little village is called Zuerichtal. In the second half of the 19th century many Catholics emigrated and founded the little village of Genduchai. The fortunate situation

of confessional separation is the reason for the fact that mixed marriages, by which the Catholic cause would have been irreparably damaged in religiously mixed communities, hardly ever took place in the diocese of Tyraspol. However those kinds of marriages were a daily occurrence in the cities of the bishopric. While the Catholic Poles mixed themselves with the Russians, the German city dwellers mixed with the Protestants. Since according to Russian law every mixed marriage with an "Orthodox" individual had to take place in a Russian Church and all of the descendants had to be raised "Orthodox" the damage can hardly be measured which was done to the Catholic religion by such unions. Not much less was the damage which took place when there were mixed marriages between Catholics and Protestants, even if the marriage took place in the Catholic Church and all of the descendants were to be baptized and raised Catholic. In such families true Catholic religiously cannot, as a rule, develop since the children are confused by the contradictory example of the parents in terms of their religious convictions; if they can even have a religious conviction. The religious life of the German Catholic colonists did not suffer any losses because of mixed marriages. However one could not speak of genuine Catholic life since the days of settlement. First of all, the immigrants had some clergy who were zealous for souls who also sacrificed themselves for the colonists and shared the discomfort and difficulty of the long trip with them but in the meantime they had to fight against dire poverty and want during the first years. However, experience teaches that in the midst of great poverty and want the religious life of the people cannot develop.

The situation of need reached unbelievable heights as the poverty was accompanied by the cold Siberian winter with its troubles and in the summer time it was accompanied by the African heat, drought and various illnesses. However after the settlers had set themselves up as farmers with difficulty and had somewhat gotten used to the climate and had established schools and simple prayer chapels, most of the German priests who were members of orders and who led the pastoral work had died out. The new members of religious orders were Dominicans and Trinitarians. All of the pastoral care was restricted to administering the Holy Sacraments, the celebration of the Holy Mass and the burial of those who had died and these sacraments were administered by priests of other nationalities. Because of the lack of ability to communicate in the language of the colonists the pastor, so to say, withdrew into the sacristy. They had too little contact with the population. For these reasons it was very fortunate that the fathers at least did not offend and to the contrary were blameless in their private lives and pious. With this type of pastoral care and with a complete lack of successful religious instruction of the children and youth and with no preaching of the Word of God in a language which they could understand a great lack of knowledge in regard to religious things became noticeable among the populace. The author of the Book of Wisdom states in Proverbs 19:2 "Where there is no insight into the soul there is nothing good."

According to this proverb evil walks hand in hand with a lack of knowledge. For this reason it should not surprise anyone if one heard of the rough sides of the customs of the German colonists as well as of drunkenness, debauchery, adultery, thievery and other crimes which previously had not taken place when the people were pastorally served carefully by German-speaking members of religious orders. To be sure, adultery and great debauchery even now seldom appear. The relatively good morality was not accomplished by a zealous care of souls but by very strict rules which the clergy . supported by the state officials used against the delinquents in the German Office and the Chancellery for New Settlers located in St. Petersburg. (Beratz, The German Colonies P. 204)

The genuine Catholic pastor must not just be in the midst of the congregation which he pastors but must live with her. It is only through close community contact that the genuine pastoral relationship between the shepherd and the flock can be established. The relationship which is found between the members of a family and its head, the father, must be copied. The German Catholic in the of the Volga regions refers to the priest in a special way. He calls him Pater because for about 100 years priests who were members of religious orders were his pastors. The Catholic member of the parish must realize that the pastor takes a warmhearted part in all of his wants and needs and is concerned in aiding the member as much as he possibly can; according to his strength. The church member must have the feeling that the pastor is his spiritual father and is not just that in name only. The first prerequisite for this is a solid knowledge of of the mother tongue of the parish members and the getting comfortable with their character. Both requirements were neglected by the otherwise very good and pious Polish and Lithuanian pastors. For this reason there was no success in leading the souls which had been entrusted to them. However the good fathers deserve to be excused in that they did not realize the importance of these challenges for a warm-hearted understanding vis a vis their parish members and they were also hindered by the German Colonial Settlement office and the Office in Odessa in corning into more intimate contact with the people outside of the "sacristy."

Both instances which have been mentioned had the duty of taking care of the agricultural and social wellbeing of the German colonists. However they were not satisfied with this and at times transgressed these boundaries in regard to their areas of responsibility and, as is common in a bureaucratic system, mixed themselves into the intellectual and religious areas of life. They always wanted to play a type of patriarchal role over the clergy. As proof of this conjecture, one regulation sent out by the German Colonial Settlement Office can serve as an example. This took place soon after the settlement of the Germans. As examples several paragraphs from this document can be viewed.

1."The Fathers and Pastors" it declares, are not only to give instruction to their congregations which will educate them and serve the well-being of their souls according to the Holy Scriptures(!) and teach the youth, but also be examples of the practical application of these teachings by their way of life and behaviour." That note, which requires that one teach according to the Holy Scriptures, is completely Lutheran, as the Lutherans do not accept the office of teaching and tradition through the Church which had been established by Christ. However the Catholic clergy never accepted this note.

5."But besides, this the clergy are not to mix themselves in any secular affairs and affairs

which have nothing to do with their office as has happened with several who feared great resentment by the powers that be, the loss of their position but also according to circumstances, that something would be requisitioned from their salary." This means that the clergy in the newly-founded colonies should restrict their activities to the church and the manse and the world of bureaucracy would take care of everything else! This is how P. Beratz quite rightly notes on P. 235

This fifth paragraph from the instruction book seems to be very strict. Since the bureaucrats who issued this order reserved the right to decide which things were worldly and not the responsibility of the clergy, the pastors needed to fear that anything which they did which was not connected to liturgical services would cause offense to the state officials and thereby be in opposition to Paragraph 5 of this infamous order. Such orders had, according to their nature, to exclude every kind of social ministry and business activity of the pastors. It seems as if the state officials used the principle that: "Only that should be done which was actually allowed by law." However, every reasonable law must follow the law which is in opposition and, to be sure, this one: "Everything can be done which is not proscribed by law." Because of such idiotic and damaging laws and rules the clergy Russia withdrew more and more to the church and the parsonage. Through this a gap between the people and the clergy was established which could only be changed if it had to do with questions strictly in reference to the church as well as questions regarding religion. Up to the present day the pastoral work in the diocese of Tyraspol still suffers somewhat because of the terrible results attendant to the estrangement between the pastor and the members of his parish in questions which have nothing to do with the church or religion. No wonder as this long period of time had made this a traditional thing!

The religious life of the German Catholics was restricted to the following activities: Easter confession and Easter Holy Communion, one knew nothing of confessional services and regular communion and in most cases only the women went to confession before the delivery of babies and there was confession, communion and extreme unction for those who were very ill and those who were dying. How incomplete and insufficient the confessions were can be easily surmised since because of a great lack of knowledge most of them could not even awaken a supernatural penitence within their hearts. The people knew nothing of the beautiful celebratim, when children received their first holy communion. This is an uplifting experience. The days of abstinence in Advent and Lent were strictly held but before Lent there was all the more debauchery in eating and especially in drinking brandy; there was more dancing and carousing and unfortunately also debauchery carried out by the young people which put shame to the Christian name and called forth memories of paganism. The weddings were especially un-christian. But it must be stated that lack of religious knowledge and the crudeness of the customs added to this evil a great deal. Right up to the most recent of times the pastors' and the diocesan leadership had to fight with this evil. When during the long days of winter (winter in the region of the Volga lasts for five months) the farmer had too little to do; he is lazy throughout the whole winter. For this reason the people in the countryside had a propensity to celebrate many holidays. Besides the church holidays they also set their own but did this together with or with the permission of the pastors. It often happened that there was a failed harvest, cattle-pest or something other plague such as the destruction of the fields by locusts. These were the spark which led to the "establishment" of a holiday in honour of a certain saint etc. On these "holidays" the pastor had to hold a festive high mass which the mayor of the village had ordered for the community. On a holiday such as this no one worked, the worship service was well attended, but in the afternoon and in the evening there was also a lot of dancing and carousing.

The religious life of the German Catholic colonists was more influenced by vegetating than by living. And it would have continued to digress in that direction with these things happening if our beloved God had not had mercy upon the unfortunate colonists and sent them members of the Society of Jesus (founded by St. Ignatius of Loyola) as their pastors.

Wherever the religious and moral life is decrepid as it was at the end of the 18th century among the German settlers in the time before there was a diocese of Tyraspol, there has to be a change. Effective means had to be used if one was to have the hope of attaining success soon and to the advantage of the settlers. The most effective means have always been the spiritual exercises or the religious devotions set up for the people. Father Averdonek knew well that this was the proper means of amelioration. Without question, the Jesuits held religious exercises as devotions in all of the parishes of the Volga Region because the people were in such low spirits. Otherwise the amazing results of their effect could not have been explained in such a short period of time.

Today after 110 years, one still notices where the Jesuits were active for only 17 years among the Catholic inhabitants of the Volga. Two special religious traits are evident which are not as publicly practiced in the other parts of the bishopric. Loyola's students either were not active at all or only for a short time in these areas. Firstly, there was special aversion toward Protestantism in all its various forms as well as the adoration of the Holy offering of the Mass. These traits have so to say become part of their flesh and blood if we want to name them. The Catholic folk on the Volga can only attribute them to

the blessed activity of the Jesuit Fathers. Their deep adoration of the offering on the altar is shown by the colonists most by thousands of intentions for masses which they reserve on a yearly basis. The bishops of Tyraspol not only had to take care of all of the clergy in the diocese with them but also could have sent many thousands of them to other areas. In fact they did send out many thousands annually which could not be held within the borders of the diocese. They were sent abroad outside of the boundaries of the bishopric to clergy who were needy. If one considers that even in the years when there were bad harvests that the stream of mass intentions did not stop but continued to rush along then one must be amazed at the great devotion toward the offering upon our altars which took place among the Volga colonists.

Even in the states of America where thousands of former diocesans from the bishopric of Tyraspol were settled 50 years ago, one could determine that there were numerous mass intentions given in colonies which orginated by the settlement of Volga Germans. The adoration and high estimation of the holy offering of the mass has been transmitted from the parents to their children.

37. The religious life under the German curates of souls

After the Fathers of the Society of Jesus withdrew, the German colonists, who had cried many a tear at their departure for the followers of Loyola who were leaving, felt as if they were orphaned in terms of religion. However the mission prefecture had sent other members of religious orders to replace the Jesuits as pastors. It was just that these did not speak German. Unfortunately there were clergy among them who handled the people with an extreme strictness and did not, according to the example of their divine Master, keep the flickering wick going but put it out. The bond of genuine pastoral love and friendship could not be knit together between them and the flock which had been entrusted into their care. Where this was lacking there can be no talk about pastoral activity which is being furthered. No wonder then that the old religious situation returned to the colonists again. Again one heard about immoral acts, extensive carousing, drunkenness, of quarrels and strife, of divisions in the congregations and even about adultery. The church attendance became less frequent, the devotions for confessional services and communion distribution ended completely, and there was no sermon and no religious instruction. This took place because the new pastors could not speak the German language. To be sure, a small part of the population lived a Christian religious life but even their group got smaller from year to year. Only a few kept the memory of the good example and the teachings of the former pastors in mind; the memory of the Fathers of the Society of Jesus, while in general Christian virtues as a whole declined.

The first immigrants who still had brought along some of the religious spirit from the old homeland had long since left for a better home in heaven. Even the first generation which had grown up on Russian soil had already followed them to the grave. Since there was a lack of Middle Schools among the colonists there was a lack of educated leaders. The result of this was that every type of communication with their old homeland including written correspondence ended among the German Catholics. There was a lack of religious literature, newspapers and even of the German Catholic prayer book. The situation was better in terms of contact with the homeland and German culture among the Lutherans. As their pastors received their education in the Baltic provinces and were always Germans the contacts with the German people and German culture were not ruptured. The Lutherans in the Volga region and South Russia always had educated leaders.

1. However there was a lack of pastors among the Lutherans at the beginning after the settlement since these did not want to share the poverty and privations of the colonists. For this reason some of them even went to Catholic clergy for marriages and for the baptism of their children. (Beratz: The German Volga Colonies)

They were able to lead insofar as they were not hindered by the St. Petersburg Colonist Settlement Office and the Office in Odessa. Then also the Lutheran cause was always preferred to the Catholic among the officials of these two entities. The unfortunate German colonists of the future diocese of Tyraspol were left to take care of themselves. This was apart from the almost fruitless leadership of souls of another heritage. There was no one who took care of their many needs in an active fashion. In such a situation they would have had to perish economically, intellectually and religiously if divine providence had not provided for the training of and education of their own pastors from the sons of the colonists. The German clergy who afterward received German education and training from the committees of educators and professors from the old home in Germany were not only leaders of souls for the Catholic folk in the diocese of Tyraspol but also reconnected them to their German forebears which, as long as foreign clergy cared for their souls, had been ruptured. Through them the old homeland with its eminent cultural development was brought closer to the Catholic colonists.

The first priests who graduated from the seminary for priests in the newly founded diocese of Tyraspol were, however, Poles and Lithuanians. However they, being surrounded by German, soon acquired a better knowledge of the German language. They were also followed by German priests and the sons of German colonists. The first son of a colonist who was sent as a priest for service to his fellow Germans was Father Johann von Nepomuk Schamne. After the seminary for priests was placed into the hands of German religious committees, he was followed by a large number of well-educated sons of colonists as has already been mentioned. After the the-spiritual greenhouse of the diocese had been Germanized under the leadership of Rector Franz Zottmann and German teachers had been acquired, there was noticeable success. The numbers of German clergy grew from year to year so that Bishop Franz Zottmann could already report in the year 1882 that the number of priests who had graduated from the seminary over a period of 25 years was 68.

With the entry of German clergy into the diocese there was a happy change for the better. The German clergy were familiar with the situation, the character, and the good and bad sides of those entrusted to them in the best way. Soon the genuine German language resounded everywhere in the entire diocese. The Word of God resounded from pulpits on Sundays and on Festival Days. The people listened tirelessly to the Germans preaching God's Word as they were hungering for it. How often it occured that the colonists stated: "I could have listened to the Father for hours." In the beautiful parable in the Gospel about the sower who sowed the good seed on his land, we hear that it was only the fourth which finally fell upon good soil. The seed also brought forth rich fruit. One saw that the unhappy people had sinned more out of a lack of knowledge than because of being evil. With Peter the preachers could speak to the people in order to encourage them to repent: "And now my brothers I know that you did it out of a lack of knowledge just like your leaders." (Acts 3:17) How deep and impressive was the Word of God on every Sunday upon the listeners. This is already shown by the fact that the sermon and its contents were often the subject of the elderly parishioners' conversation the whole Sunday through when they met for their gatherings. The people sent their adult sons and daughters to Christian instruction, to catechesis, just as diligently. In this respect one single paragraph of the law fulfilled the wish of the Church. This paragraph made it the responsibility of the single youth of both sexes to attend Christian instruction; after they had finished attending the parish school. The clergyman read the names of the youth prior to the beginning of catechesis. If someone was absent without excuse he had to pay a three kopecks fine as punishment. Meanwhile the parents were urged to attend this Christian instruction more because of their conscientious duty. Not a few of the Christian parents let themselves be told by their adult sons and daughters about the contents of the sermons on Sundays and Festival Days in order to watch them in this way to see if they had paid attention to the Word of God. The more frequent reception of the sacraments of repentance and communion is the natural fruit of the hearing of God's Word when it has been taught to them properly. For this reason one soon noted a greater zeal for the reception of such important means of grace. If the German clergy during the first years of their work had many public confessions to hold, as many had confessions in the past whose validity was suspect; they had to make up for them in a good manner now. In this regard the German Catholic people especially knew how to treasure the newly-ordained young priests. As a rule everyone rushed again to their confessional and everyone wanted to give them a confession about their life. One Christian mother once rushed to her young son who was a priest and who had been, shortly after his ordination, continually surrounded by such people who wanted to confess and told him that he should move to a colony where one did not know him so that he could be freed from the heavy burden of this work. In fact, the young priest had to follow the well-intentioned view of his mother. Otherwise he would have no doubt damaged his health. In this way the members of the parish in the city parishes are the direct opposite to those in the countryside. The former only want to have their confessions heard from older priests. However many city parishoners often do not want to receive the sacrament of penance at all.

While the pastors of other nationalities always urge the exact keeping of the rules of abstinence and of fasting, the German pastors tried to reduce these duties for their · parishoners. The German colonists had emigrated from Germany and Austria. At that time the rules for abstinence and fasting were not kept according to ancient Christian strictness. They had been lessened by dispensations. The Polish and Lithuanian clergy came from a land where the law of fasting had been observed very strictly. They had to fight a lot in order to have the Lenten customs of their homeland introduced among the colonists. The colonists did not especially care for the so-called "black" rules for fasting: abstinence from butter, fish, eggs and milk. They could not get accustomed to these rules. But in order to yet hold the absolution from sin in the Easter confession, one abstained from milk, eggs etc. for three days of the week. The German Jesuits had already gotten a dispensation for milk products for the German parishoners. The colonists believed that these "black" Lenten rules were only an unlawful burden with which the Polish priests wanted to bear down upon them. Bishop Franz Zottmann, before whom the pastors appeared for relief from the laws of fasting, was able to obtain a dispensation for the whole diocese for not having to abstain from meals with milk and eggs. This dispensation was announced annually by the German pastors in the church at the beginning of the Advent and Lenten seasons. Many of the Polish and Lithuanians pastors did, however, not want to keep these "lax" disciplines of fasting and did not only not report this rule from the bishop but announced "black fasting" from the pulpit for three days in the week to the people gathered there. By doing so, they themselves had taken away; by their own volition, three days of "black" fasting. Thus there was nothing to do they thought, than have moderation take place in this situation. Now the people clearly recognized that the heavy rule of "black fasting" was not a church law meant for them; at least it was no longer a rule for them. Thus and at last as well, the strict fasting people had to stay away from a stricter view of abstinence fasting and, forced by the people, join the rule of the diocesan shepherd.

Under the care of souls given by pastors of other foreign tongues there were often processions held regularly with the most holy sacrament. These were held in a very festive form. They were held on every main festive day before and after High Mass. The people especially loved this custom. They also loved pilgrimages to the neighbouring church on Patron Saints' Days or Church Dedication Festivals. The processions were nice and orderly with the Holy Cross going in front and with many flags. The church council members were in the middle of the long rows praying the rosary while the schoolmaster presented church litanies with the choir in the midst of the procession. The procession started from the parish church in the locality and went on for several kilometers. Having come its destination, it then ended. Then the nice teams of horses also appeared with decorated wagons which followed the procession and loaded the members of their family. Now one proceeded at a quick clop forward right up to the first cross before the neighbouring parish. This is where the pilgrims descended again and everything was arranged again as it had been before for another procession. With prayer and singing the procession finally entered the village and the House of God which had been festively decorated. Very often several processions came together from the surrounding Catholic villages to the church where the pilgrimage was being held. These processions and pilgrimages were very beloved and enlived the slumbering religious spirit among the clergy of other nationalities over and over again. Unfortunately, the young German priests showed too little understanding and zeal for these processions and pilgrimages. In some places, the young pastors, because of some misconduct which some sassy young people carried out, did away with them. For the preservation and awakening of religious life and Catholic consciousness they should be re-introduced and held again everywhere. This nice custom was however only indigenous to the parishes of the Volga region. The south of the diocese knew nothing about them.

A nice tradition is the church celebration of first Holy Communion for the children. Unfortunately the Catholic colonist knew nothing about this uplifting ceremony before the time when the sons of the people took over the care of their souls. The day of first Holy Communion was held, however, always on a Sunday or a Festival Day after Easter. It is one of the biggest celebrations of the entire church year. In all of the homes in which there is a child for first communion, work is done and things are prepared in order to make this celebration very solemn and nice. The children are dressed in their Sunday clothes with the boys in black with a fresh flower decorating their breast and the girls are in white with a myrtle wreath decorating their head. They are picked up in a celebrative procession by the priest in ecclesiastical robes while the bells are ringing and led into the church. There they all stand around the baptismal font where they received the first holy sacrament with lighted candles in their hands. In a tender address, the little ones are reminded of this important moment and called to renew the baptismal vow. There is hardly a more uplifting ceremony in the church than this one. After the children, with their hearts pumping, have had the great fortune of hearing the devotion on the first reception of the body and blood of Jesus Christ the High Mass begins in which the children walk up to the table of the Lord in pairs. By the introduction of this uplifting ceremony the German priests have grasped one of the most effective means of furthering religious life in their parishes. Many an impenitent father, whose child was among those who received communion for the first time at this moving ceremony, allowed the grace of God to reenter his heart again after many years and became a good Christian.

In earlier times the instruction for first communion was given by the schoolmasters, only that it was very superficial as these men were inundated with other occupational duties. Now the clergy who had graduated from the seminary gave the instruction themselves. This class instruction usually lasted for two months. Because of this change the instruction was more thorough and brought the pastors m closer contact with the young group of children. Since the diocese had to deal with a lack of priests under the bishops who were active until the beginning of the 20th century, the German pastors did not give religious instruction themselves in the congregational schools but had that done by one of the Catholic teachers who had been given this position by the local priest. From 1906 onward the teaching of religion was made a strict duty in all of the congregational schools by the episcopal leadership for all of the priests and their substitutes. However there were now also German pastors who did not take such an important task very seriously in that they figured that they were excused because of numerous items of parish business or other pastoral activities. Many an easy-going gentleman found the episcopal rule too hard and complained about such an expectation to their colleagues in ministry.

Since they however did not find open ears with these colleagues who had more understanding for the importance of religious instruction in school and the larger and healthier group of pastors had begun to give religious instruction they were, at the same time, still involved in the school. The Catholic religious instruction was supported by the pastors themselves by the circumstance that the so-called parish schools had been made the responsibility of the Ministry of Education (literally the Ministry of Enlightening the People) As the ministry paid the teachers of other subjects it also took over the salary of the instructors in religion. This was an encouragement for the clergy to now give the religious instruction in the schools themselves instead of giving it, as was previously the case, to a secular teacher. As long as the parish school existed, the teachers were paid by the parish or by the Catholic congregation with the exception of the teacher of religion since the parish did not view religious instruction as being the direct duty of the pastor. However not all of the congregational and parish schools everywhere were transferred to the Ministry of Education. In these cases the congregation had to come up with the salary for the teachers since the state school supervisor hired them just as in those schools. In all schools the medium of instruction was the German language. This lasted until the outbreak of the World War. The German language was even forbidden as a subject to be taught when the war started. Not even the religious instruction could be given in the German mother tongue anymore. The dignified gentlemen who initiated these draconian measures did not consider that the schoolchildren did not know any other language than German. Thus religious instruction in the schools had to be given up completely during the World War. It was only after the revolution against the first constitution that religious instruction could be given again. During the World War the military office forbade the use of the German language in those regions which were endangered by the war and in the entire south of the diocese of Tyraspol. It could not be used for sermons or even for the singing of church hymns. In many places the military office even expected the priests to give a written promise that they would not use the German language in church. Some priests also provided this written promise. This meant as much as making an end to the proclamation of God's Word as the people could not speak another language like their German mother tongue. this persecution had to naturally lead to religionlessness and to all of the things that follow in such a situation. It was just that this outlawing of the German sermon and of religious instruction w~ of short duration. The Bishop of Tyraspol protested against such religious rape before the Ministry of the Interior. The ministry promised to look into the situation more carefully and to undertake the necessary steps. In fact the military order was withdrawn but in a smart way just in the daily newspapers so that there would not be a piece of correspondence from the government that would fall into the hands of the Catholics as proof of such an illegal and terrible order. The Bolshevism which followed took the religious instruction out of the schools entirely. No wonder, for the hatred of God is a part of their system of doing things.

Despite the fact that the order not to preach in German had been-withdrawn the "all-powerful" governors in the individual provinces (gouvernements) did not accept it. They had greater power in the empire of the czar than a king in Western Europe. If no one was charged before the governor because of a German sermon then they were allowed. Meanwhile it was the Poles in the mixed city parishes who since the proclamation of the autonomy of Poland by the Highest Commander Grand-Duke Nikolai Nikolaiyovitch suddenly were transformed into Russian "patriots." Then they had to publicly show their hatred against everything that was German. They figured that they could do this most publicly when they charged their own pastor before the governor for preaching inGerman. Thus, the pastor of Astrachan who had held a speech in German and was then charged in court by a Polish lady "patriot (for now there was a close bond of brotherhood between the Poles and the Russians to the detriment of everything that was German) was commanded to leave the parish and Astrachan within 24 hours!

To be sure, the Catholic bishop preached from the pulpit of the cathedral and in German and in Polish also during the World War. Then the Polish refugees sent the priest the plea to never preach in German after the sermon in Polish but to preach only in Polish! One Polish superpatriot sent abusive articles to the "Novoye Vremya" opposing the sermon in German in the cathedral and stated that this barbaric and criminal language should be completely silenced so that the Catholic Poles would not become upset and could pray! The superpatriot tried to get the Russian government to discontinue the use of the German language in the House of God, to suppress the German diocese and to remove the German bishop! Actually this uproar was nothing more than hypocrisy. As long as the Russian state carried on with the rebellious Poles in this manner they would storm against

Russian barbarism and yet the Russian government had more reasons here to act than to be against innocent faithful citizens whose only crime was that they were the descendants of Germans. If in earlier years the Russian government had acted like this toward the Poles like these patriotic "madmen" had expected of the Russian government, then these unfortunate people would have been treated even worse.

The great success of the blessed activity of the German pastors is noted by the awesome concern of the German colonists for the quick administration of Holy Baptism for their newly-born children and the prompt reception of the sacrament of Extreme Unction for the terminally ill. What a big difference there was in the diocese between the Catholic inhabitants of the cities and the German inhabitants of the countryside! While the former, insofar as these are colonists left their children without this first and most needful holy sacrament of baptism for weeks, months and in many cases years on end, the Catholic colonists bring their newborn to church on the day of their birth so that the little citizen of the world becomes a citizen of heaven and of the Holy Catholic church. Neither heat nor cold keeps them away. If the child was born far away from the parish church then the longest trip is immediately made by wagon or by railcar. One overcomes all hindrances in order to transform the little heathen into a Christian. The colonists are also not afraid that the child will be harmed in the cold church when it is baptized. This is what the urban Catholics say in order to be able to postpone the baptism as long as possible. It has never been reported that someone to be baptized ever was harmed on such an occasion.

Also, all of the colonists eagerly accept the rule of the church to have their children baptized in the House of God and not like the Polish and Lithuanian Catholics in the Russian cities who want to have them baptized at home. How often one made serious attempts to end this bad habit in the urban parishes, but in vain. There are many situations in the city parishes where people were antagonistic and waring against pastors. This was in cases where pastors zealous for their souls would not allow a heathen name which the family wanted to add to the name of the child and because of situations where the pastor would try to convince the family to have the baptism in the church. The Catholic colonists are readily willing to accept the rules of the church to give their children only names given in the holy church. They consider this custom of the church to be self-explanatory.

Despite the continuous pleas and admonitions of the city priests, there were situations which came up again and again when families brought their children for holy baptism when they were six to ten years of age. Sometimes it seems as if the pastor has to take them out of their houses for baptism himself. But even now one would not have the children baptized if a baptismal certificate were not a requirement in order to have the child attend a school. The author of this history himself baptized a lot of children who were between six and ten years of age. In some cases, as the children were already fourteen years of age, the author had to use the rite of baptism for adults after he had awakened in them previously an act of divine repentance just as one does this with the baptism of an Indian, a Chinese or a Zulu Kaffir. This shows the pagan spirit of such parents who live in the lap of Christianity and to their own disgrace almost have nothing in common with Christianity.

Thus it is not surprising when such "Christians" also want to know nothing about the other holy sacraments. They do not go to confessions for years on end and neither do they receive Holy Communion nor do they pray and attend the worship service but under the flag of Christ live the life of someone who opposes Christ.

The life among the German pastors in the German parishes of the bishopric of Tyraspol is completely different. There were, to be sure, since the days of their settlement tares among the wheat. Yes, the tares sometimes seemed to grow above the wheat and to smother it. Through the Fathers of the Society of Jesus and since the 70s of the previous century when many parishes received pastors from the diocesan seminary, the German Catholic folk became conscious of their Christian duties again. However, in the 80s there was a change to a genuine Catholic life which showed the success of the blessed work of the German clergy. This work soon made itself especially noticeable in the care of the people for the Christian preparation of the terminally ill who waited for a happy death.

The entrance of a citizen of the world into a Christian place of respite and the departure of a Christian from this life was known by the Christian Catholic people of Tyraspol. They had been taught by the curates of their souls that these were the two most important moments in life. For this reason there was an awesome concern when these things took place. One could boldly assert that in all of the parishes of the widespread bishopric with the exception of the parishes in the Crimea that there was hardly a single case when someone who was terminally ill, by his own fault left this world without being pastorally care for. The care for the reception of holy extreme unction is so great that one often calls the pastor to the sick person unnecessarily and also often at night so that some priests had to dampen the enormous zeal of the people rather than to encourage it. With a proper view the concern to have their terminally ill people prepared for death by the clergyman is the most important thing of all. If the priest is not in the same locality as the sick person then one undertakes the furthest of ways in order to reach him. this is done by wagon and in the worst weather; by almost impassable roads in winter as in summer. One stops harvesting, threshing and important work and travels to see the pastor. One has no rest until one has brought the pastor and until the sick individual has received that "through which the Lord justifies him" (Gottesrecht). And if the gravely ill person has received the sacraments for the dying then one is almost always amazed at the wonderful peace of those dying who have an amazing way of accepting death. Often the terminally ill ask the clergyman to repeat the beautiful German prayers for those who are dying! This is truly trust in God! Such great trust in our beloved God will not go without being recompensed by the All-merciful. Rightly one can pray with such dying people in the words of the psalmist: "I hoped in you and I will not be put to shame in eternity." (Psalm 30:2) However, seldom does death takes place before the pastor arrives. What a terrible terrors of the heart are thus bestowed on the closest relatives and even the entire congregation. All are in mourning about this. If the close relatives of the very ill person do not have a good horse or a wagon for transport in order to pick up the clergyman this effort is eagerly taken upon himself by a fellow citizen in the village and this even if the way is also distant. If a fellow village inhabitant dies, the death which has occurred is soon announced by the bells ringing from the church steeple. Every person whether walking or standing on the street, if on his property or in his house or if he is doing the most important work: everything stops for a while: one makes the sign of the cross, prays the Lord's Prayer, the Hail Mary and: Lord give him eternal rest! One does this for the peace of the soul of the departed person. In the same manner the colonist does not shrink from trucing off his head-covering out in the open street when the bells ringing the Angelus (Angel of the Lord) ring in order to pray this beautiful prayer. These are also beautiful and many proofs of a genuine Catholic spirit and life among the Catholic colonists. The sons of the colonists who have graduated as priests from the seminary for priests in Tyraspol have breathed this spirit into the people and have always repeatedly stimulated and maintained their religious life anew with the grace of God. In order to do this they, besides the sermon and religious instruction, used the most important means of grace, those which the divine Redeemer left for his Church. But also various religious exercises were a part of their blessed activity and were thanks to this view. We will see this very shortly.

When the great Pope Leo XIII in his encyclical letter laid the rosary upon the hearts of the Catholic world and determined that this prayer was to be said in the month of October, the rosary was introduced in all of the Catholic churches around the world. In the diocese of Tyraspol the clergy who graduated from the diocesan seminary really instilled the love of this prayer in the people. They had prayed it already in the seminary chapel when they had communal prayer on a daily basis and had come to treasure it highly and to love it. In large groups the faithful people stream into the Houses of God during the month of October in order to honour the Mother of God with the rosary and to be blessed. In many homes one prays the rosary together if one has not been able to take part in the public praying of the rosary in church. The way of the cross is held during the times of major fasting (Advent and Lent) and every time when there are festival days. · This touching devotion is attended by all of the members of the parish. Our urban parishes are also no exception in this regard. The reflection upon the suffering of Christ always has something which is exceptionally attractive for the believing Christian soul. The devotion of the way of the cross was a part of the practice in the German Catholic colonies since the days of their settlement and was brought along by their forbears from the old homeland Germany.

One kind of devotion which has been held and which is a new thing is the devotion which takes place in. the month of May. It is known that the most beautiful month of spring is dedicated to the dear Mother of God. The May devotion is attended by the Catholic people just as frequently as the rosary devotion. These May devotions were introduced in the parishes for the first time by the German clergy.

Through the introduction and the furtherance and support of these devotions the religious Christian life among the people received great stimuli. Coarse moral failings became less frequent and in many parishes where priests zealous for the souls of people were active, they disappeared completely. In their stead, virtue and piety flourished and not only among older more aged Christians but also among the rising generation of young people who had not allowed themselves to be restrained previously.

In order to further the religious life more all the time and to keep it alive the German pastors introduced various meetings of the brotherhood such as the Heart of Jesus Brotherhood, that of the Immaculate Conception and that of the Rosary etc.
The greatest of success in piety was achieved with the introduction of the III order of St. Francis of Assisi. A very special blessing rests upon this order. The members of the order did not only distinguish themselves by a pious Christian way of life but also by works of love for one's neighbour which they carried out among the poor. They not only supported the needy with a lot of alms but they were also lovingly concerned with their souls and admonished lax Christians to receive the Holy Sacraments and to attend the worship services and to live a Christian life. They visited and watched over the poor and lonely sick people and took care of their poor widows and according to means took care of poor orphans and carried out a mutual apostleship of laymen within the congregation. One had already often had the experience that the III order of St. Francis was a strong one if not

the strongest dam or means of protection against the spread of mixed marriages and the spread of heretical faith or atheism. Wherever this order took solid root among the people the church had a field for its grand activity which had been prepared in the best possible way.

One had already often accused the German people that it lacked in terms of emotional feeling. However this does not lie in the German character showing its inner feelings to the outside world, as one can often note this with the Slavic and Romance nations. But a little kernel of truth lies in this assertion. The Germans uses fewer words than the Slav or the person from countries in which Latin-based languages are spoken. Also, the larger half of the German people, because Protestantism in all its variations has gained entry to it, lacks a warm heart and warm emotions. Despite this the German has a big merciful heart for the needs of the neigbour. For this reason there are many organizations which practice mercy and love of one's neighbour and there are pious establishments for the well-being and the alleviation of people who are suffering. The members of the diocese of Tyraspol were exemplary in showing genuine compassion for the needs of their fellow man. A poor person who was a beggar was never sent away without alms from a village where Germans resided. That is why the German villages were often and regularly visited by Russian beggars a lot. Even if one had to interrupt one's work a hundred times every day in order to look after the poor person, one still did it eagerly and willingly without any complaint.

Blind Russians led by a woman or by boys often begged in the Volga colonies by going down the streets. They made it easy on themselves and did not go into the farmyards or houses. In order to attract the attention of the inhabitants they would sing a Russian song

in the middle of the street. The people who lived in a house had hardly even heard the song when they would already send someone to the beggar with a gift. The beggars from Austria and Germany also often visited the villages in the northern and southern parts of the diocese. The author remembers one beggar from Germany who would only accept meat or bacon as alms. As a rule he would sing a very moving German melody. He was given many gifts everywhere. The colonists saw in him an old, helpless and poor comrade of the same heritage for whom everyone had great sympathy.

If there was a lack of faith-based and pious establishments of mercy for the poor then the reason for this is the absolute bureaucracy which reigned supreme. This was the case in the diocese right into the modem age and generally also in the German colonies in

Russia. The government officials often put great obstacles in the way when such institutions were to be established. The person belonging to the bureaucracy wanted to have their leadership extended to everyone and everything and this was often very distressing. By countless orders issued in the form of a circular the little freedom of movement which the citizens had was lamed entirely. One suspected political danger in every society. All of this smothered every intiative before it could bud. One had to get permission from the office of the government officials for all the gatherings and even the celebration with the Christmas tree in the school. The watchman of the state had to be present everywhere. For this reason no one should be surprised that the Catholic Church could not develop its work of social service even in the diocese of Tyraspol or· that the establishment of institutions for mercy and love of one's neighbour could not develop; at least to the same degree as in the Western European countries.

After many vexations with the bureaucrats, the efforts of the priest Jakob Scherr were successful in building the first orphanage in the colony of Karlsruhe in the middle of the 90s. The constitutions of the establishments for social aid or of the societies were generally shortened so much by the officials that the work which was proposed had to suffer. There was a more favourable atmosphere to be noted in the large empire after the Revolution of 1905. Through the initiative of some clergy in parishes, credit unions were established in many of the parishes of the bishopric. They aided the farmers who were without funds and were useful in relieving the needs associated with their farms. However there were, in the county administrative districts of the German colonists, so-called relief funds. They had been in existence for half a century already. They were established using the property of orphans who had not attained the age of maturity. After the death of the father his property as well as the property which he could sell was auctioned off by the colonial administration. The capital funds which came from this were deposited into the county relief fund account. The fund was administered by its own administrator who was elected by the community for a period of several years. These funds also aided the farmers residing in the same county with insurance for their borrowed funds at a reasonable percentage of interest.

Hospitals are present in the Catholic districts since the 90s of the previous century which were formed and kept going by the canton office which had its seat in the county cities. Catholic members also belonged to and administered it.

38. Church, parish and school

Without question Russia's greatest Czar was Peter I. History calls him the Great. He had great gifts and great love for his people. For this reason he wanted to make them happy. For this reason he left to his successors the inheritance of conquering India and Constantinople. The two centuries of carrying out this foreign policy upon the preconceived goal is which caused the great empire to end. With this idiotic idea of wanting to expand abroad, Peters' successors and inheritors omitted the most important thing: the spiritual growth of the people. There were more illiterate people in Russia than in any other country in Europe. The German immigrants had learned to treasure intellectual growth in their old homeland They also wanted to see to it that their children would inherit this inherit this in their Russian homeland. For this reason one of their big worries right after the settlement was the establishment of congregational schools. There was not a single German village in which a parish or congregational school was built next to the church.

However the first Houses of God and parish schools were very poor and simple buildings. The settlers simply had to fight for their lives during the first period of time. At first they had to form a foundation for their own existence. One must value the fact ever so much more that in the midst of all of this they did not forget the House of God, the school and the manse. The clergy while still on the journey to and through Russia with the settlers held worship services on all Sundays and Feast Days with a sermon and the teachers, in every place where the settlers took a break, taught school. After the colonists had settled in regard to their houses and their property, the poor little churches and schools slowly disappeared. In their stead large beautiful churches and near those buildings large schools and stately houses for the priests were built. Whoever visited the Catholic German colonies of the diocese of Tyraspol had to make the observation that the churches everywhere stood right in the middle of the village and that they were surrounded by the most beautiful houses in the locality. Those were the residences of the priest and the parish schools or as one sometimes refers to them; the congregational schools. However, with few exceptions the churches in the Volga region during the first

half of the 19th century were built of lumber. In the second half of the same century a large number of large beautiful Houses of God were constructed with bricks and their high and slender steeples were seen from quite a distance. The wooden churches are covered inside with stucco and are painted outside with oil-based paint. All manses are built of brick. In the region of the Black Sea and the Sea of Asov all of the churches as well as the parsonages and the schools were built of porous limestone. This is a type of material which is especially well-suited for the construction of larger churches and residences. All churches, parsonages and parish schools were built by the parish congregations themselves without any type of great help from somewhere else. To be sure, there was a special fund established in St. Petersburg for Catholic Church buildings but only two churches in the diocese received support which was of any portent. These were the parish church in Kishinev in Bessarabia and in Nikolayev on the Bug River. The churches of the Catholic German village parishes were excluded from the fund for church buildings. Both of the Houses of God mentioned are parish churches in mixed urban parishes.

In the region of the Volga all of the residences for priests were built by the parish congregations. However the settlement office in Odessa had the parsonages in the mother colonies of the Black Sea region built with its funds. With one exception, they are still all standing today: in Rastatt, Kleinliebental, Selz, Mannheim, Heidelberg; Eichwald and Josephstal. Many congregations used up large sums of money for the construction of the church. These included Selz, Mannheim, Kandel, Karlsruhe in the Black Sea region and Herzog, Kamenka and Seelmann on the Volga. The congregations considered the upkeep of its House of God as its most own responsibility. For this reason large sums were set aside for repairs to the building. For the inside upkeep of the House of God as, for instance the paintings, the altars, the pulpit, the church vessels and the sacred robes etc. the church council was responsible. It was made up of the priest and both of the members of the church council (called the syndics). The expenses which were necessary for this work came from the offerings. In the same way the congregation took care of the upkeep of the parsonage and its places of service such as the parish or congregational school. A supervisory person who was employed by the congregation had to make sure that the necessary repairs were made. This way of doing things for church buildings was held in the Volga region. In the south of the diocese this issue was not regulated very much as the rich wanted the poor to help carry the same burden of expense for the congregation as they did. This should have taken into heart the prohibition in the old convenant not to hitch the ass next to the ox because of the inequality in terms of strength. 1. Besides this, the congregations deliver heating materials to the priest: wood, coal, cut blocks of dried manure and straw for the heating of the residence and the rooms belonging to the servants. In the region of the Volga there were one or two milk cows next to each parish residence. The parish congregation would provide hay, coal and potathes according to the needs of the priest. The mother parishes of the Black Sea were given 120 dessiatines of agricultural land which did not have to be fertilized. Since this land from the beginning of the founding of the parish only brought in very little rent the parish congregations were responsible for paying their priest 300 rubles as an annual stipend. If a filial congregation separated itself from the parish church then this congregation could not make claim to a division of the land which was to be used for the support of the priest. The newly-established parish alone had to pay the salary for its pastor. The size of the salary was determined by a contract between the episcopal leadership and the respective parish congregation. Since the cost of living in Russia is low, this sum was sufficient for the standard of living needed by a clergyman. The churches of the Volga region received no parish land. Since the colonies on the Volga had to deal with a lack of land, they came to an agreement with the state that every religious worker in the parish was to be paid a supplement to his salary which was 142 rubles and 90 kopecks. But each colony could use the 120 dessiatines of agricultural land determined by the state for the church in order to come up with this sum. Since these dues (142 rubles and 90 kopecks) were also collected from the farmers in the vacant parishes, after a period of time capital in the sum of 42,500 rubles was earned and deposited in the college (directorship) in St. Petersburg. The annual interest was then paid to various clergy in the diocese and this was for the administrators of the diocese. Of this interest the ill Canon Fleck received 600 rubles annually and 250 rubles were set for the deaf priest Dovblis. 500 rubles were paid out annually by the government as a supplement for Bishop Antonius Zerr's pension.

This is the usage of that capital which the author of the History of the German Colonies on the Volga, Reverend Gottlieb Beratz discovered according to his research. He could have found out about the use of the· interest from the episcopal leadership. Instead of this he preferred to write the following note in his history: "Not a single kopeck seems to have been received by any of the Catholic clergy in the Volga region from the interest from this fund. For this reason it would have been preferable that the Catholic eparchial administration or its consistory in Saratov had cleared up any questions in regard to this issue among the Catholic clergy because many a person who was ill and needed to recuperate or priest without means would have been able to receive support from this fund."

1. Deuteronomy 22:10 and 2. Beratz, the German Colonies P. 225

39. The transfer of Bishop Eduard von Ropp to Vilna

For not quite 1 ½ years the very honoured Lord Eduard Baron Ropp held the Shepherd's Staff in the Diocese of Tyraspol. The newly orphaned diocese of Vilna needed a Head Shepherd who had the ability to lead the ship of this diocese through the waves which rolled it. For almost one century the bishops of Vilna, with one exception, had been exiled for Catholic cause. If there was anyone there who had the ability to uphold God's laws and those of the Church without at the same time coming into conflict with the state beauracracy the just-appointed Bishop of Tyraspol, Baron Eduard von Ropp.

He had studied law before his ordination to the priesthood and was then an official in the Russian Ministry in St. Petersburg. He had former colleagues among the high officials in the residence of the czar. As a priest and dean in Libau (Translator's note: now a city in Latvia) he had shown a great zeal for souls and showed great capabilities in the administration of the most difficult parish of the diocese of Kovno. For this reason Bishop Eduard von Ropp himself was a combination of all the characteristics which the Catholic Church and the Russian Government could expect from the Head Shepherd of Vilna. Included in this was that the Governor of Vilna was a special friend of his. For these reasons the Holy Father laid it upon Bishop von Ropp that it would be his desire for him to resign from Tyraspol and take over the administration of the much-tested Diocese of Vilna. However the desire of the Holy Father was a command to the highly respected bishop that the Head Shepherd should use this opportunity in order to obtain an equivalent benefit for his agreement to this posting. This was the approval of the government for the appointment of Professor Joseph Kessler as the bishop of Tyraspol whom the Holy Father Pius X had decided would be the successor to Bishop Eduard von Ropp during his last audience with Bishop George Count Schembek. There were many problems in having Professor Joseph Kessler appointed as the successor to the diocesan chair in Tyraspol (Saratov) by the Russian government. Father Kessler had been active in the Crimea since his early years as a priest. It was there that he administered the large and multilingual parish of Simferopol and he had since those early years been put into disrepute (the Black Book) by the government in St. Petersburg. The governor of Tauria, Peter Lazarev, who was a very simple-minded man, had sent complaints to the ministry against the young pastor because of the objections of non-Catholics. They considered him to be a religious fanatic. Bishop Antonius Zerr had to send Father Joseph Kessler to a German village. He was ordered to do so by Minister Durnovo so that "he could not damage other religions." This duty which Bishop Eduard von Ropp had carried out was very difficult. The government had just previously and repeatedly refused the confirmation of Professor Kessler as the supervisor of the seminary for priests. It was only when there was a personal conversation between the energetic Bishop Eduard von Ropp with the Head of the Department of "Foreign Confessions" that the state government could be won for the confirmation. When upon this occasion, Bishop Eduard noted that the state officials were open to the appointment; he had the hope of also getting the authorized supervisor of the seminary as his successor upon the diocesan chair of Tyraspol. Since the bishop had found out from Archbishop George Count Schembek that the Holy Father bad marked out Professor Joseph Kessler as the candidate for the diocese of Tyraspol he was even more determined in his request of the ministry to allow the appointment of Professor Joseph Kessler as the Bishop of Tyraspol. He even made this appointment a condition of his resignation of the position as bishop of Tyraspol and acceptance of taking over the Bishopric of Vilna. That had its effect. The bishop could hardly believe his ears when his chief the Pope agreed so quickly and asked Bishop von Ropp to appoint the professor who had not received any spiritual honours thus far to the cathedral head as a prior step to his future elevation to the cathedra of Tyraspol. Just shortly beforehand a position at the cathedral which was that of the cantor had become vacant. This position as cantor should actually have been given to the beloved and elderly supervisor and Professor Johannes Antonov. He was the second and most worthy candidate for this honour. However, because of the situation the elderly and much approved gentleman had to rank second this time. However, in order to show special favour and high honour because of his achievements and to bring them to light, Bishop Eduard von Ropp caused the supervisor, who had been appointed as the rector of the seminary for priests as well, to receive a position as a papal house prelate.

When in this manner a successor for Tyraspol (Saratov) had been found there was nothing which stood in the way of the beloved Head Shepherd to leave. The day of departure had arrived. The spiritual bond between the Head Shepherd and the flock of Tyraspol had not yet held for a long period of time and yet its unraveling was not without pains for the priests in the bishopric as well as for the cathedral chapter and the entire Catholic population. Everyone was sad to see the Head Shepherd leave and this was proof of the fact that he had won the hearts of the faithful and the clergy by his beloved and cleared-headed character in a very short time. And this was not just in a small way.

After the departure of Bishop Eduard von Ropp one asked the question: Why did you send this highly-honoured gentleman to us as the bishop if he was to be taken away so soon again? Since it is the Holy Spirit who sends bishops to the orphaned parts of the Christian flock one must confess with the Scriptures: "Who can understand His ways?" Job 36:23 However one can state at the very least that God sent Bishop Eduard to Tyraspol in order to show ways which one was to tread and in order to lead everything upon these ways or in order to give the entire administration of the diocese new directives. He set this course. He had done his duty. For this reason providence sent him to a much more important posting. Bishop Eduard was to work in a reviving way and remain there for a long time. The evil of human beings in alliance with hostile forces could not deal with his activity. For this reason his work had to come to an end. He had to share the fate of many of his predecessors upon the cathedra of Vilna. He had to go into exile.

40. The priests and the believers of the diocese

The relationship which is found between the pastor/clergyman and his parish congregation, or should exist, cannot be shown in a more poignant way than by that of the Good Shepherd. The Good Shepherd looks for the lost sheep and bears it, when he has found it, upon his shoulders and brings it back to the flock. Rightly so, the church calls a good pastor a shepherd of souls. In the diocese of Tyraspol he is generally referred to as Pater because the first pastors belonged to orders of priests. Even individuals among the people who are not pastors are honoured with this beautiful name as soon they are consecrated as priests. The curate.of souls is actually the spiritual father (pater= Latin for father) of his congregation. For this reason the Apostle states in his first Letter to the Corinthians: "For in Christ Jesus I conceived you by means of the Gospel." (I. Corinthians 4: 15).

But the curate of souls is not only called by this beautiful name; he is also honoured by the faithful as a father. This is especially true of the faithful in the southern part of the diocese as well as in the north. Out of respect the faithful kiss his and every priest's hand. All greet him with the greeting: "Praised be Jesus Christ!" The entire Catholic population of the diocese shows great trust toward him. The signs of honour are not just simply outward. They are the way in which deep and inner respect are shown. Even foreign clergy often had the opportunity to experience this child-like way of respect. It is enough to point to the witness of a French bishop who visited several colonies in the region of Odessa a few years ago. I. Even the godless efforts of Bolshevism could not tear away this respect for their priests from the Catholics of Tyraspol. Legitimate requests by the curate of souls were always considered by those placed under his car even if this meant that large sacrifices had to be made. However there were also not a few contradictions in the parishes contrary to the directives of the priest. These usually came from individual members of the parish as has been described above in a more thorough manner. Often this happened because of stupidity and irresponsible pastoral practice on the part of young and inexperienced priests. One should not forget that in a land of the most widespread and extensive type of autocracy, the inexperienced clergyman was tempted to go before officials and that this sometimes led to damage in regard to his care of souls. Others did not count on the weaknesses and defects common to man. For this reason it was a wise decision for the diocesan administration to leave such young pastors in their positions for a long time. In their new posting they could then use their acquired experience and be gentler and more careful in regard to the new people placed in their pastoral care.

Finally it is also the case that the divine Shepherd of souls also allows contradictions in order to develop character among young clergy. If a young cleric always was able to carry out his orders then his self-will would easily develop into obstinacy and stubbornness. What was lacking was something to hold him back as a necessary corrective that would have made him more receptive to humility and obedience to his superior. Experience teaches that a man who in his young years has everything go according to his own desires often becomes completely inflexible. When such a clergyman teaches others the great virtues of humility and obedience then he runs into the danger of forgetting what he learned and in this he damages himself and harms those entrusted to his care. For this reason the Apostle to the Gentiles says about himself: "I chastise my own body so that after I have preached to others I myself am not rejected."

    I. Corinthians 9:27

1. Michael D'Erbigny, Pastoral Journeys in Soviet Russia

In general and as a whole, a spirit of love and unity reigned between the priests and the members of the parish in the diocese. This good understanding was only ruined in a few situations. The many complaints on the part of the parish members against the curates of souls and those of the pastors against their parish members which belonged to daily occurrences during the first years after the founding of the diocese almost entirely ended during the time of the last bishops. The type of love and deep respect which the faithful had toward the clergy is clearly evident from the many letters sent by immigrants from the diocese that went, for example, to Siberia, South America etc. The parts of the letters regarding their situation read: "We have Catholic clergymen here too. Unfortunately they do not understand our German language and many are too worldly." However we do not want to examine the authors of these letters too carefully in regard to the comment "too worldly." This is in regard to the condition of the priests. For the emigrants from Tyraspol understand this to mean that the clergy not only wear the spiritual robe outside of the church but also a civil robe and that they are no different than those who are citizens of the world. For this reason they yearned more for the custom according to which the pastor also wore his clerical robe outside of church as the clergy were accustomed to do in the old homeland.

Humans are simply creatures who place a great deal of emphasis on outward appearances. If a person sees a clergyman in a black robe then the difference in class distinction between himself and his pastor immediately comes to mind. If the clergyman moves about those entrusted in his care in clothing which does not differ from civilians then nothing outward reminds him of his high spiritual rank. A clerical collar is not seen enough and does not set him apart enough. It does not immediately remind the person about the respect due to a priest, expecting that he first be made aware of it and used to it.

Our loving Lord often ties the first threads of the call to become a priest to clerical garb. The author can talk about this from personal experience. When he was a child of five or six and saw the first priest in a black robe, this figure and the clerical clothing made such an impression upon him that he could never forget or wipe it away. During his later years this impression of respect for priests was so strong in his heart when he was a boy that he is not able to express it. Without clerical garb these first and best-sown seeds of religious feelings would hardly have been awakened in his soul. For this reason it is genuine Catholic spirit, Catholic religious feeling if the Christian desires to see his priest in a black robe. A less solemn bishop wrote the following at the end of the century to a priest in the diocese of Eichstaett regarding the clerical robe: "In Bohemia the priests cannot be distinguished from the layman and I am not pleased with this." "Clothes do not make the man." (Latin: Habitus non facit monachum) These sayings have good intentions but one also says: "People make clothes." The clothing of the priest has to be respectable. The lack of manliness in a priest always begins with the removal of clerical garb." It is always a concession to heresies which have departed from the true Church of Christ if Catholic priests wear worldly garb which makes them the same as all the religious servants of Protestantism in all its variations.

But we will return to the theme of the love which the faithful of Tyraspol have toward their pastors. When the Bolshevik authorities, by using crazy and more inhuman acts of plundering among the farmers of the bishopric, caused them to die in large numbers and brought them to starvation, famine also knocked on the doors of the priests. In many parishes the parish rnembers gathered and decided to make decisions with the following content: "Everyone who still has produce, even if it is just a little, will deliver something for the support of the pastor. He should be the last person in the congregation who dies of starvation."

41. The Catholics and the middle schools

During the first years of the settlement of the German immigrants one was not able to consider the establishment of higher institutions of learning. All of the prerequisites were missing. The colonists had to think about their existence as they did not bring along any means of support from the old homeland. Because of their lack of knowledge in regard to the soil conditions and the different climatic situation they continually had to deal with failed harvests. The soil also had to be cleared of weeds and had to be cultivated before one could count on more abundant harvests. The inhabitants of the Volga as well as those who lived in the south of the diocese continually had to deal with economic deprivation. History reports that they were not even able to support their clergy. However, despite their poverty and need they still formed church or congregational schools in all of the villages, even if these were very small. The schoolmaster not only had to teach the children but also had to act as the sexton in the church. With two positions it is easy to think about how the school took second place. In many cases the teacher also had a teacher no a helper. Such a person was usually a person who was a village inhabitant who had received his "education" solely in the parish or congregational school and for this reason was not as adept at performing his duties. However the teaching program was very modest: reading, writing, some arithmetic and the catechism taught in German. That was all that the school could offer.

As the entire administration of the colonists was carried out in the German language, one did not even consider learning Russian. Outside of the officials and the clergy no one understood the Russian language. One could not even read or write Russian. This complete neglect and lack of knowledge of the official language was mainly caused by the geographic separation of the German colonists from the Russian population. This was something which had been planned for their settlement. In those colonies, which because of their location in terms of trade had contact with the Russian population one needed to learn Russian. There were only a few of these colonies on the Volga. Very early onward they were like smaller cities. The colonists made all of their purchases and took care of what little business they had. All of this could easily be done using their mother tongue. There were three such colonies in the north: Katharinenstadt and Seelman on the left shore of the Volga, and Balzer on the Hilly Side which was 25 versts from Saratov.

Soon after their settlement, the colonists realized that there were few institutions of higher learning. It was to be expected that they would try to change this as soon as they were able. Because of this a "county" or as one called it in the region of the Black Sea, a "central school," was formed. They were the creation of the German colonists without regard to religious confession. Lutherans as well as Catholics established a large number of stipends for the poor sons of colonists. Orphans were given preference. All of the county and central schools were built in Lutheran villages. The leaders and the teachers were Lutheran. At first the teachers were men from the provinces of the Baltic Sea because there were no colonists' sons who had been educated in order to become teachers. As the Catholics everywhere in general matters when Lutherans and Protestants constitute the majority are at a disadvantage this also took place at this time. It was of good fortune that according to the school statutes Catholic religious instruction was set up for Catholic students. As there was no instructor in religion present in the school itself the neighbouring priest had to hold these classes. This was not without a few problems. This was especially the case when the neighbouring Catholic parish was quite distant.

Sometimes the Catholic religion instruction, little as it was, had to be omitted. The Catholic students were also wronged by their fellow Lutheran students because of their faith. If by exception the director of the school was a Russian one would have expected more feeling from him for that which is Catholic than for the Lutheran position as the "Orthodox" religion is very closely related to Catholicism. Without considering this the "Orthodox" leaders always took the side of the Lutherans or Protestants versus the Catholics. All of this made it harder for Catholic students to study well in their own schools. One "Orthodox" school director went as low as to make fun of his Catholic pupils with the following Protestant slander: "As soon as the coins ring in the treasury, the soul will jump out of purgatory."

The Catholic student was forced to pray together with the Lutheran students. The Catholics had their religious instruction either before or after the regular times of instruction and this also made it harder for the pupils to learn properly. Such a rule of teaching is in opposition to the ABCs of pedagogy. This requires that instruction for the child is made as easy as possible. It should look forward to instruction with joy and eagerness. Religious instruction should especially be made as pleasant as possible because it is the most important. The same order in regard to Catholic religious instruction was held in the Middle Schools in the cities insofar as they were even allowed there. For it cost the curates of souls a lot of trouble and effort to introduce Catholic religious instruction in the government schools. Remuneration was also not paid. The priests were glad if the school officials even graciously accepted or allowed their services. According to Russian state law not even the bishop or the pastor of the parish was allowed to take the initiative in order to introduce religious instruction in the state schools. The right to do so was only given to the director of the institution of higher learning. "The Director chooses the instructor of religion and the Commissioner appoints him and the Bishop approves him" This is how the outstanding paragraph in the Russian state law reads. Right away one notes that he usurps, as only a government official who belongs to a genuine state church system could, the divine commission which Christ only gave to his Church (that is to its leaders: the apostles and their successors, the bishops) "Go and teach!" Matthew 28:19. He does allow himself to be reconciled with the teaching of Holy Scripture because he looks down upon the Catholic Church. The commissioners for education in the Russian provinces generally thought very highly of themselves and were haughty. When it came to the introduction of religious instruction in a Middle School they did not even deign to respond to the Catholic diocesan bishop who had the secular rank of a Lieutenant General and who corresponded with the ministers of state! This took place even if letters were sent to him over and over again. If the director did not take the initiative himself in order to introduce Catholic religious instruction, then all of the efforts of the Catholic clergy were in vain. While most of these bosses were opposed to Catholic religious instruction or at the very least, simply did not want to have it, they were very zealous in making sure that our children were taught to dance well! This was more important to these educators of humankind. In this situation, wise priests who had zeal for souls tried to get the parents of the male and female students to send an appeal from all of them to the educational advisors at school in order to attain the goal of introducing Catholic religious instruction. Since some of the petitioners were first class civil officials the petition was, as a rule, considered but often with the comment that the school could not waste any money on the teacher of religion because there were no funds for this! This was the way in which the urban Catholic inhabitants wanted to attain the introduction of Catholic religious instruction in the Middle Schools.

Some pedagogues especially enjoyed making the Catholic students feel ill at ease because of their religion. They forced them to attend the Russian Orthodox Church services on Sundays and on Feast Days. Many Catholic students were hindered in taking part in the singing during the services in their own parish church since at the same time one expected them to sing in the "Orthodox" church choir. It is fortunate that there were only a few of these cases. What did take place often was that in many cases all of the historical slander against the Roman popes, the Society of Jesus and against indulgences had to be memorized thoroughly. Whoever is acquainted with the Russian books used in instruction regarding history as a whole will be surprised that they were written as if they had a Lutheran and not an "Orthodox" author. All of the slander and historical lies are viewed as having been written from a purely Lutheran standpoint.

During the 90s one began to want very strict and better-prepared teachers for the elementary schools. As there were not enough teachers colleges/seminaries, and the graduates of Middle Schools studied at universities and other higher institutions of learning, there was a great dearth of school teachers who had become certified. Many schools stood empty. The Catholic priests had the children come together in the school rooms for religious instruction. They had every right to do so. Then it customarily happened that a school inspector of a county would visit the schools located in it. He would do this just when the children were together with their teacher in religious instruction. Instead of informing themselves first in regard to the situation and then give "directive" to the school inspector would stamp his feet as if he was crazy. If he did not start to speak and curse in Russian as often happened, then this was too his credit. The children were shocked because of the rage of such people so that they often fled and jumped out of the windows so that they could take off. An example of this took place at the beginning of the 90s of the previous century in the Crimea where the author of this history was the city priest. However, this kind of insanity was against state law. Unfortunately, in this nation where the officials under the absolutism of the czar were the actual autocrats instead of being the officials of the emperor, this law was not implemented. fu fact their arbitrary action was the law. Another school inspector had strictly forbidden the priest to lecture on religion in school. He could give no other reason for forbidding this. According to the law, religious instructions in schools was not only permitted but was required. Despite this the children were not allowed to learn religion because of the arbitrary action of this inspector who was also an unbeliever. For this hero, the Christian faith was a thorn in his side. The people were not to have any religion. Now it has Bolshevism. With its inventors, the intelligentsia, Bolshevism really-cleaned things up. May the unbelieving and intelligent gentlemen learn a good lesson from this!

42. The religious life of the Catholic urban population

Almost all of the parishes in the cities of the diocese of Tyraspol are mixed in terms of language. With few exceptions the Poles form the vast majority. The use of many languages causes the pastoral care to suffer. The cities are the cause of big problems. This especially true for Russia where the vast majority of the city population belongs to the state religion. While the cities in Western Europe do not have a strong Christian formation anymore (with the exception of the smaller cities), in Russian cities public life was still Christian. Nothing was undertaken which had any importance without a moleben 1 - the - prayer - Unfortunately this was only an outward ceremony among the majority of the intelligentsia. What was missing was the inner spirit which quickened and gave a person a soul. The Catholic intelligensia was also infected by this superficial religious formalism. Unfortunately there was only poor religious instruction in the Russian schools. The liberal, rationalistic, pantheistic and enemies of the faith; the Russian authors which they had to read, robbed them of their joyous faith when they were still young. The great truths of the Holy Catholic Church could not enter the hearts of the youth at school. Thus every religious conviction; also among the Catholic intelligencia had become less firm even when they were young. That which kept them somewhat religious was tradition: the Holy Catholic faith was a precious inheritance which they had received from their forbears. The female Polish intelligencia was especially faithful to this inheritance. For this reason they still attended the worship services on Sundays and on Festival Days, received the Holy Sacraments at Easter and halfways practiced the Catholic religion. The urban German intelligencia which originated from the colonies also practiced the Catholic religion where good sermons were heard. If these were lacking they; for the most part, threw their faith overboard. This was also the case with the

Catholic intelligentsia in the Crimea. A young Catholic pastor who is very serious about his religion has to fear that he will be mocked by these people as a fanatic just as by the Lutheran intelligencia in the larger Russian cities.

The average Catholic city inhabitant of all nationalities is quite faithful. As a rule he attends the Sunday service; prays with devotion in the House of God, diligently hears the Word of God and keeps the rules of abstinence. He also receives the Holy Sacraments and still lives a Christian life. He lets his children be baptized soon after birth and sends them to the Catholic parish school. This is especially true with the Poles and the Lithuanians. The German colonist becomes more lax than they are when he settles down in a city. Usually he is then despised by the people in the village because of his lukewarm religious life and his morals. The colonists want to have little or nothing to do with him. They also do not gather to hold fast to the Catholic Church in the cities. The Catholic parish church is home for the Poles and the Lithuanians in the city. For them it has to do with their nationality and their religion. The parish is the center of his national and religious life. He has full trust in his ksiadz or priest.

As a man lives, so he also dies. This is also true in terms of religion. It you live estranged from the church then you also die without the sacraments! For this reason the majority of the intelligentsia in the Russian cities enters eternity without the holy sacrament of extreme unction unless the priest finds out about the person's severe illness or if believing relatives ask the clergyman to come to the person who is dying. It is often the case that one waits until the sick person is no longer conscious. Then one states and assures the clergyman that the ill person himself asked for the holy sacraments. However, the pastor still proclaims the forgiveness of sins and gives extreme unction to the person who is dying. However the clergyman will never himself be satisfied with this type of preparation upon which all rests, for this is the most important step involved.

The situation is not better with those Catholics who lie in the city hospitals and who are dying. For first of all, the Catholic clergyman is not allowed to freely visit the ill. It is stated that "The sick person will get such a shock if he sees the clergyman that he only get much worse." This is what the heads of the hospitals state. Only if the sick person asks for the pastor can he go to see him. For this reason many soldiers also die in

Russian cities without the holy sacraments. However if the poor dying persons had asked for the holy sacraments, then they would have known how close they were to death.

43. The inner missions in the diocese

In the year 1906 Czar Nicholas sent a message to the governor of Saratov, Peter Arkadyevitch Stolypin that he was to have the office of minister of the interior and prime minister. The Czar needed to have a man who had lots of energy and was popular, and an unusual adroitness and savoir-faire in order to remove the threatening danger of the outbreak of a revolution and to bring peace to the troubled country. The autocrat of the country did something good in appointing Stolypin. The minister nipped the revolution in the bud. That he turned to the military courts and their radical ways of doing things cannot be held against this man of the state, for Russia was in such a confusing situation at that time that soft measures would have achieved nothing. However it was not only by authoritarian means but also because of higher religious reasons that the minister wanted to influence the people. For this reason he permitted the Catholic diocesan bishops of Congress Poland and Russia allow foreign members of religious orders to hold missions in their bishoprics. The ordinary of Tyraspol also made use of this permission. For this reason, in the year 1907 he firstly invited four German Redemptorist Fathers from Vienna to the region of the Black Sea. The Fathers agreed to his invitation. They were Weihmann, Janauschek, Frachessen and Hartmann. One of them preached in French and one in Italian but all of them could preach in German. I.

1. In the diocese there are two parishes with many French people and two with just as many Italians.

The mission to the people began in Odessa. The Fathers held missions in all of the parishes in the deanery of Odessa. The churches, especially those in the village parishes, were filled with the pious the whole day long. The faithful people listened to the soul-stirring sermons and surrounded their confessionals for a period of 2 ½ months. The highly honoured Fathers held 190 sermons and listened to 17,000 confessions. They were uplifted by the zeal of the German Catholics of Tyraspol. After the missions had ended, among other things, they joyfully reported to the ordinary that they had found a great deal of faith and Christian piety in the bishopric of Tyraspol. However they also got to know many of the Tyraspol clerics and bad a high opinion of them. They showed this in their correspondence. "We wish much blessedness and eternal diocesan grace to a clergy like this! You can be proud of them." This is what they said.

The Polish diocesans, who almost exclusively resided in the larger cities of the bishopric, bad missions allowed by the bishop. He invited the sons of St. Francis whom he had invited from Lemberg (L'viv). The ordinary took three Polish Fathers along with himself on a visitation. While the missionaries held missions in the cities, he himself visited the parishes in the countryside where he confirmed the faithful by giving them the sacrament of confirmation and consecrated the churches which had not been consecrated as yet. These missionaries also carried out great work which resulted in much blessing from God and revived the Christian spirit in the city parishes. The folk missions were held held in the following cities: Rostov, Yekaterinodar, Novorossisk, Taganrog, Mariupol, Odessa, Saratov, Astrachan and Yekaterinoslav.

In the same year the Polish Catholics in the Caucausus were also to receive the grace bestowed by missions. For this reason three Redemptorist Fathers were invited from Krakow. Because of a misunderstanding, the Fathers arrived before permission for holding the missions had been received by the governor of the Caucasus. As the bishop had waited in vain for permission and the Fathers had already arrived in Tolisi, he gave the visitor of the Caucasus, Lay Brother Michael Antonov, the task of introducing the three Fathers to the imperial governor, Count Voronzov-Daschkov, so that the mission could begin without specific permission. The bishop hoped that the count would not allow any difficulties to impede the missions. In the meantime, the ordinary tried to obtain authorization from the Ministry of the Interior. While the Ministry turned to the governor in this situation and wrote back and forth, the Fathers held their missions in almost all of the parishes of the Caucasus. They did this without being bothered and without permission. Finally, when the religious exercises for the people had begun in the last parish the answer came from St. Petersburg. It was negative. However the bishop reported the negative response to the Fathers only after the missions had ended. In this way missions were held in all of the parishes of the Caucasus. The diocesan bishop took the responsibility upon himself without having received permission from the state authorities. The officials were faced with a fait accompli and, as often happened in the empire of the czar, left the ordinary undisturbed.

Priests and pastors of the bishopric did not hesitate to hold missions because they were zealous for the souls of their people. This took place until the ordinary could invite missionaries from abroad. In most of the deaneries they united and made their parish members joyful with this unusual way of renewing the religious and churchly spirit without thinking of the fact that missions for the people were forbidden by Russian state law. The forty hours of prayer which had gained entry into many parishes in the diocese generally gave the pastors a good opportunity to hold religious excercises for the people.

The good fruit which the united activity of the clergy of a deanery produced was often very comforting. Every first mass said by a newly-ordained priest was always held with a large crowd of people. It often gave the curates of souls an opportunity to revive and to encourage the religious zeal of the people.

In some parishes in the diocese the festivals of the male and female patron saints were celebrated by the male and female youth in a very festive manner. In large numbers, the youth who were growing up came to their patron saints such as on the feast day of St. Aloysius and St. Agnes. They came to receive the Holy Sacraments and took strength and grace from this wellspring of life.

Many a priest in the south as in the north of the bishopric saw to it that there was good and positive entertainment and diversion held for the youth and the parish members in that nice plays were held and by setting up reading libraries for the people. 1.

Some curates of souls who had a diligent organist in their parishes tried to enable the people through the presentation of beautiful musical presentations, and in order to make them more receptive for the beautiful and noble things, and also for church hymnody.

All of this gives us evidence that in the diocese of Tyraspol genuine and true Christian and Catholic life reigned and that its pastors made much effort in that they educated and enobled and did not just build them up in terms of their religion. These people had been entrusted to them.' Even if a Catholic came from the best Catholic regions of a foreign country to the German Catholic villages of the diocese, he soon felt that he was surrounded by Catholic air. May it not be polluted by the enemies of God and of every religion - by the Bosheviks!

I. When the colonists of the Volga region celebrated the 150th anniversary of their settlement in the year 1917, a theatre group was formed by high school/college students and they presented the play "Kirghiz Michael." This was a drama which the Fathers Baratz and Hunger had written for this purpose. The hero of the drama was a young fellow from Mariental who had been taken away by the plundering Kirghiz together with many other colonists and sold. He had freed himself by trickery from slavery in Asia and fled to his homeland. The piece gave the reader a picture of the times of persecution of the colonists by the wild Asiatic inhabitants of the steppe and was a real hit among the colonists who viewed it.

44. Attendance at chapels and prayer processions

The pious Christian attitude does not restrict itself to the every-day devotional excercises required by the church as for instance the attendance at Sunday and festival masses, hearing the sermon, and the reception of the Holy Sacraments. It also wants to participate in other pious acts of worship which are not required. Silent devotions far away from the troubles of life, from the crowds and from the noise of the world are also popular. The Christian soul would like to tell its creator alone of its needs and place prayer requests in -all quietness in a solitary place which has been sanctified by the Church. This natural drive of a pious heart has been a part of the Catholic Church since the first centuries after the bloody persecutions of Christendom. For this reason, chapels were constructed in lonely places which the church placed under its protection and sanctified. Our German Catholic colonists also held fast to these pious customs and built chapels in solitary places which as a rule were consecrated to the suffering of Jesus. A long row of high crosses with scenes from the fourteen stations of the cross lead to the entrance of the oratories in solitary places. The author remembers that when he was a small boy, large groups of men and women would make devotional visits to these chapels. He remembers how they would pray the painful rosary aloud starting from the exit from the village. At the first station of the cross, which was located below at the foot of the big hill, the pious would kneel down and would begin praying at the stations of the cross. The last station was the place where a beautiful devotion was held. All of the stations of the cross were visited by slowly moving forward in a kneeling position. As the progression took place by the more pious women upon bare knees the devotion was connected with intense physical pain. These pains were sought by the pious in order to bear physical suffering out of love for the suffering Saviour. However there were so people among the Catholics who were rationalists and who would make jokes and mock this way of prayer. However, the pious did not let themselves become distracted during their devotions. The people of the Volga were very determined to keep this custom. In the southern part of the diocese this pious custom was little known or not known at all. There were also no chapels there outside of the colonies if one does not count the church or cemetery chapels.

The chapels were the goal of large processions of prayer on St. Mark's Day and on one of the days of prayer. These processions were beloved by the people. Everyone participated in them; At the head of the procession there would be a cross carried by a boy. Then there would be two rows which firstly included the boys and then the male youth; the men. These were followed by the women and girls. The processions were always led by the clergy of the parish locality dressed in clerical robes and the priests usually walked in the midst of the elderly men. Directly behind the pastor and the ministrants, the schoolmaster

followed with the choir and they sang the bidding prayers for All Saints responsively. Whereas the youth considered it to be of special advantage to be allowed to carry the church flag, they only seldom wanted to carry the processional cross. It often happened that a boy from the church council had to be forced to come just as was the case with Simon of Cyrene! The church council members who were in the middle of the long row prayed the rosary for the people until the procession had arrived at the chapel or at a cross located in front of a field. The missa de rogatione (mass of prayer) was then held in the chapel. After the service had ended the procession continued according to the previous order back to the village and to the parish church. The days of prayer with their processions as the people referred to them, were truly days of prayer and of repentance and an expression of true Catholic and religious life among the people.

The solitary chapel also attracted individuals who wanted to carry out their acts of repentance or promises. Just the fact that it was a solitary location and a hill upon which they stood or the forest by which, in individual cases, they were surrounded, exuded a certain consecration which invited communication with the creator. God speaks powerfully to the heart in solitary situations: One solitary chapel in the middle of the forest has something religious and poetic for the Christian soul. The largest colony of the diocese, Mariental, even had two chapels in the forest which were visited by the pious during the summer. When the congregation, in the years prior to the end of the World War decided to harvest the beautiful oak forest not far from the Karaman River one did not even show any respect for the two holy places in the forest. One chopped down the last trees around the chapels in a barbaric and heartless manner!

45. Pilgrimages of the colonists

Since the most ancient of times, the Catholic Church promoted visits to holy places such as Jerusalem, Bethlehem, Nazareth, Rome etc. in order to do penance. In doing so it satisfied natural and pious emotions. Christian character was moved to see those places and to honour them since the divine Saviour was born there and walked visibly among human beings and suffered and died there. As however very few Christians have the fortune of travelling through the Holy Land, God sees to it that also in the bosom of Christendom special graces are either granted through his virgin mother or by other saints to the Christian people from century to century. This takes place in a wonderful way. Thus many places of grace were established in the Catholic Church such as in Loreto, Althetting, Czenstochau and Lourdes in France. However, the diocese of Tyraspol did not have the good fortune of having a place of grace in its midst. Despite this, the faithful of Tyraspol made pilgrimages to those parish churches where one of their most beloved patron saints is specially honoured. Among these saints one counts St. Anthony of

Padua, St. Joseph, The Dear Mother of God, and there is the Holy Cross. From earliest times the inhabitants of Koehler especially honoured the Cross of Christ even though this was not the name of the parish church. During the festival of the Discovery of the Cross many thousands of faithful people come together in order to honour this holy symbol of our salvation. All of the clergy in the deanery take part in the festivities on May 3rd.
In the evening previous to the festival, all are very busy hearing the confessions of the pious. The confessionals are crowded way into the night. Here innumerable people strengthened themselves with the bread of life. For hours on end the Holy Masses are read and heard. They are held from early in the morning and the people tirelessly hear the moving words of the festival preacher. "Holy Cross Day" as the people refer to the festival is not only famous on the Hilly Side within close proximity to the colony of Koehle ~ but in the entire north of the diocese. For this reason the pilgrims undertake-taking long on journeys on foot or partially by wagon in order to reach the goal of their pilgrimage. It often happens that large steamships on the Volga are filled mainly with pilgrims and their journey takes them to Koehler to the Holy Cross. The honour which the Catholic people of the diocese bring to the Holy Cross on "Holy Cross Day" in Koehler is probably the greatest act of worship which is presented to the symbol of our salvation in Tyraspol. That just this public act of worship is connected to the parish church of Koehler probably has its roots in the following legend.

"A farmer from Koehler, while he was plowing his field in springtime, hit upon a hard object. He was already about to go over the object with the plow because it did not seem to be heavy and only one end was showing. However when he wanted to drive the horses forward he could not get them to move when he struck them. This caused the farmer to take note. He looked at the object: It was a crucifix of normal size as one kept it in the Catholic houses in the locality. The man freed the cross from moist and sticky soil, took it home where he placed it in a suitable place of honour on the wall. It was just that after a few days his family members noticed that the crucifix was missing. One looked for it in vain. Then the idea came to mind that that the cross might be found again where it had been discovered. This was a sign that God wanted to have a chapel built there in honour of the crucifix. But one also looked in vain in the field. Finally, after looking for a long time one found it in a side altar of the church. From here one took it again to the house of the person who found it. But this time it was already gone the next morning. One found it in the same place in the church. This disappearance and rediscovery took place again and again. Then one realized that God wanted to have the cross specially honoured either in church or in its own chapel. Soon a chapel was built not far from the village in honour of the "Holy Cross." However, in the vernacular of the people in the north this legend was not considered a thing of faith because it had not been authenticated enough to be such. Just this is shown by this legend. The Catholic population of the diocese of Tyraspol, following its inner religious compulsion, highly honours the saints and holy vessels and seeks support for its prayers through their mediation with God. The people readily took upon themselves the burdens and abjurations which a pilgrimage included.

Pilgrimages to neighbouring church probably took place because at the time of the settlement of the colonies and because of the lack of priests, a parish consisted of two or more villages. If one of the churches celebrated its patron saint or Church Dedication Sunday then others came to the parish to which the villages belonged "together with the Cross and the Flag." This was in a procession. Because of the gathering together of so many people in the church, and the church could not by far hold everyone; there was a big crowd. The attendance in the House of God was not always without danger for the life of the parishoners. This was especially true if the church was made of wood as all of the churches in the north were constructed before the second half of the 19th century. Thus it almost happened that there was a dangerous catastrophe during the celebration of a first mass by a newly-ordained priest. This took place in Luzem. During the holy service one suddenly heard a cracking of the beams which were holding up the choir loft. It was only thanks to the quick thinking of one of the respected men that there was no confusion among the people and that no one panicked. In 1884 the celebration of the church dedication in the parish church in Louis was not as fortunate. The church was made of wood and did not even stand upon a foundation of stone. To be sure, the church was not a wreck but much too small in order to hold the pious who wanted to crowd inside. This was especially true because a procession with many people had arrived from Mariental. The young parish administrator had just begun his sermon from the pulpit when in the back on the choir loft where the boards from the old organ house lay piled up, there was a big noise. Several young men stepped on the organ's thin walls and these broke making a lot of noise. When this happened the dust which had been gathering for years started to rise. Several of those who were afraid called out in their village dialect: "It's breaking, it's breaking"! In other words, they thought that the church was breaking apart. Many of those present falsely understood the call" It's breaking! as: "It's burning, It's burning!" Everyone became alarmed and ran out of the three exits to the church. Sensible men sought to clear up the misunderstanding by calling out. And they were almost successful if the preacher had not at that decisive moment left the pulpit and kicked out the window on the stairs to the pulpit and looked for a way to escape. This was the sign that led to general confusion. Now no one could be kept back anymore and no one could be calmed down. Whoever could not get to a door which led outside tried to climb up through the next window in order to escape what seemed to be a dangerous situation. Many young men who were on the choir loft jumped through the upper round windows down to the church yard. The parish administrator, who always wore glasses with black lenses to protect his eyes, was confirmed in his thinking that things were really burning when he thought that the dust which had been stirred up was smoke. One very fortunate thing happened during this misfortune in that no one was killed and there were no people badly hurt. Despite this the sensible people in the congregation in Louis saw this sad happening as an admonition from a loving God that it was an unavoidable necessity that a new large stone House of God be built in place of the small church. Today Louis has one of the largest stone churches in the diocese of Tyraspol. The administrator who was mentioned began the project.

46. Church hymnody

The singing which the first settlers of the diocese of Tyraspol did was not different than that in the old homeland and this was true neither in terms of the melody or the text. Even today one can hear the same German religious songs and style of singing in the churches of the bishopric as in those areas of Germany from which the German colonists of Russia originate. Since the Volga colonies and those of the Black Sea emigrated from different regions of Germany, they only had a few church hymns in common. But when the boys and the youth of the south and the north of the diocese united in the seminary for clergy the northern hymn styles spread to the south and the southern hymn styles spread to the north. A common hymnal for the entire diocese was not available until the year 1908. This is when the beautiful "Alleluja" was printed. Without question, this hymnal can compare favourably with the best German church hymnals. According to the judgement of those who are knowledgable in Germany, it is superior in some ways to the best church hymnals in Germany. Besides the most common Latin chorale chants the book also includes the melodies in notes which are more common among secular professional musicians than the notes which are used in church settings. For church use and for the Latin liturgical chants the Kantionale of the Polish dioceses was required. A big deficiency of this hymnal was that there was not a single spiritual song in the German language included. This deficiency had to be corrected with a German hymnal. The above-mentioned "Alleluja" showed its advantages in this regard.

As in all traditional customs and traditions, the German colonist of Tyraspol held fast to German hymnody. With the passage of time he was more restricted in the use of his mother tongue. Therefore he clung more steadfastly to the German church hymn. The love toward his native German church hymn showed itself especially when in several parishes of the region of the Black Sea some priests with a sense of extreme zeal and without any kind of wisdom introduced the Latin hymn into the service and did not want to allow even a single German church hymn. The battle between the pastor and the congregation continued for about 25 years and generally ended in the suspension of the organist's salary and in the most extreme of cases in the transfer of the priest to another parish. The people were prepared to make the greatest of sacrifices when it came to the retention of the German church hymn.

However this battle also had its good results. In order to make the Latin hymnody favourable to the people, the priests of the Black Sea region saw to it that good and well-educated organists were hired. It was there in the Black Sea region that the battle for German hymnody during High Mass and during the Holy Mass was passionate. As was generally the case in education and in culture, church hymnody and music from Germany had to serve as a model for the colonists. A priest in the south invited the first German choir director and organist from the Church Music School in Regensburg to visit. This first organist from abroad was a well-educated and proficient person who knew the Latin chorale and church music. In the parish church of Karlsruhe where the young man was hired, superior church music and singing was soon performed. However the farmers were educated too little in order to properly appreciate the superior achievements. To be sure the colonists had to admit that the previous singing could not be compared to the performances given by the person from Regensburg. It was just that outwardly one did not want to approve of "new things that were to be introduced." This was because the German hymnody was removed from the High and Sung Mass (missa cantata). In opposition to the will of the parishoners and with the strong opposition of most of the people the chorale and also Latin hymnody still was able to gain entry into most of the parishes of the south and in several of those in the north. In the meantime the folk songs were also fostered by the younger educated organists and was sung more beautifully than before by the church and after the mass and on various occasions. However, the cathedral church in Saratov always had the Latin chorale and chant in its High Masses and during vespers. However, when the Head Shepherd of the diocese got a priest who had received his instruction in church music in Regensburg and he had been called as the professor of hymnody at the seminary and as the choir director the ecclesiastical efforts at music had reached their pinnacle.

The development of church singing in many parishes of the bishopric of Tyraspol naturally led to the purchase of good and superior organs which undergirded the singing. These organs originate in the most superior organ factories of Germany such as Steimeier, Sauer, Klais etc. While in the south almost every church had a good organ, this glorious -instrument could find acceptance in only a few of the Houses of God· in the north. For some reason not understood, the harmonium was preferred and one often spent much money in order to purchase one.

Every church in the north as well as in the south of the diocese had its own choir. However, these choirs could not produce anything of a superior quality during the first years of settlement. Most of the singers couldn't even read Latin and had no idea about notes. Even the schoolmasters, who as a rule came from the class of farmers in the village, and were elected by them had no musical education whatsoever and practiced the choir songs b ear. One change for the better took place with the arrival of the Jesuit priests. They instructed their schoolmasters in the reading of Latin and in Gregorian chant. Among these the colonist Anton Schneider was special because he had a better education. He was active as schoolmaster for 25 years during the middle of the 19th century in the village of Mariental on the Karaman River. By tireless diligence he gathered German church hymns which had been handed down in the north of the diocese and. filled several volumes with these hymns. His hymnals, which he himself wrote down in a beautiful manner, were disseminated in almost all of the parishes. He set all of the hymns to the same way of notation and thus saved the predominant way of singing in the Volga· region. He composed the notes for the rubrics (which were not to be changed) in the Holy Mass such as the Kyrie, the Gloria, the Crede, Sanctus, Benedictus and the Agnus Dei and thus actually became the creator of all the notations which were common in several churches of the north and which were generally sung by ear. One of his mass compositions he designated as the "High Mass of Mariental." He composed various anthems as for example the one used during the Eucharistic processions and which was so beloved. This was "Jesu dulcis memoria" (Jesus of blessed memory) The melody of the "Te Deum" had changed greatly from its liturgical form within the vernacular of the people. When at the beginning of the 60s, Diocesan Bishop Ferdinand Helanus visited the north Schoolmaster Martin Schneider specifically travelled to Saratov in order to study the liturgical melodies and to set them to illustrative notations. (Figuralnoten)

In the south of the bishopric, church hymnody in the first years after the settlement of the colonists was not better than in the north. However, there were several families of schoolmasters there, just as in the north, among whom the knowledge of notes had been retained. One had taken along hymnals with notes from the old homeland. The Fathers of the Society of Jesus who were the first pastors in this area could not effectively influence the development of hymn-singing because they had to leave Russia after a period of eight years· of activity. In the north of the diocese church singing completely died out after the first and second generation had passed away. Whoever could scream the highest notes was· considered to be the most qualified. In many parishes the so-called "transposers" were loved a lot. But this unbecoming style of music was abolished when a mocking article about these "singers" appeared in the "Klemens." It had compared them to hawks "who always rise higher and higher in the air." However in the south the church hymnody did not turn into wild screaming. Despite this, there was also improvement needed there. The way was paved for this by the opening of the seminary for boys in Saratov in the year 1857. However, it was only 25 years later that the beginnings of an actual reform were initiated. The priest of Karlsruhe in the south earned a special place in the diocese in arranging this. This active young priest was Jakob Scherr. He let a diligent church musician by the name of Edmund Schmid come from Regensburg in Bavaria. Within a relatively short period of time during his stay in Russia, he was able to bring about excellent results. The organists who graduated from the school soon spread better church hymnody in the south of the bishopric while little was being done in regard to this in the region of the Volga. Special merit was achieved by Edmund Schmid by presenting and teaching church chorale singing. 1brough him one first learned to appreciate this type of - hymnody. The church singing first blossomed forth in the cathedral and in the seminary under the choir director and singing instructor, Father Leo Weinmaier, in the year 1910. Father Leo Weinmaier had attended the Church Music School in Regensburg and had been educated in a thorough knowledge of church hymnody and church music. Under his leadership in the seminary and in the cathedral the most beautiful creations of music · dedicated to St. Cecilia and even old masters such as Palaestrina were performed. "This choir" said a highly-educated Western European, "can perform everywhere in Western Europe and expect great acclaim." It is to the merit of the seminary that church hymnody in many parishes of the diocese attained a state which had never been reached before. Until the outbreak of the World War, it continued to be brilliant.

47. The relationships between the government and the church

The relationship between the Russian State and the Catholic Church in Russia is in the state codex, which came to be under Czar Nicholas I. Part I of Volume XI of the codex has to do with this. Apart from some some generally damaging paragraphs toward the rights of the Catholic Church and religion, the Russian state law is generally favourable toward the Catholic religion and church. The most damaging attack upon the rights of the church is found in Paragraph 17 in which the free and direct communication of the diocesan bishops, priests and believers with the Apostolic, See is forbidden. All correspondence of the diocesan bishops with the Holy See, it made no difference if this was official or private could only take place through the Ministry of the Interior. The correspondence in Latin always had to be prepared in duplicate and with an exact Russian translation. It had to be addressed to the Ministry of the Interior with the application that it be sent on. The contents were studied completely in the Ministry and if something did not please someone the correspondence was not sent to the Holy See and the bishop who wrote it was considered responsible. From time immemorial the Russian czars swore allegiance to the principles according to which the state did not recognize any power, not of the conscience and not even the power of the divine For this reason there were offensive and troubling attacks upon the rights of the Church and the rights of God.

Through the cowardly subjection of the schismatic Russian church to the absolute power of the state and its comradeship with the same, the state and its government were even strengthened in their false principles: That which also added to this was the pernicious influence of the Western European and especially German Lutheran philosophers who taught the absolutism of the state and set up the principle that might makes right. The hindering of free correspondence by letter mail of the diocesan bishops with the successor to St. Peter naturally led to the fact that the bishops had to carry on their correspondence with the Holy See in a roundabout way. Because of the close comradeship of the Russian Church with the state, various "misdemeanors" against the "Orthodox" church and religion were viewed as misdemeanors against the state and resented. According to state law no one could convert an "Orthodox" believer to another religion. A Catholic who was about to enter into a mixed marriage with an Orthodox believer before the priest could not be denied the sacrament of absolution or have absolution pronounced upon him because this was punished as a state crime with removal from office or exile for the priest. This could not be done if he had been excommunicated because of benefits bestowed by the schismatic church or if he had fallen into the trap of heresy as this was a crime against the state especially since all of his descendants were lost from the Catholic Church. Besides this the clergyman involved would, as a rule, be marked for life and was especially watched by the criminal police. And the latter carried out, as in no other place in the world, its "debt to the state. The Ministry of the Interior had its own department which was used to watch the "Foreign Religious Denominations" more and to protect "Orthodoxy." This was the department of "Foreign Religious Denominations." Non-Russian, that is non-schismatic religious denominations or religious societies were not viewed, as the name of the department already implies, as belonging to the Russian Empire! According to law, political questions were not allowed to even be touched upon in general expressions during the sermon. The Russian civil office especially and carefully watched that the prayer for the Czar and the Imperial Family was said after High Mass on Sundays and Festival Days. One Polish priest allowed himself to pray other prayers instead of this one and he did this in a mumbling, incomprehensible manner. He was denounced by a personal friend. For months on end the investigators and sheriff's officers chased about and one could have thought that it meant as if all of Russia was going to be saved from destruction! Thanks to the able defence of the priest by a highly thought of mayor/head of a council whose name was Dobler, the priest was saved from severe punishment. Woe unto the clergyman who left out or forgot the line for the czar in the petition during the chanting of the petitions!

All of the inheritors' estates made in a will which were left for Catholic churches, social religious institutions or religious foundations had to, even if they were very insignificant be sent to the Board in St. Petersburg where these sums were administered under the chairmanship of the Catholic archbishop of Mohilev. In the cases where donations for the benefit of churches and oratories exceeded 1,000 rubles, they could only be withdrawn with the permission of the czar. Public church collections of money outside of the parish were forbidden. New parishes with congregations could only be established with the permission of the Ministry of the Interior even though the state provided no subsidies for the establishment of such new parishes with congregations and provided no salary for the priests. The permit for the establishment of a new parish always had a clause added to it that the government would not pay any parish salary. The parish congregation would have to come up with this itself.

Despite these restrictions of free movement, in many ways the Russian state law was still more favourable toward the Catholic Church than most of the laws in Western European countries. If the czar's government would have fulfilled or allowed fulfillment of the paragraphs favourably inclined toward the church then the situation of the church would have been much better. It was just that the laws which were not liked by the ministers of state were often laid aside and made invalid by circulars. The latter were often not even made public. If the bishop pointed out a paragraph in the law which was favourable toward the church then one responded with a circular which replaced the paragraph involved. As a rule, the offices which were under the ministries responded with the words: "We have conflicting ministerial rules." In such a situation the arbitrary action of the officers was given free reign. Until the beginning of this century all of the bishops' pastoral letters were subject to censorship. It was only after the opinion of a censor who was a clergyman but who was, however, a Russian Orthodox priest had been given that the pastoral letters could be published. For this reason there were very few pastoral letters from the bishops until the outbreak of the revolution in 1905. From that time onward they could be printed but could be issued by the publishing house only after censorship. The publishing house had to concern itself about the expedition of the censorship. Even the church directory list of church personnel (the latter had to be issued in the Russian language) was subject to a strict censorship every year as if one had to do with a book which was dangerous for the state. In order to do this the manuscript had to be sent to the Department for "Foreign Denominations" in St. Petersburg. From here the manuscript went to the Board where it was recently subject to an examination! In the year 1916 when the personnel directory issued the notation that at that time 150 years had passed since the

settling of the German colonists in the Volga region, the acting chairman/representative of the emperor (Prokurator) of the board, Von der Flaas, considered it necessary to strike this notation. A sensible reason for this "act of the government" cannot be determined. Did it perhaps seem dangerous for the state to the man because of the panic which had been caused by the Germans (Translator's note: the Germans who were at war with Russia)? Another time the ministry asked for the personnel directory to even be examined a second time! Those Russians whom the government had employed in the Department for Foreign Denominations for the protection of "Orthodoxy" can become this petty while the Russian on average is inclined toward generosity.

With this restriction of religious freedom no one can be surprised if the visitatio liminum, the pilgrimage of the bishops to the tombs of the princes of the Apostles, to Rome was forbidden until the beginning of this century. Bishop Kahn never went on this pilgrimage. His first successor, Bishop Franz Xavier Zottmann went just once secretly. Bishop Antonius Zerr visited the sacred city only once when Czar Alexander III sent him in regard to the issue which Kroze had; in order to defend the Russian government before Leo XIII in vain against the "slander" and distortions of the Polish-Austrian press. Bishop Antonius used this favourable opportunity to make a pilgrimage to the tombs and to visit the Holy Father Leo XIII.

The Russian government did not even like to see that the bishops were doing visitation trips in their own dioceses. None of the first three diocesan bishops visited the bishopric completely. Bishop von Ropp was only in Tyraspol for a short period of time. He was not able to visit the entire diocese. The government placed no hindrances in the way for the visitation of the bishopric by the author of this history. In the same way he allowed him to visit ad limina two times and even once to the 23r Eucharistic Conference in Vienna in the year 1912. The times have already changed some things for the better. More liberal ideas had affected the people since the first revolution; that is of 1905. The absolute state in the East could not completely ignore these ideas.

A Latin proverb states: "Audacem fortuna iuvat." "Fortune is the benefit of the bold." This saying often proved to be true in the leadership of the diocese; especially in dubious cases. If there was a doubt concerning the meaning of a paragraph of the law then it was

the senate's matter to undertake the clarification of the paragraph. The competence of the senate was also subject to the explanation of those laws which had to do with spiritual or religious matters. In fact, however, things were kept differently in regard to these laws. The Department for "Foreign Denominations" brought this explanation to its tribunal. But no one could expect an explanation or a decision in favour of the Catholic cause from it since it had been established for its suppression and not its well-being. Therefore it was advisable to never turn to the government; that is the Department for an explanation in dubious questions but to go ahead without hesitation. If the government had to do with something that had transpired, it very often was accustomed to closing one eye and to not bother the ordinary of the diocese any further. He who has only fleetingly gone through the archive of the diocese must have experienced that the tone of the correspondence between the Ministries or the Departments and the Bishops of Tyraspol, from the establishment of the bishopric until most recent times before the World War has dropped in severity and in the most recent times become very mild and mannerly. While the first bishops even received threats from the Ministers, these almost completely ended since the 90s of the previous century without considering that the bishops of Tyraspol did not count on the Ministries as anxiously as the first Head Shepherds of the bishopric of Tyraspol. One single exception in this case was made by the letter of Prime Minister Stolypin from the year 1909 in which the Ministry of the Interior demanded the sending of the circular of the Ministry opposing the papal decree "ne temere" (not to fear) explaining that all marriages of Catholics with people of other faiths which were united before non-Catholic servants of the church in the future, would now be valid. However the bishop had to deny the sending of an explanation contradictory to the decree to the clergy despite the threat by the state government.
.

Moreover the Bishop wrote to his clergy that his consistory would in short order and by means of a circular inform them that the Ministry would like to have the mentioned mixed marriages considered as valid but that the Ministry's will could not be given any credence and that only the Holy Father is to decide in such matters and that therefore all mixed marriages between Catholics and those of another faith which were performed by non-Catholic clergy are null and void.

If despite this one example the relationship between the church and state in Russia became better, then the spirit of the times brought this about which tried to remove every kind of coercion. Just the fact that both of the first bishops were foreigners had determined and influenced the aristocracy. One was of the opinion that foreigners would let themselves be influenced more by threats than native-born people.

Despite this, the relationship between the government of the state and the bishops of Tyraspol was always a much better one than between the bishops of Poland and Lithuania and the Russian state. The German colonists were always faithful citizens and subjects of the czar, which could not always be said about the Poles and the Lithuanians. The rebellions in Poland in Lithuania gave a clear signal in this matter. If South Russia had also been strongly populated by Poles, then the Russian state would have hardly ever have committed itself to allow the establishment of a dicocese which was for them.

According to the explanation of the Russian government the bishopric of Tyraspol was founded for the German colonists and therefore was a German diocese. During the World War when the political and national hatred between Russians and Poles suddenly, as a result of the promise of the Russian Head of Command Nicholas Nickolayevitch to give Poland autonomy, changed to friendship, the Russian government seemed to have changed its opinion.about the German character of the diocese of Tyraspol. For when the ordinary of Tyraspol wanted to appoint a German supervisor and professor at the seminary, the government which had, shortly before the World War, driven out and exiled Polish priests and bishops from their parishes and deaneries wanted to grant this position to a non-German; that is to a Polish or Lithuanian clergyman! The same government now did not watch even the greatest misdemeanours of Polish preachers such as the comparison of the Russian state with "a bear which with its heavy paws destroyed the Polish beehive, that is Poland, would scratch out the honey and now would lick it off!"

On the other hand, the Ministry approved of the administrative removal and expulsion of German priests by the governors, despite the fact that their only · "transgression" was that the proclaimed the Word of God as previously in their mother tongue to the German parishoners in parishes of mixed nationality. This was because "the Polish members of the parish could not keep their devotional posture and pray when they heard this barbaric language." Pharisaism or hypocrisy can easily be driven to a higher pinnacle. Some Polish national fanatics stooped so low as to demand the removal of the German bishop of Tyraspol in the leading public daily newspapers and to have a Polish Head Shepherd appointed in his place. In the same manner the cathedral chapter, the seminary and the entire diocesan administration was to be given over to the Polish clerics. It was just that the Russian government was less cold-blooded and kept its view of what was right and wrong in the middle of hatred toward nationalities and the din of war. By means of the highest army command in the south, it even initiated the withdrawal of its order against German sermons when the bishop of Tyraspol protested.

The relationship between the Ministry in St. Petersburg with the German Catholic bishops and the church was already also always a better one before the World War than that of most of governors and the officials who were subject to them. If the governor was a fair and friendly man then the situation of the clergy in that region was bearable, yes good, and it was not dampened by any kind of persecution or pressure. But the exact opposite was the case if the governor was a "somodyeryetz;" that is an autocrat who always wanted to have his subjects· and especially the Catholic clergy feel his power. This was how the narrow-minded governor of Tauria, Peter Lazarev, who was an inveterate enemy and hater of everything that was Catholic. 1. "If I was governor here for twenty years," he assured, then "There will be no Catholic left in my gouvrnmement." The tyrant acted according to this premise of bringing Catholicism to extinction in the

1. Under his influence he sent the head of police, who was a retired captain, to the young youthful priest in Simpferopol in the year 1895 to confession in order to investigate if he was blameless in terms of politics; The captain was a schismatic (Orthodox).

area of his authority. As a true autocrat be interfered in all the religious matters of the Catholics and the administration of the sacraments was not exempt. Unfortunately there Were nominal Catholics here and there who called upon the "power" of this tyrant against their pastors. Fortunately there were such violaters of their own consciences only in the cities and among military personnel.

In the year 1906, all the circulars of the government, which had no foundation in state law, were declared null and void by an ukas (proclamation) of Emperor Nicholas II. The relationship between the Catholic Church and the State became a friendlier one. One year previous the Orthodox, by means of a dispensation from the czar, had received permission to convert to another Christian religious denomination according to their own desire. In the diocese of Tyraspol about 2,000 schismatics also accepted the Catholic religion. They were mostly those who originated from mixed marriages with Russians. However, the government held fast to the law, according to which all children of mixed marriages with the Orthodox had to be baptized and raised in Orthodoxy. Not even the Republican government of Russia could decide if that should be changed. It had well proven itself to be an excellent way of Russification.

The German Catholic clergy of the diocese of Tyraspol regarded Russia as its homeland. The clergy had been born and raised upon the soil of Russia, educated in the schools of Russia and from the age of boyhood been occupied with learning the national language. Just like its parents, it was always a true citizen and subject of the czar. Its relationship to the authorities of the state was that which the Apostle to the Gentiles lists in the 13th chapter of his Letter to the Romans. Since the establishment of the bishopric and the seminary for priests no one among the clergy of Tyraspol could be proven to be politically untrustworthy or incorrect. All of the clergy of Tyraspol were always concerned: "To render unto God that which is God's and to render unto Caesar that which is Caesar's. 1. Matthew 22:21 If sometimes however, demands were placed upon them by government authority which opposed divine commandments, then they always found the courage to reply with Peter, the Prince of the Apostles: "One must obey God rather than man." 2. Acts 5:29

48. Relationships of the different language groups of diocesans and clergy to each Other

The question of nationality always played a very important role in the history of the Church and it also showed itself in a loveless way. The Acts of the Apostles report of misunderstandings which occurred between the Jews and the Greeks. 3. Acts 6:1 If the soil which the Holy Ghost especially moistened with dew and the sun of grace resulted in the weeds of jealousy, should this not happen today even more when many enemies on earth attempt to sow weeds among the wheat? Because of the confusion and spread of languages, people on earth are dispersed but through the unity of faith, and the bond of Christian love which is to hold together the Church of Christ around the nations, a unified Christian family is to be established under the headship of the invisible Head Shepherd Jesus Christ and also under the visible successor of St. Peter. This was the entire content of the High Priestly prayer which Jesus Christ sent on high to his Heavenly Father on the evening before his suffering: "Holy Father, keep them in the name which you gave me, so that they may be one as we are one!" 4 John 17:11

Among the non-German Catholics; the Poles formed the largest percentage within the diocese. Until 1972 the Cathedral Chapter and the Leadership of the Diocese and the by far largest number of the parish priests were Polish. Now things were to be transferred into German hands. The Poles had to withdraw. However this was a blow which had to be sorely felt. This change could, of course, not result in any kind of friendly relationship. It is the result of the influence of the suffragan Bishop Vinzentius Lipski if the relationship between the professors who remained at the seminary and their German colleagues soon developed into one of friendship. Between the German Catholics and the Polish in the city parishes, a certain tense relationship held sway. The more ponderous character of the Germans could not be reconciled with the lively Polish character that set itself ahead of others in the House of God. The singing of the Godzinki liturgy was wrongly protested by some German parish members in churches of mixed nationality. However the German parish members did not leave the House of God during the Polish sermon in order not to bother their Polish parish members while the Polish members never remained in church during the German sermon. Since Poland borders on Lutheran Germany, the Poles get to know the Germans only as Lutherans or Protestants. German and Protestant means the same thing to most Poles. For this reason they cannot understand how German parish members in the cities of the Diocese of Tyraspol can be true Catholics just as they are.

This false idea is caused mostly by fault of the fact that the Poles try to repress their fellow German parish members. This is even more serious because they identify nationality with religion. Polish and Catholic are one and the same just as German and Lutheran are one and the same. The differences of religion among the Poles and the German Lutheran members are thereby caused to a large degree by the fact that Germans and Poles stand in opposition to each other in the bishopric of Tyraspol. Confessors of the same Holy Catholic Church; children of one and the same mother of the Holy Catholic Church should have a warmer relationship with each other. For this reason, one of the main tasks of the urban pastors is to always work towards removing the differences of opinion between the Poles and the Germans. The relationship between the German and Polish clergy of the diocese also leaves something to be desired. The political pressure of the German Lutheran government upon Greater Poland and the pressure of Russia upon Congress Poland; especially since 1863, caused the Poles to become more unified. One result of this was that the Polish clergy of the bishopric pulled back from their German spiritual brethren. This was even more natural as the Polish clergy since the 70s headed the pastoral care in the cities of Tyraspol. German and Polish clergy had, for the above reasons, contact which was restricted to a minimum. The Christian and priestly love could not reach a point where the national differences were bridged. Neither the German nor the Polish clergy can be exonerated from this accusation. Without a doubt the young clergymen showed too little friendship toward their Polish and Lithuanian brethren. this took place not because they considered them inferior or wanted nothing to do with them but because of a lack of tact. In the colonies and being apart from other nationalities from the time they were the age of boys and raised with the closed walls of both seminaries, the German priests of Tyraspol had too little polish and experience with life. This lack of experience is more or less shared by all graduates of the Tyraspol Seminary. Firstly, the Tyraspol academics and graduates of foreign universities had a good chance of making up for this deficiency. Among the Polish clergy of the bishopric, Dean Nikodemus · Czerniachowicz showed the most brotherly concern and tactfulness toward the German brethren. He understood, as no German dean could, how to gather and to influence the clergymen who surrounded him in his deanery. It only seldom happened that a festival was celebrated in his deanery where he himself did not appear or participate. By his superior tact and love, the prelate won not only the love of the German Catholic people, but also the love of its clergy. Canon Xavierus Klimaszewski, the cathedral priest who had even been left behind as the vicar general by the ordinary in Saratov for the north when the diocesan seat was moved to Odessa, was beloved by all in the same measure whether this had to do with clergy or with German parish members. When he was elected as a delegate by the cathedral chapter to the College in St. Petersburg, and said goodbye to his parish, the Germans and the Poles saw him leave with deep sorrow.

If at the time of the founding of the bishopric almost all of the parishes with German colonists were served by Polish and Lithuanian priests, then since the close of the century the pastoral care of the German and Polish parishes as well as the nationally mixed deanery was, with few exceptions, carried out by German clergy. In ever decreasing numbers did the German pastor, when he took over a parish, first need to learn the Polish language. Since all of the clergy had mastered the Russian language, the learning of Polish was not very difficult so that pastoral care suffered very little. The German priests proclaimed the Word of God and gave religious instruction in the school and middle school by means of the Polish language and prepared the children for their first confession and first communion in their mother tongue. In most cases the faithful Polish people were very satisfied with their pastors. In the rarest of cases there were complaints against one or the other pastor heard. The German clergyman who had a heart for his parishoners was also treasured and loved by them. How much the Polish parish members were attached to German pastor was especially demonstrated when a priest was transferred to another parish. When the farewell speech was given there was usually not an eye without any tears.

49. The relationship between the Catholics and their Lutheran compatriots

Since the Catholics were separated from the Lutherans in their own groups of villages, close contact between the two confessions was not possible. Because of the separate settlement; according to the Russian government, religious conflicts were to be avoided. Among religiously mixed communities of farmers this would have been unavoidable. The confessional separation of the Germans had other advantages for the Catholics. Firstly, they were thereby saved from religious influence, religious liberalism, indifference and religious uncertainty. Experience teaches that, for example, in Germany where the people live in mixed religiously, the Catholic religion always loses members of those who confess the faith. The most effective way of making people Protestant and causing disinterest in religion is the mixed marriage. These cannot be avoided in cities and villages where Catholics and Protestants live together. If the German colonists had been settled together with the Lutherans in the same villages, then today there would not have been very much left of Catholicism in the German villages of Russia because of the great lack of pastoral care by German clergy. Sad evidence of this danger is found in those small villages of the Crimean Peninsula before Catholic priests were sent to those localities. There were more mixed marriages there than in the entire diocese of Tyraspol. Among the Catholics religious confusion was prevalent. There was nothing more common than the participation of that which is prohibited by the church; namely communicatio in sacris; the participation in the religious ministrations of those of other Christian denominations. In large numbers the Catholics attended the Lutheran devotions the sermons of the pastors and participated in the funeral services of their village compatriots and were also godparents when the sacrament of baptism was administered.

In the same manner, the Lutherans also participated in Catholic services. Among not a few Catholics and Lutherans the religious differences were completely obliterated. "Oh," was stated when the pastor spoke on teachings which differentiate; "Oh, we all have the same one God!" "Everything is over." How far the religious confusion had gotten ahold of some Catholics can be clearly described by giving an example which the author himself heard from a German priest who had led a parish in the Crimean Peninsula as a pastor for several years. His parish consisted of the village with the parish church and several smaller villages (filial congregations). Several times a year the priest visited all the little villages in his extensive parish in order to serve the Catholics. He could not leave the most Holy Sacrament behind in the small oratories because there was not enough security for it or for the eternal flame. After the last Holy Mass an elderly little mother announced her intention for oral confession. "Her confession;" as stated by the pastor "I can hear her confession but I cannot give her Holy Communion because the tabernacle is no longer in the chapel. However I cannot remain here until the morning in order to hold another Holy Mass in which she would be able to receive Holy Communion then. For this reason she has to wait for Holy Communion until I return again."
This news caused the elderly lady great sadness and she then said to the priest: "But Reverend Sir; go over to the Lutheran pastor and he will lend you a one;" that is a holy host. There was a Lutheran parish with a pastor in the neighbourhood. However the pastor explained to the lady that the Lutherans do not have Holy Communion like the Roman Catholics because Martin Luther had gotten rid of the ministry of priests. As the lady fanner was of a good temperament, she believed the explanation of her priest and was satisfied with this response. Perhaps some Catholics, because of religious confusion or a lack of knowledge, even received "The Lord's Supper" in Lutheran churches. It is

only a step from such a religious view to complete apostasy from the Catholic religion.

For this reason the Lutheran pastors in the Crimean Peninsula were convinced that within a time not too distant the Catholics in the Crimea would convert to Lutheranism. This hope was thwarted by the fact that German clergy were soon sent to the parish in the Crimea. Under their leadership the Catholics were again conscious of the joy of being Catholic and began to hold fast stronger to the Holy Catholic faith. It was not as easy to win the nominal Catholics in the cities for Holy Catholic truth again. Through continual contact with rationalistic, atheistic Russians and Lutherans and through mixed marriages with them, they had lost the Christian faith. For this reason they stayed away from the church and its means of grace; the holy sacraments, and did not give the poor Catholic churches, which were completely dependent upon the generosity of the good people any type of offering. However they sometimes gave offerings of a considerable nature for schismatic and Lutheran religious causes and often had a very bad and hostile attitude toward zealous pastors. However, the middle school had led to the loss of the Christian faith among the educated because the school was godless and without religion. This was a big influence among the "nominal Catholics." When, according to the report of the Holy Scriptures the descendants of pious Abel became unbelievers by contact with and marriage to the descendants of godless Cain who were evil like their father and then themselves became godless; then no one will be surprised that close and regular contact and especially the marriages with those of another faith made them lax, liberal and godless in the end. A proverb states it this way: "Tell me with whom you have contact and I will tell you who you are." Experience teaches well enough that evil emanates from evil people and enters the good people whose will is bent and taken over until the good, faithful Christian himself has no religion and is godless and finally ends up in complete. faithlessness. For this reason Jesus warns specifically in Matthew 24:4: "Watch that no one leads you astray."

The German Catholic rural population thus seldom had contact with the Protestants. This was the case in the north as well as in the south. There were even fewer contacts between the Catholic priests and the Lutheran pastors or the Russian Orthodox priests. The religious differences between the Lutherans arid the Catholics were too great to think of having friendly contacts. One was not used to covering up one's religious convictions in the land of the czar. In public, one was completely open with one's faith and religious confession. Until the beginning of the 90s of the previous century the German Catholics of the diocese of Tyraspol did not have their own daily Catholic newspaper while the Lutherans in the north and in the region of the Black Sea had such a newspaper. The Odessa Newspaper had a strong Lutheran direction and occasionally even allowed itself invectives against the Catholic religion and its servants. The editor generally did not print any refutations of these attacks. When the editor refused to print a Catholic refutation for an article against the Catholic worship of Mary the Mother of God the priest in the parish of the colony of Franzfeld, a special character among the Cappucins, Father Beda Sebald, journeyed to Odessa. He arrived with the insulting article against the honouring of the Mother of God in hand and when he came into the editor's office he called out in his own peculiar tone of voice: "Where is the editor? Where is the editor?" Finally, when everyone in the editor's office had gotten excited, the editor appeared. He was a little thin man and introduced himself to the excited priest: "I am the editor and what would you like?" The priest stated directly to him: "You are the editor! You look miserable enough to be him. What did you print here as an insulting article against the Mother of God in your dirty paper? I expect that you retract it in your next edition with this article which I have brought along. If not, then I will go to the Russians who also venerate that which we also venerate." In saying this, he gave him his retraction. In order to avoid the greater punishment which the Russian state law had set for insulting articles against religion and the veneration of saints and especially the Mother of God, the editor took the article of the Reverend Father and published it in the columns of his paper.

Another time, when P. Beda Sebald was an assistant during an examination on the Catholic religion he met with several Lutheran pastors in the Central School in Grossliebental and a pastor asked him: "Are you as I heard; a Bavarian," the Reverend Father replied: "Yes, I am a Bavarian and still a very solid one too."
The German clergy in the countryside hardly ever had any contact with the Russian Orthodox clergy, since the German villages were separated from the Russian villages by long distances. However several Catholic city clergymen had friendly relations with one or the other Russian or better said educated, Orthodox priest. This did not hurt the Catholic cause and quite the contrary was only of benefit. The Catholic city priest who completely removed himself from all Russian Orthodox clergymen was always in danger of being decried as a religious fanatic among the Russian populace. Also, the religious differences were not that great. It was possible to establish a relationship of cordiality between the Catholic and the Russian Orthodox clergy. The contact between the Catholic colonists in the countryside was not more frequent with the Russian population than the contact which the rural clergy had. For this reason the German farmer, especially the one who lived in the Volga region, was not able to speak the Russian language, but he learned it if participated in military service. In the Black Sea region most of the German farmers speak the Ukrainian dialect which they learn from their workers and maids. The contact with the Russian servants is the entire limit of contact with the 'Russians.

50. The construction of Catholic houses of God

According to Russian government law, the Catholic congregations were allowed to build churches, prayer houses, and chapels if a House of Worship had stood there before. Only when the first new construction of such a building took place, did one need the special permission of the government. The permission for the same was given by the Ministry of the Interior. By means of a ministerial decree, during the second half of the 19th century extensive repairs, etc. were prohibited for church buildings. Only in special cases of emergency was application by congregations for the construction of new buildings allowed. Even the "Orthodox" bishop, within whose bishopric the building was to be constructed, had to give his approval for the construction. This was a requirement of a paragraph of the law when a church building was first built. Under Czar Nicholas I, the permission for such a church building was given to the diocese of Tyraspol without any special problems. As a rule, the Ministry of the Interior took care of the situation so that the respective Orthodox bishop gave his assent. It was different under the regime of Alexander II and especially under Alexander III and under Nicholas II until the year 1905. Under Alexander II, the fanatical procurator of the Holy Synod, Pobedonoszeff, had such an influence upon the government of the ·empire that even the Ministry of the Interior had to deal with him. The new construction of church buildings was not allowed at all for the period of a quarter of a century. Even extensive repairs were, as a rule, refused in the strictest of ways. Generally, the denial upon the part of the ministry was given as: if the congregation desires and has the need for something like this, then it should attend the services in the neighbouring parish! One did not take in account that the neighbouring parish was very often 10 or more kilometers distant and that the elderly and the children were not able to travel this far. This was the case even when one did not have to count on bad weather or the cold of winter. Several parishes, among whom are Grosswerder in the Don region and Alexandrovka in Tauria; begged for years in order to receive permission for the construction 0£ a new building. Finally, the congregation of Grosswerder obtained permission for the construction of a house of worship, but without a bell tower; while at the same time everything was rejected for Alexandrovka. The government continued to hope for the backsliding of the weak church believers, the Czechs, who were members of this congregation. And yet the construction of a house of worship for Germans and Czechs in the congregation was so important and would have also been beneficial for the state, as both nationalities were continually at odds with each other. The author of this diocesan history was the first person to influence the Ministry of the Interior to allow the construction when, shortly after his consecration, he presented the issue to the ministry. The first request of the German bishop of Tyraspol was not to be rejected. However, the church construction was not hindered as much as in the other dioceses of the Poland and of Lithuania. For this reason the German bishopric also had the most church and prayer chapels in the empire of the czar. Among these are, also such which can, at least in terms of the interior, compete with the most beautiful churches of God in Western Europe. Examples of this are the beautiful Ascension of Mary Church in Odessa, the churches in Nikolayev, in Seelmann, and in Karlsruhe. Tyraspols churches are largely constructed in the Gothic-Romanesque and Renaissance style. However one sees the lack of education and the lack of a sense of artistry with the architect involved.

One notes immediately when a Protestant architect or foreman from a Protestant school carried out the work. In almost of the churches the sacristies are too small. One big problem was that most of the churches were built by young clergy who often did not have an ecclesiastical view of artistry and who lacked the necessary experience. Some even lacked in terms of necessary virtue when it came to humble moderation. They figured that they knew everything better and because of this took no advice from anyone. Most churches are built much too low in size. A lot of mistakes were also made in the interiors. Ever since Tyrolean master craftsmen have been working in the diocese, much excellent work has been done in terms of the inner decoration of the houses of God. Among the most beautiful are the raised (stufelesserischen) altars of Selz, Kamenka, Seelmann etc. Also the pulpits, creches, stations of the cross etc. The German colonist cannot come to terms with churches which have three and more naves because the pillars hide the view of the altar. He wants to see the sacred acts taking place upon the altar. He is right in this regard, but the size of the building itself often causes the pillars or arches to stand as supports for the building as a whole. The common man cannot and will not understand this. If the congregation in Kamenka had built the House of God with three naves rather than just one, as the then pastor wanted to have it, and had built this with arches made of masonry, the church would have largely been consumed by flames. The wide length of the arch needs to have a weaker; that is a wooden arch. However this burned because of the heating system so that only the masonry remained. When churches were built, the respective priests generally had to deal with great opposition from the people. They always cried out: "No churches with pillars!" However, the congregations loved to build large balconies because the young men liked to participate in the services "from above."

One was willing to construct churches with single naves and made the greatest of sacrifices for them. The taste of the colonists, especially in the Volga Region, demanded rich gold ornamentation of the altars, the pulpit, and the stations of the cross. The large statues behind the high altars of the churches in Mariental and Graf were famous in the entire region of the Volga. They covered the entire rear of the apse and made a powerful impression upon every visitor with the gold overlay and carvings. Unfortunately, a young parish administrator who had a lack of education in regard to church artistry had this beautiful wall painted with scenes removed from the church in Mariental and replaced by a poor-looking wall of mediocre gold-coloured bars done by a Lutheran bungler. The bare, poorly-painted church walls in the apse now glare at the visitor without any effect. The gold only really shines properly when it has a white background and does not show properly on a yellow or aged oak surface as is the case with most of the altars in Germany. The German colonists are proud of their church. One village competes with the other in building a beautiful House of God. The church built upon an open square in the middle of the village should be a place of beauty. With few exceptions, the churches of the German parishes surpass the Catholic city parishes in terms of size and sometimes in terms of interior fittings.

It was pointed out above that unfortunately in. too many cases, young priests with little experience in Christian architecture constructed churches in the diocese. One such pastor in a congregation of the region of the Volga allowed the construction of a large stone church contradicting the plan to build the steeple close to the houses of the neighbours. Of his own accord, he thereby cut off one long street so that both the property owners had to tear down their houses and had to move their yard far back into the property so that the House of God had enough room to extend its space into the property. The House of God now stands with its main facade situated in a corner! The young gentleman did this without any rational consideration and contrary to the wishes of all of the members of the congregation aided by a friend who was a provincial governor! Unfortunately the young pastor did not even inform the leadership of the diocese! This bad placement of the House of God resulted in general protest and even hatred against the pastor. All of this happened so that the priest had a direct way to the sacristy in the church! Other clergy entrusted the construction of the church or church altars to Lutheran foremen without considering that these people did not have the right idea or the right taste for a Catholic House of God. According to the spirit of Lutheranism, these foremen constructed the ceiling or the arches of the churches of wood instead of stucco which was then painted with very ordinary colours. By doing this, every kind of decoration of the ceiling with paintings was prevented. As is known, Protestant churches do not allow images of the saints.

It was, as everyone can see, something which belonged in the realm of the diocesan administration that this situation be changed. For this reason, the diocesan leadership of Tyraspol sent out an order in the year 1910, according to which there was to be a building committee in each deanery under the chairmanship of the dean. Two clergymen from the deanery were to be advisors. The duties and agenda of this committee were to set up a temporary and simple plan for the House of God so that a report could be sent to the diocesan leadership. It was only then that one could begin to build according to the original plans for construction. In the same order, the building and the placing of orders for altars, pulpits and organs was regulated so that the architectural plans or drawings of these items could-be approved by the diocesan leadership. Then they could be ordered.

As the construction of churches or prayer chapels was only allowed by the Russian government with great difficulty, there were many examples in the large diocese where one or the other village church which was far away from the main parish church built a prayer house "of its own volition." However, this was affected by the lawlessness of the corruption among the Russian officials; especially as concerns the police. If the police made for problems then the farmers said that we will come to terms with them. In saying this, they meant that they thought they would put a large sum of money into their pockets and would solve the problem in this manner. It often occurred that the Russian state law caused such action because it created so many difficulties when a prayer house was to be built. If the higher authorities heard about the construction of such an illegal prayer house, then it was important to get good advice. Generally, church services were not allowed to be held in such a building. This is what transpired with 'the construction plans in the little congregation in Dyamin on the Crimean Peninsula The tyrannical governor of Simpferopol heard of the illegality of the building. He sent an Uryadnik and had the house locked. It is noteworthy what the simple but believing official did after the closure of the entrance doors to the prayer house and said to the saddened Catholics: "You can build a tavern, but you are not allowed to build a prayer house!"

Every reasonable state regime should, once and for all deeply imprint upon its memory and on its heart never to take away the ability of Christian people to gather for common prayer or worship.

51. State "methods of conversion" among the Catholics of Tyraspol

Besides the German Catholic rural population there are, since the middle of the 19th century, also many Ukrainian and Czech settlements in the area of the Black Sea. Some originate from Volhynia and the Czechs come from Old Austria. While the Ukrainians farmers settled in Tauria, the Czechs in part settled together with German Bohemians on the Crimean Peninsula. During the settlement of Ukrainians, Catholic parents who only had male inheritors were settled with parents belonging to schismatic confessions who had daughters. The later were preferred. Through this order the Russian state planned to quickly mix the Catholics with the "Orthodox." The Catholics were to be hindered in this way. Because of a lack of Catholic girls, the Catholic youth had to marry schismatic girls. Since according to Russian law, all the descendants from mixed marriages with the "Orthodox" had to be baptized and raised as such, within the not too distant future the communities which were mixed Catholic and Orthodox would soon become entirely Orthodox. Yes, there is the example of a purely Catholic village where the government regime settled only one single "Orthodox" family with seven daughters. Today, through mixed marriage, the majority of the inhabitants are schismatic! The "conversion" of hapless Catholic farmers also happened more quickly because of a lack of pastoral care. For in none of these villages was it possible to build a prayer chapel; the only pastor for all of these villages had to reside at a respectable distance from his parishoners so that no one would hinder the "conversions." As the place of residence the priest was given the town of Perekop. There was not a single Catholic in this town and it was 25 kilometers distant from the next little Catholic village. That village which was furthest from the clergyman's residence could only be reached after a trip of two days. If one considers the impassable ways, the rough wintertime and the far distance to the parish church, then one has to admire the heroism of the poor Catholic folk in this parish. It was only this which gave it the strength to fetch the pastor for the ill and dying and to attend the parish church at least a few times a year in order to receive the Holy Sacraments and to bring the newborn childr7n for Holy Baptism etc. Such draconic and tyrannical methods were employed by the Russian government in order to attain its goal; that is the Russification by means of the State Church which had debased itself in order to become the accommodating means of attaining secular advantage. The history of the last Revolution and of Bolshevism showed the world what absolute state power can accomplish by violating the conscience.

The religious situation was not much better among the Czechs and the Bohemian Germans in the Crimean Peninsula. However the Czechs caused a lot of this. But the Bohemian Germans cannot be completely exonerated either. As long *as* the Czechs and Bohemian Germans were poor, passable unity reigned. After they came to enjoy a good standard of living, they began to cause enmity against one another in those congregations in which they lived in common *as* was the case in the village of Alexandrovka. The national enmity went so far that they consecrated two prayer chapels. The government had enough opportunity to learn about the weak faith of the Czechs; a long time previous many sympathized with "Orthodoxy" *as* the "Orthodox" had more rights in the government. One Czech denounced a German co-habitant to the Russian police and stated that he had blasphemed the "Orthodox" religion. The situation was brought before the county court in Perekop. The question of the schismatic judge, *as* to whether the Czechs were favourably inclined to join "Orthodoxy," was answered with a clear yes by the litigant. With the encouragement of the civil authorities the "Orthodox" bishop of Simpferople sent the Czech Marschalek, who himself had fallen away from the Catholic religion and become a lay brother in a monastery to Alexandrovka in order to prepare and to cause the Czechs to convert *as* schismatics. The governor of Tauria was supposed to act as the patron when the schismatic church was to be received by the exarch (bishop). It was just that the Czechs demanded several civil advantages as recompense before their conversion and, at the same time for their leaving their old (Catholic) religion. They had namely heard from their compatriots in Volhynia that big promises had been made but after the conversion to "Orthodoxy" had taken place, the promises had not been kept. The missionary replied: "No." "'Become Orthodox" first, and then the government will give you various privileges." And thus there was dealing back and forth *as* if one had to do with the purchase of a cow! Finally the faithless Czechs let themselves be fooled and gave their assent and affirmed this with their signatures. Among these faithless people there was also a Lutheran who gave several children of his deceased Catholic wife over to the heretics while he himself did not change his religion! 99 people were to become members of the "Right-Believing" church. The efforts of the priest, who had his residence in Simpferopol, in other words 75 kilometers fr.om Alexandrovka, were able to influence them, after he had encouraged them to get their promises and signatures withdrawn. One had really made a mistake. The missionary showed himself to be very immoral. A Russian official, who came to the village by chance, discovered the crime and investigated the situation. The result was that Marschalek used immoral experiments upon himself in order to mislead his young female students. The governor and the school authorities immediately fired him and the schismatic bishop sent him to repent in a monastery. Thus the "mission" of this rascal ended with scolding and shame for the schismatic Church and the Russian clergy. Later the Czechs remained faithful to their Holy Catholic faith and almost all immigrated to North America.

The governor did not forgive the pastor from Simpferopol because he lost a high decoration which he certainly would have received because of the favours he would have gotten because of the "conversion" of so many people to the state religion. Since he could not however blame the pastor because of the scandalous result of the "mission," he waited for another opportunity. This would soon present itself. A schismatic officer, who had married a French Catholic countess, took the pastor to court before the "all-powerful" governor stating that his wife had not received absolution during confession because she had married a schismatic. The self-styled ruler of Tauria reported the Catholic pastor's "crime" to the minister of the interior. Immediately the diocesan leadership received the command to send the young "fanatic cleric" _to another parish and, to be sure, to transfer him to a German village parish outside of Tauria. Shortly thereafter, the pastor shook the dust off his feet and moved to the village parish of Sulz. Besides this, he was placed under police observation!

In Western Europe, Russia, although it is a European country, is less well-known than America. This is no surprise because it had cut itself off from the rest of Europe because of fear that the social and governmental movements for revolution would not find a way in. However, this isolation was only of a physical kind which could not hinder the entry of damaging ideas and teachings. The gates of the czar's empire were always completely open for these teachings. Exceptions therein were the Catholic principles and teachings and all the works which were a part of this religion. While the works of Voltaire, Renan, Chamberlain and all kinds of religious nonsense and immoral dirt could pass the censor's eye, these actions or works which had devotion for the Sacred Heart of Jesus (pictures of Jesus with his heart) were sent back. The same fate was shared by devotional books, prayer and religious material for the growth of spirituality during the reign of Alexander III. The Russian censor expected a prayer for the czar in the prayer and devotional books. It was not sufficient that there was a prayer in the prayer books for the prince of the land,

for the king or for the emperor; no, it was a requirement of the censor that the name of the ruling czar not be referred to with the abbreviation N.N. as it is always the case. It had to be printed exactly. When the czars changed, a new prayer with the new czar's name had to be printed in the prayer books in all the different languages! For this reason, Bishop Zottmann wrote his own prayer for the czar of Russia, Alexander III. He had it printed by Herder and had it glued into all of the books sent to Russia's colonists. The requirement of the Russian religious censors was, however, just as idotic as arbitrary. For the lord censors should have realized that German, French, Italian etc. prayer books which generally were meant for the Catholic inhabitants of Germany, France and Italy etc. were also printed for them and could not include a personal prayer for the Russian czar who did not have anything to do with these countries and their inhabitants. Such a requirement implies in advance that the Russian czar is also the prince or ruler of all of these countries and this is most laughable when this is emphasized. The German booksellers now started to glue the prayer for the czar not only into all of the prayer books destined for Russia, but in all printed material. After the title page, the prayer for Czar Alexander III followed and after his death a new edition of the prayer was printed because the name of the Czar was no longer correct. Thus a prayer for Nicholas II appeared in various publications of the press and also on the first page! This seem to be demanded of all the readers, that right after opening the book; for example the table of contents of a theatrical piece, or an historical book or of a journal etc. One was to first pray for the Russian emperor! Thus the Russian religious censors made themselves a mockery in all of Europe with their illusory and burdensome demands; if not to say contemptible.

But not only Catholic religious literature was prohibited entry to Russia at the border. No, also within the imperial. borders one had the goal of destroying specific Catholic works or to take them away from the Catholics. When books were transported it often happened that if a piece of literature regarding the adoration of the sacred heart of Jesus, the primacy of the pope, or the infallibility of the pope or in regard to purgatory was among them that you had to be afraid that they would disappear. Rosaries as well and other devotional items did not always get to their place of destination within the empire. The state Orthodox leadership patronized in the extreme while all of the dirty, godless and immoral false teachings were allowed entry everywhere and were allowed to be spread among the people without any problems. In fact, they were also taught by many educators of the people. The complaint which Jesus once made to the Pharisees was also pertinent for most of them; within whose hands the fate of Russian people existed. Matthew 23:24 "You blind leaders, you who see the fly but swallow the camel."

52. Church property and its administration

According to Russian state law, the clergyman and the designated church authority (or authorities) had the power to acquire liquid and fixed assets and for the church and congregation (Translator's note: this probably means the diocese and its bishop because of the particular governance of the Roman Catholic Church) and to administer them. The "church account or treasury" according to a paragraph of the law, is a part of the share which belongs to the parish and is administered by the clergyman with the aid of the congregational members in the parish." The paragraph, because of its unclear composition, often led to large misunderstandings between the clergyman and agitated members of the flock in the city parishes. In general, the law in regard to the administration of church assets is very hazy and unclear and it even has contradictions. As long as the Catholic Houses of God in the city parishes were without any notable assets, many very intelligent Polish and sometimes nominal German Catholics let the priest toil alone and pied poverty in order to provide the poor church with as little support as possible for its existence and further development. If the priest, by means of tireless care, many curtsies, and above all by his spirit of enterprise and talents secured the future existence of the house of God, then "Catholic gentry" appeared out of nowhere. They tried to take over the administration of the House of God. As they did not succeed in this, they stirred up the ignorant class of the Catholic population, wrote letters of complaint to the diocesan court, demanded lay control over the income and expenses of the church, and a "more suitable" administration of church assets. If they got nowhere with the diocesan court, then one was not ashamed to send lengthy complaints signed with many signatures by "dissatisfied" people to the ministry and even to the emperor himself

In regard to this way of doing things, the Church of the Assumption of Mary in Odessa attained quite a bit of fame. It often occurred that the leadership often did not support the priest according to the letter of the law in the administration of the large amount of capital which belonged to this church in Odessa. They laid claim to rights which according to canon and state law belonged only to the priest or they resigned from their position. The work in their position was even once illegally passed on to one of their people in training. This man, a nominal Catholic, took the entire administration of the church capital into his hands when there was a weak priest and "administered" it just like an "autocrat." When the diocesan bishop intervened in this illegal procedure, and pushed the man aside, he tried to justify his arbitrary action and autocratic dealings in the newspapers, whereby he even slandered the Head Shepherd of the diocese in a rough and idiotic way.

Things were rocky in Odessa and, as a rule, also when elections for the congregation's leadership took place. According to the bylaws of the Russian state law the priest called upon parishoners who were 21 years of age and over to vote and was the chairman for them. Whoever did not appear or vote then gave up his right to vote. The priest had the right of nomination and he had to nominate four practicing, good men who were esteemed in the congregation. This was done in a congregational meeting. Of these the congregation had to elect two men to the church council and the two who were not elected were their future candidate successors. If someone attained a majority of the votes, then the election was valid. Meanwhile, those elected were allowed to begin their period of office in the church council only after confirmation by the episcopal leadership council. The election law was obviously favourable toward the Catholic Church. That was the reason why so often lax and liberal Catholics opposed it so vehemently. One always tried to tear away the right of nomination from the priest with the public intention of bringing men who were weak in faith or even men who were immoral into the church council. With that one would have satisfied oneself with something that worked. Then one would have tried to push the priest aside and so "administered" the church capital so that by these means the church would have had to have been destroyed! However, the church revolutionaries did not push ahead with their plans; not with the czaristic government or with the episcopal leadership. In order to make their standpoint clear concerning the administration of the church capital to the diocesans and above all to the anxious individuals, a pastoral letter from the Bishop of Tyraspol was published in the Polish language in the year 1910, in which Russian state law was brought in harmony with canon law regarding the acquisition, the owning and the administration of church capital and the right of the church to administer its capital independently. Then the thing would have returned to divine authority. This pastoral letter was accepted by all good-minded Catholics and especially by the Catholic clerics within and outside of the bishopric of Tyraspol. It was accepted with great applause and also spread outside of the diocese of Tyraspol.

In the German rural parishes there was almost always no dissension because of church capital, since at the time of the establishment of the parishes and in agreement with the episcopal leadership and the congregation everything had been determined clearly and explicitly. The churches in the north owned no real assets besides the parsonage.

However, those in the south had from 33 to 120 dessiatines of agricultural land. 1. Those of Rosental on the Crimean Peninsula had several acres of oak forest. But this real estate was not subject to the administration of the church council but subject entirely to the administration of the respective priest. The church had been allotted it from the government at the time of the establishment of the parishes for the support of the respective priest.

The election of the syndikus or church council members always took place in a peaceful manner according to the statutes of the state and canon law. Since there were almost never differences which occurred between members of the parish and pastors or between church council members and the priest, the priests did not even think about having the church council confirmed by the episcopal leadership. Since however these men bore a certain responsibility toward the state and church, an episcopal decree from the year 1910 required their confirmation by the episcopal leadership and the ordinary. According to this rule an arbitrary removal of church council members by the priest or parish administrator was to be prevented. The history of the diocese had some arbitrary removals by young pastors to note which harmed the reputation of the clergyman and also that of a church council member and these did not pass by without much vexation.

1. This was only the old mother churches.

53. Immigration to America

According to the manifest of July 22, 1763, paragraph VI, n: I 4, whereby Empress Catherine II, had invited the German colonists, these were to be forever exempt from military service: "Such settling foreigners in Russia are, during their entire sojourn here, apart from normal agricultural service, not to be taken into military or civil service against their will." For 100 years the German colonists were glad because of this privilege. However, when military conscription was extended in the year 1876 to include the Russian nobility and the Russian merchant class of the first estate, the colonists also had their privileges taken away. However, the government gave them an alternative: either emigrate or serve in the military. Thousands of colonists in the Volga region, particularly Catholics, decided to emigrate. The emigration became the topic of daily conversation. Everyone cherished the desire to leave Russia. This was proof of the fact that the German people in Russia did not feel at home. If the Volga Germans had been able to come up with the necessary funds, probably only a few would have remained behind in the Russian homeland. Nevertheless, the removal of the military privileges would have not caused this general attitude to be brought about. Its causes lay deeper. At one time the colonists felt themselves to be foreign in the empire of the czar as one always looked upon them as being foreigners. The Russian does not consider all non-Russian citizens as having equal rights and as loyal subjects. He always sees them as being foreign invaders. When during the war, a German colonist, a member of the imperial duma held a speech concerning the welfare of the fatherland, many from the rows of Russians called out: "Which fatherland; Russia or Germany?" How often did the

German colonists, ever since they stood in more regular contact with the Russian population, experience how very much they were envied and even hated because of their higher standard of living? The consciousness of being envied and hated by the great mass of the Russian population did not easily allow the German colonist to have the feeling of equality with the other citizens. If for this reason, there was a lack of devotion to the fatherland on the part of some colonists, then the fault must be looked for not so much in them but much more in the general population of the country. A second cause, why the German colonist never felt very good, lay in the different psyche of the Germans and his Russian surroundings. By nature, the German is open-hearted, rugged, hardy and without guile. The exact opposite is found in the character of the Russian farmer. For this reason the Volga colonists invented the saying: "The Russian has a Russian in his breast."

However, proverbs originate from the deep conviction of a people and are based on general experience. The third reason why the desire to emigrate and to leave Russia took hold of almost all of the colonists was the poor judicial system. As long as the guardianship office and the offices made decisions concerning the legal issues among the colonists, the colonists had enough legal protection. The leaders of the communities and the administrators had the power to bring serious crimes to court and to pass judgment upon them. The administrators had the power to sentence brutal criminals with corporal punishment. They could even have people punished with rods. With the introduction of the "Russian rules;" that is since 1876, these rights were withdrawn from them. The judicial cases were handled in the county cities, or in the case of important issues, even in the gouvernements. Corporal punishment was abolished. Russian justice often even let the serious criminals go without punishment. The people were convinced of the fact that the judges allowed the thieves to go without punishment so that they could steal even more and could divide that which was robbed with the judges. As a result of the poor handling of justice, whole bands of horse thieves were formed who often drove away all of the livestock belonging to the farmers. No complaint, no protest to the government official solved anything. With this state of affairs, the people turned to self-defense. Murder and killing of the thieves and swindlers was not unheard of in some of the colonies. Actually the lack of legal protection was one of the main reasons why the best colonists left Russia. Together with others, it even caused Balthasar Brungardt, the leader of the emigrants from the colony of Herzog, to say farewell to Russia forever, as the aged gentleman himself told the author of this diocesan history while he was visiting America.

Even the Jesuits, who led the pastoral ministry among the colonists for about 18 years in the Volga region, suspected that the Germans would not remain in Russia forever. In case of an emigration, they taught the colonists to leave just after sunset and not after sunrise.

Without a doubt, they were referring to America and not to the old homeland of Germany. Since the Russian state needed the Volga Germans as a human bulwark against the assaults of the wild nomadic peoples of the East; the Kyrgyz and the Kalmucks, the priests could not speak directly and openly. With the term "toward sunset," one could also have meant the old homeland. But the colonists could return to the old homeland. This was not considered to be a crime by the Russian state. The elders now were reminded of the advice given by the "Jesuviter," as the people called them. According to them, it had to be better in America than in Russia. Considerations such as these affected the Catholic German farmers in the Volga region. Nevertheless, the Catholic colonies of the Meadow and Hilly Sides (on both sides of the Volga) decided to send scouts to North and South America. These were to explore the land to see if it was suitable for agriculture and to enter into negotiations with the government officials concerning the allotment of sections of land. Those so authorized travelled through many states of North America, Brazil, Argentina, Paraguay and Uruguay. According to the report of the authorized delegation, the conditions for immigration were most favourable in the states of North America. For this reason, the first stream of Catholic emigrants from the Volga region poured into the United States of North America. A second movement from the Catholic Volga colonies went to Argentina. In the year 1926 the colonies in the state of Kansas celebrated the 50th anniversary of their settlement in the new world. However, Kansas is a state in the middle of the states which often suffer from a lack of rain and therefore from failed harvests. Nevertheless, as the author of this history witnessed personally during his visit to America in the year 1922, the valiant fellow brethren of the same heritage, by means of diligence and prudence have set themselves up so well in such a short period of time that they helped to still the hunger of their unfortunate relatives in Russia by generous gifts given to them in the years of famine caused by Bolshevism. Once again, let me heartily thank the dear benefactors for their kind and willing cooperation and the dear reception which they prepared for the author and his ministerial travelling companion!

Since the year 1876, many immigrated at various times to the new world from the south of the diocese of Tyraspol; mostly to the United States of America. Most of them settled in North and South Dakota where many, despite the short period of settlement, have established themselves well. Some have already attained a high standard of living. By means of their great courage, prudence and diligence they will soon be better off than in their former Russian homeland. The author was very glad to have met many of the former members of his diocese in North Dakota, also members of his parish, and even students from the parish school. At this point in the book, he also thanks these dear brethren of common heritage as best as he can for their kind reception and the generous donations for the starving! Our dear God will reward them for their great acts of compassion. The dear Americans often saved on their own meals in order to just have their starving brothers in Russia fed! We will always lovingly remember the benefactors. However the famine could not be truly alleviated since the same one affected everyone upon the territory of the diocese of Tyraspol, so that the proverb "Many brethren but few possessions," was fulfilled.

54. The Catholic military chaplaincy

Russia had finally conquered the Caucasus shortly before the establishment of the diocese of Tyraspol. That which had been won by so many heavy and bloody losses, in the long term had to be secured for the empire of the czar. Strong military occupational forces had to be posted and quartered in various places among the wild war-like population of this mountainous land. Since the Russians were much-hated by the ethnic groups of the Caucasus as the hostile conquerors, numerous Polish officers and soldiers were sent there. Even in the years before the World War, the forces of military occupation in Ciscaucasia and Transcaucasia counted no less than 25,000 Polish and Lithuanian troops.

The Russian military office allowed two chaplaincies for the pastoral care of the Catholic soldiers. There was one established in Timir-Chan-Schura (Translator's note: now Bujnaksk in Daghestan, Russian Federation) in the year 1843, and another in Manglis (Translator's note: now in Georgia) a few years later. The Russian state seems to not have given one kopeck for the construction of churches in the cities which were mentioned, for in all of the records it is expressly stated that both of these Houses of God were built by the generous gifts of the faithful. However, one could at least thank the Russian military officials that they considered it to be their duty to pay the salaries for both army chaplains. Nevertheless, the number of soldiers in these army parishes were much too numerous for two ministers. The priests had to spend the entire year in the confessional booth in order to hear the confessions of all just once a year. Only completely healthy and youthful clergy were capable of handling such activity. Notwithstanding that, the religious situation of the Catholic soldiers in other regions in the large diocese was even more difficult. These troops did not have their own chaplains. The local Catholic clergy had to care for their souls which often restricted the effectiveness and care spent in the parish which supported the priest through its charitable donations. This made it impossible to have any kind of orderly pastoral work. One example out of many of this kind will be presented here.

The city of Sebastopol had about 1,000 parish members and
more than 2,000 Catholic soldiers who required more care than the parish itself and this took place to the detriment of the regular parishioners. The city of Simferopol and other cities on the Crimean Peninsula had just as many Catholic soldiers as the city noted previously. For 22 years, the priest in Simferopol, who was also the priest in Sebastopol, and of the cities where the other 2,000 soldiers were stationed, had to pastorally serve 4,000 Catholic soldiers besides the parish with a membership of about 5,000 souls! They were scattered over an area of 4,000 square kilometers. Therefore, he served 9,000 souls alone! If he wanted to hear confessions once from all his congregational members and all of the soldiers, this was a job which even the healthiest human being could hardly master. In the case of such overload even the most pious priest is tempted to fall into a rote way of bureaucratic functioning. Because of this, a young curate of souls, upon whom the burden of the mentioned ministerial acts were placed by the diocesan ordinary, himself turned to the head of the 7th army corps who was headquartered in Simferopol, and asked if he might apply for the establishment of a military chaplaincy for his Catholic soldiers. It was just that his petition received a negative response. The reverend found greater understanding for the spiritual welfare of his troops with the head of the 13th division, General Dochturov/Dochturoff, who had his headquarters in Sebastopol. Finally, after many applications to the government in St. Petersburg, this energetic general was finally

successful in creating military chaplaincies for Sebastopol and Odessa, so that the priests in Simferopol and Odessa were relieved of their overload. In regard to this matter, the courageous general had personally travelled to St. Petersburg in order to revive the idea which had been in danger of being ignored. The head himself, who was an "Orthodox," but right-minded gentleman, was completely vexed concerning the fact that the poor Catholic troops were so very neglected, whereas each "Orthodox" regiment had its own chaplain.

55. Huge problems in regard to pastoral care

If the vineyard has not had the caring hand of the gardener for many years, it will only produce wild and sour grapes instead of good, sweet grapes. The grape vines and its branches need to continually be pruned anew. Only then will they produce good grapes. It is also like that with human beings. If the young German ministers came upon many bad situations in their vineyard after many years of neglected pastoral care and, in order to remove them, often dealt with great problems, then no one should be surprised. The most difficult was the battle with the termination of invalid marriages as a result of a marriage hindrance which separated them. Also the marriage hindrances of a public nature were kept secret from the pastor. The people could not be convinced and this could not be understood; that a marriage that had been entered into with a hindrance which separated, was invalid. The people were of the false opinion, and perhaps even of the conviction, that by the act of marriage itself, every obstacle to marriage had been removed and that the sacrament was valid in the eyes of God. Because a financial tax was collected when there were petitions for marriage dispensations, the people held the view that this was actually a permit for marriage which could be purchased. For this reason one often heard this statement among the colonists: "If it can be done with money, then one should be able to do it without money as well." In stating this, they wanted to say: If the marriage is to be valid after money was paid for the hindrance to marriage, it must then also be valid without paying any money. When one looks into the situation more deeply; in doing so, the people actually wanted to state their conviction that one could not purchase grace or something of a spiritual nature with the value of money, so that accordingly, the hindrance to marriage did not have any annulling power. The first view held by the people was actually correct; unfortunately their assumption that it had to only do with a matter of money was wrong. Seemingly, this false idea had taken root among the people because of a lack of proper teaching. This false view was even brought about or perhaps caused by the offense given by some Polish and Lithuanian ministers.

The old colonists told the story of how one priest or another declared to the bridal pair that there was an obstacle to marriage between them as, for instance, if there was a blood relationship in the third or fourth degree (Translator's note: This refers to third or fourth cousins) and that for this reason, he could not marry them. However, after they gave the clergyman a gift of some sacks of barley for his pigs or chicken feed for his poultry, he would perform the marriage without further ado. And unfortunately one had to believe these stories because their truth was authenticated well enough because even the first German clergy, as young boys, had been witnesses who saw and heard of this method of pastoral care of some greedy Polish and Lithuanian clergy. Money and other important gifts of natural produce such as wheat, barley, oats, hay or poultry such as geese, ducks, chickens etc. caused some of the miserly priests to clear up obstacles to marriage which normally hindered or delayed them. Here is just one example: The brother of a German priest, who was a boy of 12 at that time, was to get married. He appeared before the parish priest with his bride, before whom, in accordance with the custom even back then in the diocese of Tyraspol, the marriage engagement had to be made. Upon this occasion, the young bridal pair was required to be examined concerning teachings from the catechism. It was only after the examination in the necessary truths of religion and its prayers was passed that the cleric announced the banns in the church. According to the directive of the diocesan office, the priest received one ruble for publishing the marriage banns. Even before the beginning of the examination, the bridegroom laid the ruble (it was several silver coins) on the table in front of the minister. Vexed, but without saying anything, the aged man wiped the coins from the table to the floor, so that they rolled around in the entire room. The same thing happened with the second ruble which the bridegroom laid on the table. The donation (stipend) *was* too little for the aged priest!

After such an unpleasant beginning, it was to be feared that the examination would not be successful. In fact, the priest spoke in an overbearing tone and said: "Get out of here, you don't understand the catechism." Saddened as a result of this decision, the bridal pair went away. Several days later the bridal pair went to the priest again "in order to give their promises to one another." This time the old priest received them in a very friendly manner and the examination concerning the catechism was very successful, even though the young people were certainly not better prepared than they had been before. Several sacks of barley and white flour which the well-to-do bridegroom, upon the advice of his father, had transported to the parsonage the previous day had removed the obstacle of a lack of knowledge of the religious truths with one single act! Nevertheless, to the honour of the Polish and Lithuanian clergy, it must be emphasized here that there were only very few greedy ministers in the diocese of Tyraspol. Just a few such examples of this kind are enough in order for stories to be spread around in the large diocese and for generalizations to take place. Christian people will forgive a clergyman all weaknesses and faults more easily than greed or miserliness. Whenever the miserliness or greed of a Catholic priest and minister affects his work, the curse of God appears. The offense of some miserly characters in priestly robes had robbed from the people the binding power of canonical obstacles to marriage. Perhaps the priests in the diocese had received the authority from the bishop's office to grant dispensations in cases of less important hindrances to marriage, as this is customary in mission dioceses, and without explaining this to the bridal couple after they had received substantial gifts, gave the couple a dispensation. Nevertheless, because of this assumption, the marriages would have been performed in a valid way, but with a poor application of pastoral wisdom. Doing this would have hindered any kind of offense if the people had been enlightened in that which was necessary. The battle which the German clergy had fought against the concealment of the less important obstacles to marriage had already continued through two generations in the diocese. Now finally the battle is over. Today no marriage bond is formed with known obstacles to marriage. Today one believes in the power of the Church to establish impediments to marriage which divide and forbid.

The brutalization of the adult male youth also created huge impediments for the pastoral ministry. Experience taught that in the rough northern climate all of the vegetation bears the marks of the wild; the character of that which is ignoble. In the same manner, in a state in which the whimsical arbitrary actions of the officials rule, instead of the wisdom of Christian laws and the ennobling power of the Christian religions lies in fetters, a noble character cannot easily develop. The poet has already stated: "Where wild power rules without reason, no (Translator's note: educational) formation can take place." Since the male youth was supervised too little by their parents during the long days of winter which were without work, and the parents themselves chattered away in the social gatherings (Maistuben), their boys and their male youth grew up more on the village street than at home. One comrade often sought to outdo the next in terms of roughness and dissoluteness while on the streets of the villages. If the parents then harvested the fruits of the negligent child-raising from their wild, unmanageable sons, then the minister was supposed to help them. For this reason not a few colonists generally desired a cleric who was somewhat strict with the youth. Because they neglected strictness and discipline at home, they figured that the strictness of the minister or the curate of souls would correct their omissions. However, this is a wrong idea and a wrong view of the. calling of a curate of souls. Nevertheless, while the priest can act with more love, this love dare not deteriorate into weakness. Where the beneficent, loving hand fails, the leader of souls must at times also resort to more serious means. Not a few young clerics, especially in the north of the bishopric, went too far in regard to the strict treatment of the adult youth. By this method of pastoral work, they damaged their reputation as a priest without even winning a single, uncivilized young man for more honourable feelings and morals.

Many a zealot for order and discipline dared to go out at night on the streets and alleys of the village in order to catch the noisy youth and bring them to the village police for punishment! In doing so, these inexperienced, young ministers forgot that when they were ordained as priests, their hands were anointed in order to offer up and to bless but not to arrest crude people or people who broke the silence of the night. However, the examples of such imprudent zealots of the soul were counted a rarity. The older, experienced priests sought other, more effective means in order to stop the wildness of the youth. They themselves gave religious instruction in the parish schools. By the way, the ordinary in his personal pastoral letter at the beginning of 1906, strongly urged the curates of souls to do this. Diligent instruction in religion by the minister himself often improved young hearts. How often could the clergyman who was a teacher of religion, when he described the piety of saintly children, boys or youth, see bright gladness in the young, little eyes of the children. At times, it even occurred that the little ones shed tears of emotion. That was proof that the good seed had fallen on fertile soil in the kingdom of this world. However, there is also no dearth of examples where more mature, undisciplined or half-wild youth got rid of their original crudeness. The teachers did not neglect to commend their male and female students into the hands of their patron saints.

It was a huge defect that young, newly-ordained priests had to be assigned to care for a parish too early because of the great lack of priests. As in some cases the priest or dean lived to far away from the young curate of souls, the young priest could not get advice in problematic or difficult issues. Because of being independent too early, the young, inexperienced priest was also in danger of developing a character which was rigid and obstinate. This had to be damaging to himself and to the congregation which he led. Because of this, the one would practice too much strictness while the other became too indulgent. Thus one very pious curate of souls became so rigid that he gave absolution only to a few people who came to confession. Another saw an offense when a head scarf made of gauze was worn on hot summer days during the worship services. Without any mercy, he ejected all adult unmarried women with this type of head covering from the church. Once he even got into such great discord with the village mayor because he had evicted his daughter from the House of God that he did much damage to the good work of the Lord. Others did the foolish act of appearing on the dance floor at the occasion of a wedding in order to stop the dance. Everyone had to acknowledge that one could not forbid hot-headed dancers from dancing, whose passions had been aroused by wine or brandy and who thus found themselves in such a state of frenzy. It is incomprehensible how young priests objected that boys and youth kneel on one knee, as the knees had to be allowed to rest in turn during a worship service which lasted for a long time. Others again interfered with the boys as they left the House of God in that they looked to see exactly that everyone bowed his right knee down to the ground before the tabernacle. This is the duty of the members of the church council.

The election and employment of an organist was the common cause of great discord; or the sexton or schoolmaster, as one referred to him in the Volga colonies. Since the congregation paid him, it also demanded the right to choose him, even though it was not even capable of making a proper decision in regard to his ability for this position or his suitability. In the Volga colonies his suitability was judged according to his singing. A good "singer" was also a good schoolmaster! This was not the case in the region of the Black Sea. Above all, there one demanded that he be able to tolerably play the organ and everything else was insignificant. If there was a candidate for a schoolmaster or an organist in a parish village itself, then he was preferred above all others since he would ask for a lesser salary. In his place of birth, he was able to doing some farming on the side. In some parishes the congregation set the salary for the schoolmaster below that of the cowherd. If the congregation was not happy with the organist or schoolmaster, then the clergyman had to hold masses without music for months on end. Every festive celebration ended until the congregation had agreed with the minister in regard to the appointment and the salary of the schoolmaster.

Some priests, tired of worship services without singing, paid a diligent organist out of their own meager salary or begged for the salary from loyal members of the parish. Thus the clergyman and dean of Seelmann on the Volga paid his organist, who had come from the School of Music in Regensburg, significant salary until the congregation, which had been stirred up by enemies and opponents of the Latin chorales, came to a better conclusion and reimbursed the entire sum which the dean had paid to the organist. However, the dean had also won an even greater victory. The congregation had gotten accustomed to the Latin chorales so that it agreed almost unanimously that the "new way of singing" continue. Another honourable clergyman in the Black Sea region was not as fortunate as Dean Loewenbruck. The opponents of church singing were his personal antagonists and these they stirred up many members of the congregation. Discord between the curate of souls and many members of the parish, which continued for years, damaged the religious life of the parish. Because of this, the priest preferred to bid adieu to his parish, in which he worked for almost 25 years in a model way and have himself transferred to another position as a pastor. The ordinary of Tyraspol bestowed the title of honourary canon of the diocese of Tyraspol upon the minister in the year 1919. His name is Father Jakob Drobrowolsky. Following this, the pious gentleman, who had already been functioning as a dean since 1905, was decorated by Pope Pius XI by being appointed to be a papal chamberlain.

Rich farmers in a parish caused many problems for the curate of souls, who did not give them more attention than the poor members of the parish. In general, pride increases as a person becomes wealthier. The wealthy person also figures that because he is rich, he is smarter than the poor villager, tries to have his views accepted, wants to be right in every situation and often rule over the poor members of the congregation. In this, he does not even stop when it comes to the clergyman. The history of many parishes in the diocese of Tyraspol shows many examples where a rich "village king" caused huge obstacles for the work of the minister. If the curate of souls got into conflict with such a "congregational leader," then he could no longer remain in the parish if he did not want to have his life embittered. However, one cannot always absolve the clergyman of all fault in such matters, especially if he was still of a young age and he lacked the necessary experience in order to "please" the rich stuck-up fellow. These then did not shrink back from any means of trying to get rid of the pastor from his parish. The poor people in a village were stirred. up against the clergyman more than others. These people, who were dependent upon the rich opponent of the cleric for their income, would finally and after many underhanded dealings on the part of their "patron provider," be seduced into signing unjust petitions of complaint against the curate of souls. However, they did this without conviction and with a heavy heart but also not without a certain amount of cowardice. However, they comforted themselves with the idea that the bishop, to whom the complaint for the purpose of transferring the clergyman was directed, knew the minister, and would not grant any credence to the complaint. Indeed, these complaints and the demand for the transfer of the reverend did not accomplish their goal. Some opponents *of* the minister did not even shy away from submitting a complaint to the government. Wealthy troublemakers in Seelmann and in Brabanter in the Volga region, and in Josephstal and in Odessa did this. Without exception, all complaints submitted to the diocesan bishop or to the government demanded the removal of the priest from his parish posting and his transfer to another parish and therefore one of the worst punishments for a clergyman. To be sure, complaints registered by Polish members were never sent to the government, but to the archbishop and even submitted against the German bishop personally if he did not make decisions which favoured them. It was thought by these people that an archbishop could call a diocesan bishop to task. It frequently occurred that Polish members of the diocese detoured around their own diocesan bishop and directed themselves to the Polish archbishop when it came to the appointment or the transfer of a curate of souls. In fact, the Catholic bishops of Tyraspol were not recognized by many Polish "patriots" as "genuine Catholic" bishops because they were Germans. Reports were immediately sent to Warsaw when there was a change in bishops in Tyraspol or a new one was to be appointed. These were sent by various mixed city parishes and they only reported negative things about the German head shepherd.

So it was said that he did not love Poles or he was made the target of people's jokes when it was stated that he did not speak one word of Polish. The first assertion was always fabricated and the last one was not true in some cases, as several bishops of Tyraspol spoke Polish well because they had studied under Polish colleagues for years. As the last bishop of Tyraspol published and sent out his pastoral letters in the German and the Polish languages until the World War, and preached in Polish everywhere in the large cities, the incorrect newspaper reports concerning this finally ended. I.
1. Besides this, his Polish colleagues from the time when he had his academic studies contradicted the false newspaper reports in that they wrote that the bishop spoke Polish well.

Also, several pastoral letters from the bishop of Tyraspol were published in the Polish periodicals. However, the opponents of the bishop were more Polish than Catholic and they did not want to have a Catholic Church in the diocese of Tyraspol but a little piece of Poland. Even if there were some Polish Catholics who were not favourably inclined toward the German bishops in the c☐ty parishes, then the head pastor of Tyraspol found great affection in the few Polish villages in the bishopric. The author can speak from personal experience. When he said farewell to the congregation of Gregorievka/Gregorieffka in the county of Perekop and wanted to climb into the carriage in order to drive away, he was surrounded by such a large number of devout folk that it seemed as if they did not want to allow the head pastor, who had also consecrated their church, to leave. Everyone pushed toward him in order to kiss his ring and his hand one last time and to receive his final blessing. When the bishop sat down in the closed carriage and the carriage started moving forward, one had to use great caution in order not to drive over anyone as many continued to place themselves in front of the horses in order to keep the bishop from leaving. Many fell on their knees upon the road and adults and children cried. When the carriage finally drove ahead and left the village behind, a large multitude of people ran behind it crying and lamenting. The bishop and his chaplain and the clergy who accompanied him were moved to tears by this emotional scenario. Once again the head shepherd exited the carriage next to an open field and directed some more words of comfort to the crowd, blessed them once more and drove off. Whoever has never seen or experienced such a scenario himself will hardly be able to imagine something like it.

To their great joy, the head shepherd promised these faithful members of the diocese their own priest, who according to the directive of the government, had to reside outside the parish in the little city of Perekop, where not one member of the parish lived. He was to now live in their midst. Because of the bishop's promise, Gregorievka built a parsonage with its attendant buildings. Before the year had ended, the priest moved from Perekop to Gregorievka because of the order given by the bishop, without having previously applied to the government for a change of its regulation which did not allow this. The ordinary kept them ignorant of this fait accompli.

The obstacles which worked contrary to the effectiveness of the curates of souls also were sadly felt in the headquarters of the bishopric; in the office of the diocesan ordinary. All of the nerve endings of a spiritual organism run together and reach the diocesan bishop just as they do in the heart/mind of a human body. The bishop takes an active part in all of the pastoral joys and sufferings of his entire flock. That is why he can say with the apostle to the gentiles (Translator's note: this is St. Paul): II Corinthians 11:29 "When anyone is weak, am I not weak too? When anyone is led into sin, don't I feel a burning shame?" It causes him great grief when a clergyman, especially a curate of souls, shows, by means of an way of life unbecoming of a priest those entrusted to his care, not the road to heaven but the road to hell, and leads there when he lives a life of vice; when he becomes an alcoholic or is even in immoral relationships with persons of the opposite sex. Then the bishop has to take hold of the strict duty of dealing with the situation in order to rescue and so save it. Some alcoholic clergy caused Ferdinand Helanus Kahn and Franz Xaverius Zottmann, the first bishops of the bishopric, great distress. For their betterment and repentance, they were summoned to the curia where they were supervised so that they could not get any intoxicating drinks. Through sobriety or non-drinking of alcohol for many months they were to be weaned off of the curse of alcoholism and put on a better path. Some even had a strong desire to do so: during the first while when they took over a position they did not drink any alcoholic beverages. However, no one was ever really cured. How often did Bishop Zottmann hear complaints about the alcoholism of some clergy when he got greetings for Christmas or for Easter. These clergy had just carried out acts of repentance before the curia. He said once that this destructive bad habit was a part of life in Russia. While in private company, he once complained about a person who drank much. I. This man had a indestructible nature which was connected to a large and energetic body: In closing, he stated: "My priests, all seem to drink tea with a few drops of brandy (cognac), but I have one, a giant, who drinks cognac with a drop of tea!" This was stated by the clergyman in order to amuse the company at hand. The clergy knew this gentleman and could not keep from laughing. The old Greeks said: "Where Bacchus drinks, Venus also gladly appears." Unfortunately, this also held true for one or another alcoholic clergyman. Their standing in the office of the ministry was repeatedly suspended and they were called to repentance and amendment of life. They willingly submitted to the former and latter punishments of repentance and punishment for delinquents which were given by the bishop. Until the year 1905 the bishop and diocese had no defections from the priesthood which had to be regretted. At the close of 1905, a sexton renounced his priestly vows. He was the secretary of the pious Bishop Eduard von der Ropp, who had left his immediate successor, after the successor's induction into the office, this secretary. I. This serious case, which had never happened before, was caused by continual activity in social circles where there was no lack of young women. All of the admonishments of his bishop were answered with rudeness. The unhappy young clergyman wanted to marry. However, as Russian state law did not allow a valid marriage apart from valid church law, he also fell away from the Holy Catholic religion and became a Lutheran. Thereupon, he let himself be wed to a younger Polish widow in the Lutheran Church in Saratov. The apostate did not shrink from showing himself to the Catholics with his concubine. This was what he did with the Catholics in whose presence he had once celebrated holy mass, to whom he had preached and from whom he had heard many a confession. It was proven here again that the fall into sin of the clergyman caused the loss of the feeling of modesty. This offensive-causing example soon was emulated by several copycats who openly admitted that they considered the Catholic religion to be the only true one, but that they wanted to enter the estate of matrimony. As the Catholic Church does not allow this for priests, they were forced (!) to fall away from the Catholic religion and Church and embrace Lutheranism and enter into "marriage" before a Lutheran pastor. Several, through rude acts, even attempted to force the diocesan bishop to suspend them from their spiritual estate so that this so-called "unjustified action" on the part of the head shepherd would be considered

1. Albeit only as a result of the request of his predecessor, who did not know him well enough.

as a reason to fall away in the eyes of society. As the bishop saw through their ulterior motives, he did not punish them. When they realized that they could not attain their goal in this manner, they still threw away their priestly garments and followed their lower passions. After his prostitute suddenly died without the sacrament (Translator's note: this seems to indicate last rites or the sacrament of the altar), one of these pitiful clergymen returned to the Church again. Soon afterward the poor man became ill of appendicitis, was operated upon in Saratov and turned into a corpse five days later. Under the godlessness of Boshevism, hardly any of the errorists will find their way back to the Church.

A young vicar caused much offense in the Volga region. Without a doubt, he suffered from a fixation. Contrary to the clear prohibition of the bishop, he took it upon himself to supply wheat from the southern part (Translator's note: of Russia) where he originated for many farmers in the Volga region. For each chetvert he took one ruble as a down payment and the remaining sum to be paid after the next harvest. The clergyman partially squandered the money which had been collected. He used another portion for the construction of workshops in Mariental. The large project could not be completed because of his addiction to wastefulness and his swindling. He was veryi ndebted and everything was auctioned off. Nevertheless, the vicar could not pay his debts. The bishop placed him into a correctional monastery where unfortunately, he could not be reformed. During the Bolshevik Revolution he got involved with Jews in business dealings and disappeared without a trace.

56. Menacing dangers for the way of life of the German colonists and for the bishopric

While Europe's states occupied the best lands in America for their surplus population in order to create a new homeland which saved their mother tongue, their nationality and culture while still remaining connected to their motherland, the princes of Germany waged war against each other and revolted primarily as a result of religious innovations (of which there can be none in Christianity) which suited their own special goals in opposition to the emperor and his empire and, by alliances with enemies abroad, even threatened the continuation of the German state. Before the Thirty Years War, which was mainly a mess caused by religious innovations, German had a population of 17 million inhabitants and after the war there were only four million left! · That was the "blessing" of the "Reformation," and honestly stated of the ecclesiastical-religious revolution. Given this sad situation, how could the German empire have acquired colonies in the New

World for its surplus population? If today, there are about 20 million Germans spread around in every possible corner of the world where they as a guest people, oppressed by he native peoples, envied and often hated, if 20 million Germans shared the fate of the Jews and if way over half of these people have already been assimilated by other peoples, and, if in the near future yet many more millions are assimilated in this great mass of peoples, then these are genuine "blessings," which resulted because of a monk from Wittenberg and most of the German nobility.

Since Russia had, in advance, offered the best conditions for the retention of the German way of life, culture and language 27,000 streamed into the country from 1764 to 1767 in order to obtain a piece of bread by honest labour during the rule of Catherine the Great. Abo tit the same number came to the land of the czars during the reign of Alexander I. Until the present, the descendants of these emigrants to Russia completely retained their Germanic way of life. And as peaceful relations reigned between Germany and the Russian state until 1914, the situation of the German colonists, even if it was not always a happy one, was generally passable. It could be predicted that if peace was broken between both neighbours that the German colonists in Russia would be at a great disadvantage. In general, Russia's German-speaking population experienced the outbreak of the World War with fear and trembling. This was especially the case when war broke out with-Germany. The colonists feared that the Russian government would view them as enemies of the empire and traitors. In this they were not deceived. On December 13th of the first year of the war, a decree (Translator's note: the Russian word is ukas) of Czar Nicholas II caused all of the colonists who were within 100 versts (kilometers) of the western border of the empire to lose their property. This decree was followed by a second on February 2, 1915 which extended the expropriation to all German citizens in the southwest. A third imperial proclamation of February 3, 1917 declared that all colonists were to forfeit all of their fixed and liquid assets. All of the German citizens of this gigantic empire were thus condemned to vacate house and home and property and all which they possessed and to disperse within the huge empire. It was just that a set time had not been given. The terrible disciplinary regulation was even more horrible since the entire male population had to fight against the enemy on the front together with the Russians and only the elderly, women and children were left at home. Those who were thus condemned would have hardly found a sanctuary or refuge among the Russian population, as every place was filled with refugees from the theatre of war. Those who were expropriated were namely to receive state documents entitling them to 4 % of the value of their property and they were to live off of this interest! The state bank was to cash in these bonds after 25 years; that is after all of the colonists had perished by famine and misery. According to the officious explanation of the "Selski Vestnik," the czarist government had purposely decided to deal a death blow to the German colonists. For the bonds could not be sold or mortgaged/pawned and not be sold in any way "so that the colonists could not help themselves in any way." The colonists were to be hindered in taking part in "economic rivalry" with the remaining citizens. This was the explanation given by the "Selski Vestnik." Its declaration was even stamped on top by the sign of the

Russian eagle!

In February of 1917, shortly before the outbreak of the revolution, when the author of this diocesan history was called by the Ministry of the Interior to participate at the consecration of two Catholic bishops for the diocese of Zhitomir (the Polish bishops themselves were afraid to invite a German bishop to the event), he dropped in on the chairman of the "liquidation committee" in regard to the assets of the colonists. He was accompanied by Canon Klimaszewski. The head shepherd hoped to at least effect a moderation of the intentioned horror. It was just that he was very mistaken in this. After just a few spoken sentences, which he exchanged with Mr. Stischinski, he realized that he was dealing with a mortal enemy of the colonists and that he could achieve nothing.

Minister Stischinski himself called the ordinance against the colonists in Russia "horrible; but justifiable." 1. He stated that it had been a "great mistake" of our government to have accepted the German colonists. "We want to correct this mistake." The author found more feelings of justice and humanity in the head and vice-regent of the department for "foreign denominations." After he had vividly described the imminent, terrible and cruel fate of one and a half million colonists and the dissolution of the bishopric of Tyraspol, the head of the department confessed that: "Yes, your situation is terrible." Thus far, all of the colonists had been loyal citizens and valuable subjects of the czar. If the regime of the czar had not been overthrown, the diocese of Tyraspol would now have been dissolved and all of the German colonies in Russia would have been destroyed and their former inhabitants would now have become slaves insofar as they had not already perished as a result of poverty and misery.

The czar's government also wanted to pay for the Houses of God or at least the movable assets in these places: the bells, the chalices, vessels, clerical robes etc. They wanted to pay for them with bonds that yielded 4 %, which however could not be cashed in until 25 years had passed! The state officials repeatedly asked about the value of these consecrated items. The diocesan curia reported to the officials that consecrated items could not be valued in terms of money nor be sold.

While unfortunate Emperor Nicholas II signed one decree of annihilation after another and even printed a label on the journal of the ministerial decrees announcing: "Wise and praiseworthy measures; I will give instruction in regard to their implementation," the Ministry of the Interior looked for reasons in order to remove the Bishop of Tyraspol, who as the sole German still had such a high position, from his office. A welcome denunciation, which originated in Saratov, was delivered to the ministry. Although this summons had been sent under the pseudonym of a man called Knorre, the ministry still decided to then send Visarionoff, the director of the department of police, and Schemetillo, the head of a division in the department for "foreign denominations" for a thorough examination of the diocesan administration and the seminary. Of course, the ministry would have discovered what it wanted to find. The diocesan bishop would have been removed from his office, exiled to Siberia or to a Russian city in the far north, the council (consistory) would have been dissolved and the seminary and the diocese dissolved. It was just that the wise providence of God watched over the bishopric and its head shepherd, who had already administered it for 13 years under numerous and great difficulties. The revolution broke out in St. Petersburg on the same day when both investigators were to start their journey to Saratov.

I. According to the foundations of Christian morality, cruelty can never be justified.

Nota Bene: The czarist proclamation of expropriation was nullified by the Duma (Translator's note: the Russian parliament). It was just that Stischinski told the author of this book that the government would still carry this out on the basis of infamous paragraph 85 of state law.

The initiator of the telegram which had been sent to the Ministry of the Interior was, without a doubt, a clergyman who was working at the seminary. He was also a friend of the rector, because he had called upon the government to hinder his taking over its leadership. He had gotten wind from the police that he would become the rector. Since the government expressed its regret in regard to the interruption of life at the seminary, of which there was no record in the telegram sent by the person with the pseudonym, the minister must have gotten the news in some other way.

57. Establishment of the "Deutsche Rundschau/German Review" and the "Deutsche Stimmen/German Voices"

Since the beginning of 1897, the diocese of Tyraspol had its own periodical called "Klemens." At fust it was published every two weeks, but it was not very comprehensive. Already during the second year it took on a more significant form and the contents were expanded. Prelate Joseph Kruschinski was the editor and founder and at the same time, he lectured at the seminary. The major publisher, Schellhorn & Co. took care of the printing of the paper. The weekly was published in Saratov, the centre of the bishopric, but had its largest number of readers in the south. Many diocesans of the south wanted the periodical to be published in Odessa, near to where they resided. Saratov lay too far away for them. More and more, the desire was expressed for a political and economical daily newspaper in the form of the Lutheran Odessa newspaper which had many readers among the educated Catholics of the south. Wanting to fulfill this desire, Edmund Schmid, previously the organist in Karlsruhe, founded a daily newpaper named "Deutsches Leben/German Life," which was published in Odessa. This paper was, as Editor Schmid made known, a paper meant for everyone; for Catholics and for Lutherans. Because of this, if it wanted to have Lutheran readers, it was dependent upon following a liberal way of thinking. It did indeed produce many offensive articles which could have damaged the Catholic cause. Without delay, steps had to be taken in order to transform the "Klemens" into a daily and to distribute it on Sundays with a religious supplement. In order to place the publishing of the daily newspaper upon a solid footing, the author of this diocesan history founded a society of supporters which he himself led. This society purchased a printing press, took over the "Klemens" from Schellhorn & Co., and published the paper "Deutsche Rundschau/German Review," together with the Sunday supplement twice a week. A daily edition would not have served any purpose since the colonists only received mail twice a week.

The first business manager and editor of the "German Review" was Father Philipp Becker. While this clergyman was a skilled business manager, he proved to be completely unsuitable as the editor of a daily paper. In the meantime, the liberal "Deutsches Leben/German Life," with the help of some clergymen from the region of the Black Sea threatened to win the southern circle of readers/readership. Incomprehensibly, these patronizing clergy had even asked the bishop to restrict the "Klemens" to purely religious matters and to leave the realm of politics and industry to the "Deutsches Leben/German Life!" For this reason, it was high time to transform the "Klemens" into a political-economic daily and to transfer the editorial staff and publisher to the south. Odessa was chosen as the place of publication. From 1907 onward and in this city, the "Deutsche Rundschau/German Review," which had been founded in Saratov shortly beforehand, began to appear with the Sunday paper "Klemens" as a supplement., "Deutsches Leben/German Life" soon became insolvent as it was unprofitable. Its editor and publisher completely fooled himself in his expectations of winning the German colonists in Russia, either Catholic or Lutheran, as subscribers and readers. Everyone was used to holding fast to his religion and to practice it publicly. Hazy liberal views were hated by the people. Editor Schmid, who was a German from the Germany, had not counted on that "Deutsches Leben/German Life" was forced to end its publication during the time when the "Deutsche Rundschau/German Review" moved to Odessa. The necessary financial means were lacking in order to keep it solvent. But the financial state of the "Deutsche Rundschau/German Review" was also not favourable. In Saratov, where the cost of living and employees were much less expensive than in the large, progressive port city of Odessa, the paper was just as unprofitable as in the south. The surplus from the publishing house, which had always been given work by the large publishing house Schellhorn & Co., kept the daily afloat. In Odessa, this work was no longer there. The business manager had unwisely rented a place for the editorial staff and the printer on one of the most expensive streets in Odessa The expenses there for "room and board" for the new enterprise were insufferable. The enterprise had to go into substantial debt. Finally the World War began. The Odessa Command of the army forbade the publishing of German-language papers. The "Rundschau" and its "Klemens" supplement had to be terminated. After the overthrow of the czarist regime, the paper was resurrected for just a short period of time. In order to rescue the paper, the Society of St. Clement donated the services of a certain Mr. Boehm for the paper and for the publishing house with the condition that both papers be continued as all societies were forbidden by the state. Bolshevism finally requisitioned the publishing house and suppressed all further papers which did not follow Bolshevism.

As long as the "Klemens" and the "Deutsche Rundschau" were published in Saratov the Catholic inhabitants of the Volga region did not value the papers in the proper manner. For this reason they were not widely read in the northern colonies. But when the papers and the publishing house were moved to the south a great desire for their own paper awoke among the northern inhabitants. In the interest of the Catholic faith and good Catholic morality, this desire had to be met half-way. A paper had to be founded which appeared twice a week and even more so because of the founding of the "Deutsche Rundschau" in the south, which was no longer owned by the clergy but had been given into the hands of a layman and could not cause any reduction of readers in the north. For this, substantial pecuniary resources were needed, and they first had to be procured. With the permission and blessing of the diocese, a Catholic Day was held for the members of the diocese of the Volga region in Seelmann during the summer of 1917. Among other important issues, it was decided to publish a paper which was to appear twice a week. The publisher of the paper was to be the "Volksverein/People's Union" which had been founded during the Catholic Day. Before the Catholic Day ended, many thousands joined the Volksverein since the leaders of the Catholic Day had set low annual dues of only 50 kopecks. If the Catholic population of the Volga region joined the Volksverein in such large numbers, then this was, above all, attributed to the fact that of how important it was for it to join together in order to end the economic and social grievances which Russian mismanagement had caused. The people felt that a People's Union was a very necessary requirement. If the repeated attempts to establish societies in the south did not succeed in the south of the diocese, then the reason for this was the fact that there the people had generally attained a high standard of living because of the milder climate, the greater fertility of the soil, the nearness of foreign borders {Translator's note: referring to foreign markets) and above all because of the much more favourable system of economic management practiced by the southern colonists. However, their prosperity was made possible by the large estates of noble landowners in proximity to where they lived which they could lease for low rent, and by prudent and diligent economic management attain a high standard of living. All of this was lacking among the colonists of the Volga region. 1.

After the close of the Catholic Day, the leaders of the People's Union purchased a printing press without delay and published the "Deutsche Stimmen/German Voices" twice a week. In order to distribute the paper as widely as possible among the people, its subscription price was kept very low. The largest German colony of the bishopric, Mariental on the Karaman River, was chosen as the place to publish and print the paper. Florian Klein, a young and diligent university graduate, was hired as the editor. Just as the enterprise began so brilliantly and continued in the same manner, unfortunately it still did not have a long lifespan. Bolshevism, which was an enemy of the truth and religion, began to persecute the editor because of his Christian convictions and even to threaten his life. In order to save himself, he had to flee to Germany. It was no better with the second editor, Father Augustin Baumtrog, formerly a graduate of the University of Innsbruck, who had been appointed by the bishop to this position. The red haters of Christ and God suppressed the paper during his time and outlawed him as the editor. In order to save his life, he had to go into hiding for a long time. The German

1. These are the real causes why the colonist in the southern lands was able to enjoy a higher standard of living than the colonist in the north. This was not the result of the greater diligence, prudence or ability of the former rather than the latter as many journalists eagerly emphasized. Whoever knows the north and the south really well and does not allow himself to be indoctrinated by feelings of region, jealousy, or even pride, has to admit that the fields in the north and the south were cultivated equally well. In this regard, differences could not be determined.

"Soviets" removed the printing press and had it brought to Katharinenstadt (Translator's by the Godless rampaging people, every trace of justice and every trace of humane freedom was destroyed. All that which had been done involving so much trouble and such great effort was destroyed. In the land of the Bolsheviks only that which is evil can be published. The language which this movement speaks is known around the world. It is a language of lies and wrongful accusations and of hatred toward humankind and the

Most High, the creator of heaven and earth, as well as everything which is holy, which is sacred and is opposed to every religion and the divine Saviour Jesus Christ. And since Bolshevism enslaved everyone, no one can dare to be so bold as to defend himself or God or that which is good against its unjust, defamatory or blasphemous attacks. Among these murderers of men this signifies a counterrevolution! For this reason, all who seek to repulse such attacks, even with just one single word, are condemned to death!

58. Two memorandi sent to the diocesan bishop

One has called the 20th century the century of great inventions. One could also rightly call it the century of revolutions. It caused the demise of almost all of the constitutional monarchies in countries. The spirit of revolution toward the existing governmental and social order also made great efforts to topple the hierarchical order given by Christ to his Church. In the diocese of Tyraspol there were also views expressed which demanded that the parishes were to have the right to elect their own priests, and not have them appointed by the head shepherd of the diocese as had been the case until then. In some parishes one did not want to accept the curates of souls appointed by the bishop. In one parish a threat was made, though by a small part of the parish locality, to receive the appointed priest with pitchforks for manure!

The same spirit of opposition against spiritual authority had also affected some clergymen. Since the beginning of this century this spirit has, so to say, permeated everything. For this reason, Pope Pius X of blessed memory expounded strict regulations concerning this presumptuous spirit in his famous encyclical "Pascendi" (Translator's note: reference is made here to the encyclical on the doctrines of the modernists). In it was written that the "bishops should in future only allow meetings of priests in the most seldom of cases. If they did allow such meetings, they were to be held with the proviso that nothing would be discussed which belonged to the realm of the bishop or that of the Apostolic See so that nothing would be presented or demanded which would cause the disruption of sacred authority. Complete silence was to be observed when it came to anything that smacked of modernism, Presbyterianism or laicism."

On August 8, 1917, in contradiction to this papal directive, about 20 clergymen met in Odessa in the Church of the Ascension upon the occasion of a county gathering of Lutherans and Catholics in which they had taken part, in order to send their ordinary a memorandum concerning the situation of the seminary since the year 1915. However, one of the former professors of the seminary was present at the meeting who, to be sure, calmly spoke after the report of the dean, but by his presence already caused the volatile tempers to be inflamed even more. The meeting was called into being only because of the promise of its leaders, who today are all deceased, to petition the bishop for the holding of a diocesan synodical assembly. This promise was the bait with which the clergymen were moved to participate in the meeting. However, there was no mention of this assembly after the leaders, after a stormy session, had in part gotten the signatures of the clergymen. Half of the priests had, without having personally given their signature, rushed to the departing steamship and to the train station. Others had perhaps signed as their proxies. During the assembly, some hotheads, who though they had not heard the view of the diocesan shepherd and only the view of the opposing side, yelled repeatedly: "We have to do something ourselves!" If it is already frivolous to take a position in opposition to the diocesan bishop, without knowing the situation properly, then it is even despicable when clergy, at public meetings, who are strictly prohibited by the head of the Church, by the pope himself, get involved in things which belong in the realm of the bishops or of the apostolic see such as the appointment of educators and professors for the seminary for priests.

As everyone realized, for those meeting in Odessa, the situation did not have to do as much with the seminary as with three leaders and a priest who was present, who just like the dean did not allow his signature to be forced. The document to which the signatures were attached was something which very much insulted their diocesan bishop. Whoever has been able to examine the archive of the modem period has to agree with this comment of the priest. The infamous memorandum reminded the diocesan shepherd very rightly and vividly of the words of our dear Saviour, according to which the apostles and their successors, the Catholic bishops, had to drink the cup of suffering together with their divine master. Matthew 10:24 "A pupil isn't above his teacher."

Yet another memorandum had been sent to the ordinary earlier by 14 clergymen from the ranks of the above-mentioned group from Odessa. This document dealt with the content of the "Klemens," which the bishop had shortly previous to this taken over from the firm of Schellhorn & Co. Edmund Schmid, previously organist in Karlsruhe and Odessa, had founded a daily newspaper in Odessa called "Deutsches Leben/German Life." The paper . steered a course so that Catholics and Lutherans would subscribe to it. Its name was "German Life" and it was to be a liberal daily in regard to religious issues. For whoever wanted to utilize his head had to realize that Lutherans would not read a Catholic paper according to the old principle "Catholica non leguntur/Catholic things will not be read." Edmund Schmid was surely one of the first who knew exactly that his paper could only count on Lutheran readers if his Catholic convictions were not revealed in it. Of course . he also watched that. Meanwhile, in order to have prospects for a more widespread sale of his paper; that is among the diocesans of Tyraspol, it was important to him that the "Klemens" limit itself solely to purely religious issues, but that which was secular be left for "Deutsches Leben/German Life." At a meeting in Odessa, Edmund Schmid knew how to win 14 clergy from the south for his plan. For the benefit of "Deutsches Leben - German Life," a memorandum was composed for the diocesan bishop and sent to the episcopal curia in Saratov. However, the petition of the 14 clergymen was roundly rejected by the bishop as a Catholic publisher and editor of a daily newspaper was no guarantee that it would follow a Catholic course of thinking for its readers. As Schmid admitted, it was to be "for everyone" and had to take a liberal direction in order to win readers among the Lutheran population of Southern Russia. In fact, several times the newspaper had already allowed a liberal spirit to manifest itself. In comparison, it is much less dangerous to read a paper which is edited by an anti-Catholic editor than a paper "for everyone," which is edited by a Catholic. For in the first instance our Catholics would always read articles with some apprehension and distrust if they dealt with religious issues or questions in which religion played a role. In the last instance they could be consoled that the editor or publisher was Catholic and had viewed false religious teachings as being Catholic.

59. Transfer of the bishop's see to Odessa

On October 28, 1917, after three weeks of street to street combat by the citizens, the city of Saratov fell into the hands of the Bolsheviks. Without delay, the rebels started to "requisition." Armed bands searched through all the houses and the businesses in the city with the pretense of determining the supplies of provisions, but in truth in order to requisition all the armed weapons belonging to the citizens. The residence of the bishop was visited by the new "authorities" on an hourly basis. As a rule they were Jews and included women who would even use their (Translator's note: Yiddish-speaking communists would be able to understand High German or the German dialects and so were sent to German localities) jargon in order to communicate with each other. If you did not let the visitors in, they would try to break the door open. With their caps on their heads they made attempts to examine every corner of the house without taking even the slightest notice of the owner of the home. Finally the commissar of the council for residences personally appeared in the company of a woman and two officers. They "requisitioned" the bishop's residence to be a children's home. They left a small room as a residence for the author. When the author explained that he could not live with children because his occupational work would be disturbed, one of the officers yelled so vehemently at him that the worst possible result was feared because of his rage. There was no thought of remaining in Saratov. The episcopal see had to be transferred to the south of the diocese where the Bolsheviks could not gain entry because of the German occupation. This view was shared by the remaining members of the cathedral chapter and the seminary professors. In the meantime the requisitioning, which was actually the rape of the city's citizens, continued to advance. The rulers of terror charged through the streets of the city with a car every night at 10:30 p.m. A large company of soldiers who were galloping wildly followed them around. They hunted "suspicious people" and rich citizens and threw a large number into jail. The prisons had been previously emptied by the rebels: they used these proper comrades in order to establish Bolshevism with their help and in order to make them into commissars. Those rich and prosperous citizens, who were not taken to jail, were removed from their homes and quartered in small cottages on the outskirts of the city. The proletariat, that is the poor people, then moved into the nice homes of the rich. In the best of cases, the Soviets left a small room in their own dwelling for the rich to live in. They were to live together with the proletariat! Of course the red czars did not stop from going into the sanctuary, into the church and its property.

The seminary was requisitioned for a hospital and the beautiful new school building behind the cathedral, since it was located in the middle of the city, was declared to be an office for commissars (a police station). In the same way, the consistory (the ordinary's residence), the residences of the professors and the members of the chapter were confiscated. Because of this situation, there was no alternative but to transfer the episcopal see south to Odessa.

August 14th according to the old time was set as the day of departure. After the head pastor of the diocese held a quiet mass, the last to be held in the cathedral, he addressed the numerous faithful who had assembled, in the German and the Polish languages, admonished them to remain steadfast in the holy Catholic faith, warned them of the threatening dangers to the faith and to Christian morals and stated the apprehension that, should no change to the better appear in regard to the civil and social circumstances, the episcopal see would be transferred to the South.

Despite the fact that the departure of the diocesan overseer and his attendants did not in any way resemble an escape but took place as a public departure with the permission of the "college" and the city's Bolshevik commandant, it would have been desirable for the travelers to have left anonymously. It was just that the public did not allow this to take place. For the faithful had gathered in great numbers at the railroad station in order to receive the bishop's last blessing and to say goodbye to the head shepherd and the members of the chapter.

By overcoming great hindrances, our group of travelers arrived in Kursk which was the last large city before the neutral border area between Russia and Ukraine. Here the group had to wait for three full days in order to obtain exit visas from nine different commissars. And after we had received all of these, we were still not able to leave behind Greater Russia; the land of the Bolsheviks. We had neglected to generously "bribe." But when we had generously used this universal means with which the Bolsheviks functioned with the senior commissar, we could finally depart from the Bolshevik "paradise" with an evening train freight car (there were no others). On the eleventh day after our departure we arrived in Odessa. Here, under the German occupation, life returned to normal regularity once again. From this point at least the larger southern part of the diocese. could be administered. The members of the chapter and the. professors from the seminary took residence next to the beautiful Church of the Assumption of Mary. One story of the large parish school was furnished as the refectory for the students of the clergy seminary and set up for lecture rooms. Because of a lack of space the boys and youth of the "pro-seminary" in the dormitory of the high school/college were billeted in Karlsruhe. There they were to do their preparatory studies until such time as normal conditions would return. As it was not easy to find a residence for the bishop and the episcopal secretary, in the churches of the city, the head shepherd and the secretary took up residence in a separate home beside the Franciscan monastery in close proximity to the Black Sea. Henceforth, the Church of the Assumption of Mary had to serve as a pro-cathedral. Also, a bishop's cathedra was situated here in the presbytery, which was somewhat small as well. Here, all of the pontifical worship offices/requirements could be carried out in a nice manner according to the rule. Thanks to the favorable conditions in the most important city of the diocese, the diocesan administration, the chapter and the seminary for clergy could be accommodated and nothing stood in the way of the highest church institutions to again resume and continue their former occupational functions for the welfare of the diocese.

60. The persecution of the vicar general of Tyraspol

When the bishop, together with the members of the cathedral chapter, had departed for the south of the diocese, Canon Xaverius Klimaszewski, who had been left behind as the head shepherd, began his ministry on August 14th. He was, since he was at the same time the priest at the cathedral, the only Catholic clergyman in the city 14 days after the departure of the bishop, a heavily armed band of Bolsheviks appeared in front of the - bishop's residence. The Bolsheviks had left two small rooms, for which rent had to be paid, in the rear of the residence for the priest. The band wanted to take the bishop to court since he had not appeared after the summons had been issued. It was just that the person sought after was already in Odessa, Ukraine which was occupied by Austrian and German soldiers. Because of this, the terrorists could not get hold of him. With special rage they then pounced upon his general vicar, Xavierius Klimaszewski. While he was absent from his domicile carrying out his pastoral duties, they forced entry with duplicate keys and hid a revolver, bullets and hand grenades in the rooms and waited for the return of the canon. The inhumane fellows immediately stormed after him into the home and accused the clergyman and while grinning stated: "Oh, there you see with what you occupy yourself, you have murderous weapons. You are a counter-revolutionary. Admit that you obtained these weapons and had them at your place." At the same time a murderous rogue held a loaded revolver to his ear. "If you don't confess," the terrorist cried out, I will pull the trigger." --- "And if you shoot me right here," replied the clergyman, "I cannot confess what I have not done." After they repeated this threat, they took the canon away. Without any trial and without a verdict from any court, they threw the poor man into a horrible prison in order to break him. In his absence, the poor parish which even then after the exit of refugees from the west, had about six thousand souls, was vacant. There had been over a dozen clergy here previously. Now the cathedral, where the worship service once been celebrated so beautifully and so solemnly, stood empty.

The clergyman, Father Sauer, who had been relieved of his position because of illness, came from the hills around Saratov to the church on Sundays and on festival days and held a holy mass. Then he returned with his pitiful carriage to his garden where he lived in a miserable state keeping body and soul together together with his elderly maid. After the Bolshevik robbers attacked, murdered and burned the unfortunate soul one day together with his maid and his house, there were no more offerings brought forth in the sanctuary. There reigned, as the prophet Daniel expressed himself "of these abominable things" (editor's note: part of Daniel 9:27), for the holy of holies was also gone, the Bolsheviks had the keys to the beautiful House of God! The red terrorists made moves to turn the church into a public Bolshevik institution if, in the meantime the freed vicar general had not declared Father Adam Desch the priest of the church and the congregation. Now we will return to our Vicar General Klimaszewski.

The jail into which one had thrown the unfortunate person did not have a single window, no chair, no bench, nothing upon which one could have sat down or laid oneself to rest! As well as this, the floor was made of cement. There, on the hard, ice-cold floor, in murderous temperatures during the winter and covered in his fur coat but almost stiff from the cold, lay our crouched together martyr priest. The same situation was present even at the end of the second month after his seizure. Only because of his youthful state of health could he survive such torment. During the third month they transferred him to a heated cell with a chair and a place with a bed. Then he also saw the beautiful light of day again.

In the meantime, the time of imprisonment for Father Klimaszewski did not continue much longer under humanitarian conditions. Toward the end of the month, around midnight, the door to the cell opened. In walked two armed servants of Bolshevik "righteousness(!)." They ordered the canon to follow them. The prisoner believed that this would be his last walk in life in order to be informed of his death sentence and to be shot right after that. In fact, his first thoughts were confirmed in that he was presented to the sinister Soviets. How great was his astonishment but also his joy, when the Bolshevik companions explained that he was free and able to leave. As the clergy residence was locked, a well-known Catholic family took him in and kept him for the night. Great was the joy of the parish family because of the setting free of its beloved vicar general.

Not long after the setting free of the vicar general Xaverius Klimaszewski, the war broke out between the Bolsheviks and Poland. Since he was a Pole, his freedom was threatened a second time. At any moment the red thieves could have snatched him. Therefore there were signs that he should take flight. But where could he flee to in order to escape the red czars? It was a difficult situation. At first glance it seemed to be very advisable that he go to a German village. Dressed as a Gentian colonist, in a yellow sheepskin coat, as the German farmers of the Volga region wore during the winter, the clergyman proceeded to the Catholic colonies on the Hilly Side. You didn't have to wait long for the pursuing commissars. Canon Klimaszewski had hardly left the city of Saratov when the search began for the Pole. The persecutors determined that the clergyman must have fled to the German villages. After the pursuing cops searched the German villages without having found him, they looked for him in the forest s of the Hilly Side. In summer a thick deciduous forest provides an excellent hiding place but not so in winter when the forest, now without leaves, allows a view far into the woods. And it was winter. Human tracks were clearly visible in the snow. For this reason the refugee gave himself away. The persecutors seemed to have found the clergyman's trail in the forest near the colony of Schuck. At dusk they came very close to the locality where the clergyman had hidden himself. He had namely crept into· a deep sandpit from which the farmers used to fetch their sand. But the commissars checked all the hidden spots and holes fastidiously. They also came to the sand pit and even looked into it but did not discover the clergyman who was shivering in fear because the yellow sheepskin coat had the same colour as the sand. This fact and the half-darkened dusk allowed him to find refuge. The police spies went away without reaching their goal of capturing him. It was not without the special protection of God that Canon Klimaszewski got to his old homeland of Poland.

61. The clergy martyrs of the diocese

There is probably not a single priest in the large extended diocese who was not persecuted by the rebels because of his holy Catholic faith and his faithfulness to his responsibilities. The large majority were thrown into prison where they suffered great deprivation and especially from hunger if members of the parish family or merciful souls were not allowed the possibility of bringing them noon or evening meals. The forcible separation from their beloved parish family, from the House of God and the impossibility of presenting the most holy sacrifice of God caused them not a few pains. But the apostle to the gentile peoples could have told them that when he wrote to the Hebrews: "1!1 your struggle against sin you haven't yet resisted till blood has flowed," that is; against the enemies of Christianity. (Hebrews 12:4) Just eight clergy in the diocese had to shed their blood and lose their lives. Among them are several true martyrs as a result of their holy calling and faith or because of their Christian righteousness. The first priestly martyr was Father Jakob Duckart, the administrator of the parish of Katharinental in the county of Odessa who had only been ordained as a priest three years previous. In 1919, when shortly after the harvest the Bolshevik soldiers retreated in a northerly direction from Nikolayev robbing and pillaging throughout the German Catholic colonies in the Berezan, entire villages fled. The young curate of souls from Katharinental also fled with them. The escape took them over the Bug River. The refugees followed the militarily armed Bolshevik bands along the river by foot. Near the ferry, which could only hold a small number of people, the bands were able to reach the German refugees. Because they wanted to cross over the not very wide river, they were met with heavy resistance by a military group of the White Guard which had taken positions on the other side of the river.

A short but intense battle followed. The Germans on this side had taken refuge in the barns and other buildings in the Russian village near the ferry. Father Jakob Duckart was among them. Suddenly a grenade struck a barn which killed several persons and wounded many more. Father Jakob Duckart comforted the unfortunate ones and provided the sacrament of extreme unction (last rites). This angered the Bolshevik soldiers. They forbade the clergyman to carry out the holy responsibilities of his office. However, the priest did not obey the godless Bolsheviks. So a brutal soldier suddenly tore the clergyman away from the dying, dragged him out into the yard and ordered him to stand against the wall in order to shoot down the priest who had been faithful to his responsibility. Without even opening his mouth for one request, without any sound of complaint, patient like a lamb, the victim obeyed his inhuman murderers. With his arms crossed before his breast and appealing to the heavens with open eyes, the servant of Christ was the recipient of the deadly shots. More precise information is lacking as to what happened to the body. Only one thing is certain: the soul of this youthful witness who shed his blood is present with its godly master according to the promise of the same: "And where I am there will my servant be also." (John 12:26)

The members of the parish family from Katharinental who were present and saw this sad scenario and the acquiescence to the will of God. of their beloved curate of souls, wept, forgetting their own misfortune, tears of godly compassion because of the death of this priestly sacrificial offering and stated: He is a saint!

A second priest who was a victim of Bolshevik inhumanity was the newly-ordained priest Klemens Weissenburger. He had received a chaplaincy and vicar's position in the northern part of the diocese. When the bishop moved his see to the south, he joined the followers of his head shepherd in order to visit his widowed mother in the colony of Selz. When in the summer of 1919, the Bolsheviks, without investigating the facts, without a trial and as a result of vengeance for the defeat suffered near Gross and Kleinliebental, drove the people together on the church yard (We note that the congregation had just assembled for a consultative meeting.), many inhabitants wanted to flee either in wagons or on foot. The priest Weissenburger was also among this group. The rough bandits seized him, drove him together with the others to the cemetery where he, together with the others, was shot down by machine guns. At that time 107 men died and among them were several men from Str'1Ssburg, Baden and Kandel. All of these executed men were the sacrifice of a righteous cause. They are also entitled to the comfort of the godly redeemer: "Blessed· are those who are persecuted for doing right. Theirs is the kingdom of heaven!" (Matthew 5:10)

Father Johannes Hoffmann was the third sacrifice of brutal savagery. While fleeing, he was martyred in the most brutal manner at the railroad station in Kurman-Kimeltschi in the Crimean peninsula by the thieving bandits of the famous Russian robber chieftain Machno, who, together with his gangs even attacked large cities such as the city of Yekaterinoslav, terrorized and plundered. The hostile peole cut him into pieces and threw them around on an empty field to be ravaged by the birds and the wild animals. According to a rumor, Father Hoffmann is supposed to have replied very unwisely to a question asked by a Machno bandit as to where he came from and why he wasn't at his home, that is in Heidelberg in his parish, that: "I am fleeing from the thieving Machno gangs." He had thought that the armed men asking the questions were Bolshevik soldiers. His response caused the bandits to go into a blind rage. For this reason the robbers carried out their atrocities. On the one hand, it is possible that an unwise response set the robbers into a rage. Reverend Johannes Hoffmann was a completely intelligent and because of his many experiences a sharp clergyman who certainly, in the dangerous situation in which he found himself, was very careful. For this reason, he would have hardly stated the impudent statement which was suggested. The Machno bands had attacked the villages in the Molotschna and had especially singled out Heidelberg but were repulsed for a period of many days by the colonists residing in the Molotsclina. They had suffered serious losses in their ranks. This defeat filled the bandits with irreconcilable hatred toward the Germans. The envy toward the prosperous colonists also played a very important role. When the ammunition ran out among the Heidelbergers and among the Germans in general, they were forced to flee in order to 'save their very souls. During the escape they seized the clergyman of the rich village of Heidelberg whom they considered to be one of their greatest enemies. For this reason they were enraged and vengeful toward him. Those are the three priests sacrificed by Bolshevism and the Russian thieves in the south of the diocese. The northern part of the diocese even mourned the sacrifice of five priests, and among these was Father Georg Sauer who was murdered by robbers.

Everyone should have believed that the lives of the clergymen in the Volga region would have been less endangered than in the region of the Black Sea. The German colonists lived in greater isolation and were separated more from the Russians than in the south. The colonists do not benefit from such a high standard of living and not a few among them are poor like the Russian population which surrounds them. Finally, the number of the northern colonists amounted to about 750,000 souls. While in the south three priests had to give up their lives, the north even had five to mourn. All five died in the year 1921 as a result of the rebellions of the German farmers who had defended themselves against giving away their last piece of bread. It was a defense which was caused by the utmost emergency, in other words literally a situation of self-defense. In almost all of the Volga villages, there were local officious Bolsheviks. They reported every farmer who still had some grain to the foreign Russian or rather Jewish and Lutheran commissars. They were the instigators and leaders for the complete plundering of the unfortunate local population. This fact must have moved even the best intended of colonists to become angry and even moved them to a type of rage against these Bolshevik village residents who seem to have lost both heart and mind. As the colonists saw that the "requisitioning" had no end, that all were destined for certain death by famine, they tried to neutralize the corrupted members of their communities, albeit in a horrible way. One morning, nine dead Bolsheviks were found in the streets of the village of Mariental. One had murdered them during the night. In Marienberg one had made a hole in the ice at a dam outside of the village and stuck the local Bolsheviks down under the ice. In Graf and Herzog similar means had been used in order to get rid of the noxious members of the community. One or another of the surviving Bosheviks reported the crimes committed to the commissars in Kosakenstadt (Pokrovsk). The Soviets immediately sent a regiment of their fiercest soldiers in order to exact revenge against the colonies. The male population of Mariental prepared for defensive action. Many who joined the local defensive guard stated: "Better to fall by the sword than die of agonizing famine." To be sure, they were armed with some weapons which their sons had brought home from the World War but only in desperation could a man risk confronting a regiment of experienced soldiers who were armed to the teeth and could not run out of ammunition and who even brought along artillery. The men of Mariental defended themselves like lions. In the meantime, even the greatest courage had to fail in the face of a more powerful enemy. 230 men died in the battle. A trial which was a farce was held for all the other men of the village. These men were driven together like wild animals into the schoolyards. A witness whose testimony was valued above all others appeared. He was the thoroughly Russian postmaster Sinjegin/Zinyegin who was a sullen hater of Germans. 270 men were condemned to death and among them was also the priest, Dean Nikolaus . Kraft. He was the first priest sacrificed in the Volga region. His vicar, Father Peter Weigel, was declared innocent, perhaps in order to give credence to the farce of impartiality or justice. Thirty condemned men at a time were taken across the river in the direction of the "Lemberg" and were shot during the night not far from there. Better said, they were mowed down with machine guns. It is very dubious if all were always killed. Meanwhile, in the darkness of the night, they were thrown into the deep trench close to there. In disdain, several bodies were buried in the "manure trench."

A second victim of Bolshevik rage who must be named was Father Gottlieb Beratz, the curate of souls in Herzog. He was the famous well-known author of the history of the "Colonies on the Volga." As a result of an unjustified denunciation by local Bolsheviks, the Bolsheviks had thrown him into jail and condemned him to be shot. The condemned person appealed to the higher Soviet. Notice was also received that he should be set free. Only the vindictive bandits placed themselves above the judgment of the high authority and led the minister to the riverbank, put him against the high, steep edge of the same and mowed him down with a round of gunfire. The martyr had raised his arms and his head to the heavens and awaited the deadly rounds of fire. His lifeless body fell down the steep bank while his pure soul rose up to be with his Divine Master.

Jakob Kayser, a young priest, who had just celebrated his first offering of the mass five years earlier, also gave his life as a sacrifice to his creator and was thus the third priest to do so. The Christian people who saw it even said that he was seen surrounded by a bright shining light when he died. This was perhaps only a pious delusion but it is certain that he was a godly priest. He was shot in his parish of Marienberg. The "Catholic"

Bolsheviks here were also guilty in his execution.

In Kamyshin the Bolsheviks shot Father Josef Baumtrog, the brother of the subsequent canon and apostolic administrator Augustin Baumtrog who is in jail at present since he is supposed to have received money from abroad for the clergy of his administrative district!

A fifth priest was, to be sure, not shot by the Bolsheviks but despite this fact Bolshevism is responsible for the death of this minister. Father Georg Sauer was his name and he lived with his aged housekeeper in his garden not far away from Saratov. During the night, bands of robbers attacked and murdered him and his housekeeper and after they had taken his few pitiful possessions they set the impoverished premises on fire and burned both bodies so that later one found them in a charred state.

These are the victims whose lives, according to the providence of God were brought by those people to God. They were priests who daily discharged to the most High God the sacrifice of his only begotten Son. These were, however, in comparison to the Polish diocesans few but very sensible, painful and bard to replace victims.

62. The persecution of Christianity and the church

According to the witness of history, all of the revolutions within the pale of Christendom directed their attacks against the throne and altar of the status quo. The Bolshevik revolution was the first one to attack everything which had existed up until that time and was directed against everything that had been tested and true in all of human society. Christianity and the Church were pounced upon by the Bolsheviks with selective rage. "Religion," so stated the father of the socialist upheaval, "is opium for the people." On the one hand, this foolish person accordingly wants to save the people from "destruction," but brings himself into the most crass of contradictions since he himself gave the statement: "Russia has 170 million inhabitants and we want to attempt to introduce communism even if 40 million people are annihilated in doing so." Thus the tyrant was not concerned about the welfare of the people. The inhumanity of the Bolshevik leader is publicly revealed by its own statements and cold genocide of millions of people and the immeasurable misery which it brought to the unfortunate nation of 150 million. What helped the unfortunate Christian people of Russia to yet bear this dreadful misery, that which was still able to comfort them, their Christian conviction, their religion, its uplifting worship service, its supernatural means of grace: all of these were to be taken away from the people and everything was to be robbed from them. Bolshevism is not satisfied with having destroyed every bit of happiness in one's life. It also wants to block the way for the Christians to a better life in eternity. The poor person was to remain unhappy for time and for eternity!

After the leaders of Bolshevism had established their power they did not wait long in order to issue their first law fur the "religious societies." It was named the "Standard regulations for religious societies in regard to: .... "

These statutes consist of only 23 paragraphs. Paragraphs 24-34 deal with the revision; actually regulatory commission, in regard to the property and the abolition of the religious society. The red czars of Moscow attempt to force all existing religions of Russia to comply: the Catholic, the "Orthodox," the Protestant and Schismatics of all kinds, the Jewish and the Muslim.

So that everyone has a clear picture of the entire dissolution of the Christian, above all the Catholic religion and Church in Soviet Russia by the Bolsheviks, here follows an exact translation of these regulations.

I. Purpose and duties of the religious societies.

1. The purpose of the religious society is the satisfying of the religious needs of its members, which are connected by the unity of the faith in the being of God and by the one spirit of love toward the neighbor.

2. Its duties are: a) The holding of general worship gatherings in the church buildings designated for such as well as in other closed premises; b) The distribution of religious mysteries (sacraments), ceremonies and religious ceremonies which are not in opposition to the state laws and proclamations or to the regulations of the local administration which are decreed for the preservation of societal peace and order....

3. The society has the right: a) to freely confess its faith and to conduct the worship services and religious ceremonies which are associated with it; b) To participate in conversations, 1. readings, and lectures of a religious nature; c) to organize lectures and explanations of the main teachings of their faith.

Notation: Those items presented under b and c are not to be public events.

4. The religious societies do not have the rights of a juridical person.

    1. Probably gossip!

5. Since the religious societies do not represent a juridical person, they do not have the right to obtain any kind of wealth or property, be it fixed assets or otherwise. They are not able to make contracts in their name, participate in agreements, present cases-in court and to defend themselves ....

All assets which are granted to the society for its use or are donated by its members are the property of the state and is to be given to it for its use for an undetermined period of time. The same holds true for church buildings and items pertaining to the worship services.

6. The society does not have the right to use a seal. The documents, extracts copies and notarized documents which are prepared for its members need to have a notarized document in order to be valid in a court of law. The same holds true for the determination as to their authenticity.

7. The religious societies are not allowed to unite in assemblies or in larger units of organization. They are not subject to any hierarchical powers even if these are provided for in the in the laws of the respective Church. The society, in its activities, must hold exclusively to the regulations of the general assembly of the members of the religious society and to the rules of this statute with the confins of the state and local laws ....

II In regard to the members of the religious societies

11. Members of the religious society can be: persons of both sexes who have attained their 18th year of life, without regard to their occupation, nationality and religious confession(!). Notation 2 A wicked or offensive way of life can in and of themselves

not be viewed as a hindrance to reception as a member of the society.

12. The religious society is not allowed to have less than twenty members.

III. The general meeting

19. The general assembly of the members of the society has the responsibility for all of the matters pertaining to the same: a) in regard to the character, form and order of the worship service and those serving the church as well as in regard to the language of worship; b) in regard to the determination of the clergyman when one is needed from their ranks or from people outside; c) in regard to the setting of the amount of offerings for the support of the temple and its employees.

IV. The administration of the religious society.

20. The administration is the office which ratifies the society. It consists of five persons and two candidates and shall be elected by the general assembly for one year's duration. The minister of the society counts as a very important member and has voice but not vote, if indeed there even is a minister present.

23. The members of the society in their activity are responsible for keeping the existing laws and decrees. They are especially not to allow any person under the age of 18 to come their meetings, conversations, lectures, readings or presentations regarding the teachings of their faith. A transgression of this paragraph describing this law will be punished according to the code of law.

Now follow the paragraphs in regard to the supervisory commission, the financial ☐ affairs and the liquidation (dissolution). Unfortunately these are missing and they can be guessed at without great difficulty.

These Bolshevik statutes remind one of the early statutes for the welfare societies, which had been issued by the old regime. They are concerned only with a religious organization which resembles a large sack in which all kinds of things find their place. The statutes know of only one God; one redeemer Jesus Christ, one work of redemption, there is no Christian Church mentioned in them, but it refers in paragraph 2 to mysteries (sacraments)! Thus it refers to sacraments without Christ. Complete idiocy! What are sacraments for if there is no original sin, no sin, of which there is none, even among the leaders of Bolshevism. Paragraph 3 refers to main dogmas. What kind of dogmas are they when, as the Bolsheviks maintain, there is no supernatural revelation?

Paragraph 2 restricts the distribution of the mysteries, ceremonies or religious ceremonies in one area. According to this, these are only allowed when they are not in opposition to the laws of the state and local community bylaws. How these rites can be contrary to state laws· or local bylaws cannot be determined. However, because the little word "existing" was left out in the wording of the paragraph, one must conclude that the Bolsheviks, when they proposed the statute already had the intention of forbidding all religious ceremonies in the future as this has now, in large measure, already happened. If a priest desires to baptize a child or marry a couple, he must, in advance, pay the commissars a considerable sum of money. If he cannot pay the money or if the respective Catholic cannot do so, his child will not be baptized and the bridal couple will not be wed. If the curate of souls still carries out the holy rites, he will be thrown into prison.

In all of Russia and also in the Diocese of Tiraspol, there is hardly a single minister who did not spend time in prison for religious rites "which were not permitted." In complete disregard to this, paragraph 3 of the Bolshevik statutes refers to freedom of the confession of faith!

The statutes forbid the societies to obtain any kind of property. They are not allowed to defend themselves before a court of law and are not allowed to lodge a complaint in court. Through these restrictions the Bolsheviks took away freedom from the religious societies, which is a part of the very being of every humane society. By doing so, the so-called religious societies have been placed on the same level as animals which do not have the right to own property. The right to lodge a grievance and or to defend oneself in a court was taken away on purpose. By doing so, the religious societies are at the mercy of the limitless arbitrary action of the red tyrants.

Paragraph 7 removes any hierarchical authority from the religious societies. This measure is directed against the Catholic episcopacy 1. and thus against the shepherds placed at the head of the church by Christ himself. This is to serve as a deathblow for the Christian! and the Catholic religion and Church. For only through episcopal succession can priests continued to exist according to the order of the Divine Founder of the church. Where there is no bishop, there are also no priests, no sacrifice of the mass, no sacraments, no sermon and no Christian teaching. Where this all ceases to exist, the Church must perish. And since the Church is the guarantor of the Christian religion, Christianity will die with her. Indeed, in a country or in a comer of the world,

Christianity and the Church can be exterminated by the rage of satanic forces. Only the universal church cannot be exterminated by any power from hell and the Bolsheviks are in the service of this demonic power. Jesus Christ himself. Jesus Christ himself has given the assurance of its continued existence: "The forces of hell will not overpower it (Matthew 16: 18). He promised to be with his Church forever. He will not forsake her for even one day: "And remember," he says: I am with you always till the end of the world" (Matthew 28:20b).

Bolshevism, in order to spread its tyranny among the consciences of human beings even more successfully, sticks to the law of the principle of division and of separation: "Divide et impera" (divide and conquer/rule). For this reason the statutes forbid the individual religious societies from uniting with each other. For this reason all of their property belongs to the government.

The entire piece of poor work in these statutes forms a religious society which is led by lay people and therefore it is not necessary to even have a minister be a part of it as can been seen from paragraph 20. If however, a minister is in the council (administration), he only has an advisory position! The hammer of the law is used in these "religious societies" of lay people as often as they let a boy or young person or girl under the age of 18 into their meetings. According to paragraph 23, all persons who are not yet 18 years of age must remain uninfluenced by the Christian religion and Church and remain a part of the new or Bolshevik. heathendom.

In harmony with paragraph 7 of its statutes, the leaders of Bolshevism had directed their attacks toward the bishops of the Church right from the start. All who were located within reach of their authority were condemned to death. It is only thanks to the special protection of God if they were saved from the execution of the death penalty. 2.

1. Indeed also in opposition to the ministry in general.

2. According to a report in the Osservatore Romano, all of the clergy in the Volga region were thrown into prisons at the beginning of August, 1930. --- Suffragan Bishop Frison and the other clergy of Tyraspol disappeared without a trace. According to the most recent news reports, the Bolsheviks are supposed to have thrown the bishop into the sea near Sebastopol.

The Bolshevik statutes that deal with religious societies are actually a mockery of every kind of religious conviction. Not even a Jew or a Muslim will be able to submit to them, let alone Christians, Catholics, Schismatics or Protestants. The Russian poet Kryloff/Krylov, in his collection of nice fables has one about a swan, a jackfish (pike) and a crayfish. These three determined to pull a goods wagon together. After they had harnessed themselves and wanted to move the wagon forward, the swan winged the wagon up to the clouds, the jackfish pulled it into the water while the crayfish walked backward: All three used all their strength so that it seemed they would kill themselves and yet they did not get the wagon to move one inch. This fable should have been taken notice of by the stupid Bolshevik authors of the statutes. Catholics, "Orthodox," Lutherans, Protestants, Gregorians, Calvinists, Jews and Muslims, all who believe in

God, are to be able to join this society according to paragraph 11 of the statutes and according to paragraph I of the famous statute, to satisfy their religious needs! Only those people who want to mock every possible kind of religious conviction and every kind of religious feeling could have produced such foolishness.

How the Bolshevik commissars view the Christian religion has been shown innumerable times to its citizens by the way it views marriage. If two marriage partners who have been married in a church want to end the marriage, there is nothing simpler than that. They appear before the commissar (as a rule this is a Jew) and explain that they are going to separate and the marriage, in the view of the Bolshevik state, has come to an end! It is just as easy for two separated persons to get married again to other persons. A declaration before the commissar is sufficient and the issue is resolved! In the last while the Moscovite Bolshevik chieftains have taken even greater steps toward human depravity. Every man can separate himself from his wife when he will and as often he wills. Every man can marry as often as he wants and even if it is three or more times per day. He can also divorce himself from his wife the same number of times! The same holds true for the wife. And this does not have to take place, as was the case earlier, before a commissar, but doesn't even have to be applied for! By doing this, the Bolsheviks have diminished an institution which was established and blessed by the Creator himself to a relationship which, we do not state, is present among animals, but which rules among the lowest kinds of animals: the Moscovite "despots" could not debase human dignity lower than that which is found among dogs and pigs and other animals. The marriage bond, marital faithfulness, love of the married couple for each other, things upon which are based the foundation of all of human society, which forms every union and establishes every act of faithfulness among human beings has been undermined by the Bolshevik "despots", destroyed and led to making each human attempt to raise children an impossibility.

According to Bolshevik principles, children should not be raised, they are to grow like trees in a primeval forest and evil tumors are not to be cut away from the children with the pruning fork of God's gardener. They only have the right to conceive and bear children to feed them and to clothe them; the Bolsheviks want to take care of everything else. For this reason, the parents are not to teach the children or let them be taught any religion or any prayers. The children are not allowed to obey their parents but only the Bolsheviks or the Bolshevik pedagogues and teachers. The "Bolsheviks and their school do everything possible in order to separate the children from their parents, to make. them their enemies, to not recognize God, to blaspheme Him, to trample upon his 'commandments and to raise them as enemies and haters of God. In every possible way, the children and the young people who are growing up are to be robbed of every positive feeling.

God, the Divine Redeemer, his religion, his Church are a hindrance to the· Bolsheviks in the attainment of their pernicious goals. For this reason there is a war waged against them. However, since the Christian family and especially our Catholic family is based upon God and the divine Saviour and his holy Gospel, Bolshevism **is.** bent upon destroying this. Not long ago a European traveler reported about the demoralization which Bolshevism had already visited upon the character of the Russian family. This demoralization is to have only damaged specifically the Catholic family a little because of the strong discipline which has ruled in its midst from time immemorial. Such a report from an eyewitness is very comforting for a Christian heart. But this fact alone does not offer any assurance against Bolshevik corruption for the future. That the unfortunate Russian people cannot free themselves from the iron chains without help from abroad is not questioned anymore. Who can guarantee that also in the near future many children of German Catholic parents will increase the numbers of those child robbers who make the cities insecure and today number in the millions? In the face of this nameless perversion which the Bolsheviks have visited upon Russia and will continue to do, we must direct the words of Jesus which he spoke to the rabble who arrested him to the Bolsheviks: "But this is your time when darkness rules" (Luke 22:53).

In the standard Bolshevik statutes which already appeared on January 23, 1918, the church is robbed of its right to own property and all church assets; fixed and liquid, including Houses of God are declared to be the property of the state. The usurpers also did not neglect to put paragraph 5 into force. Above all, they occupied the religious teaching academies and they threw the clergy out of their residences. If they allowed someone to retain a room in the home, then only if they paid a high rent as compensation. The Houses of God were left for the use of the "religious societies" for an undetermined period of time but often for the payment of rents which were unaffordable. Some religious societies which could not afford the payments were set out on the street and the churches were changed into clubs, meeting places or dance halls! This happened to the churches in Bachmut, Konstantinovka and in other places. Lenin and his associates caused irreparable damage to the Catholic religion and the Church in the diocese by dissolving the educational establishment for priests. If former professors of the seminary for priests wanted to give young people instruction in the spiritual disciplines in their rooms and in this manner train and prepare them for consecration and introduction into the Catholic priesthood; then paragraph 23 of the Bolshevik statutes stood in opposition to this whereby young people who were under the age of 18 years were not allowed to be taught or raised in the doctrines of the faith nor in morality. The instruction and even the permission to participate in 'the same was viewed as a criminal offence and punished as such by the Bolshevik tyrants! But since the Bolsheviks have their spies everywhere, secret instruction is impossible. The youth are therefore condemned to languish in paganism without any kind of Christian instruction until their 18th year of life! Under these circumstances, who will be found who will begin instruction in the spiritual disciplines and would want to choose the occupation of a priest? As anyone can easily read, paragraph 23 of the Bolshevik statutes condemns the priesthood in Russia and in the diocese of Tyraspol to extermination. Even now, after Bolshevism has been introduced to Russia for ten years, the curates of souls are missing in a dozen parishes of the diocese. The year 1920 also brought a completely failed harvest in the diocese of Tyraspol. The red rulers used this circumstance to "requisition" the silver and gold vessels of the Russian churches which are often imbedded with expensive precious stones pretending that the starving population needed to be fed with them. In fact the amount realized by the sale of the consecrated items slid into the pockets of the commissars and their Jewish-Freemasonic agitators who they sent into the whole world.

Of all of the inhabitants and citizens of Russia, no people suffered as badly under the Bolsheviks as the Germans and especially the German Catholics of the diocese of Tyraspol. In the year 1918 the red despots bad already made attempts to remove the curates of souls from the Catholics in the Volga region in order to force them into the ranks of the Red Anny. Only energetic protest from the Catholic population was successful in freeing them. The church family could not prevent the clergy from being forced to carry out secretarial work on all working days in the village offices of the Bolsheviks. The priests were only allowed to take care of their pastoral duties on Sundays and festival days. Fortunately this violent intrusion into church work lasted only several months, that is until the commissars who were Jews and Freemasons had, according to Lenin's statement, and all of whom were responsible people, had established the Volga German Republic. One utilized those who knew German better, the German clergy, for the preparatory work for the "Volga German Republic" which followed. According to popular rumor, "Lenin's responsible people" had the privilege of establishing a "German" Volga Republic by purchasing it for 50 million rubles from the Bolshevik czars in Moscow and then sought to recoup it by plundering the colonists. In fact, the commissars of Katharinenstadt took the last grain from the granary, the last flour from the bowl, the last horse, the last cow or goat, the last pig, the last sheep; everything including the last hen. Whoever turned against the robbers was shot dead without mercy. Thus the sons of Lenin and Trotsky carried out extensive blood baths in many villages such as Mariental on the Karaman River, in Graf and in Marienberg. The southern part of the diocese also had to suffer the effect of Bolshevik inhumanity. The great blood baths took place in Selz, as was mentioned previously, in Sulz where 27 of its best citizens were shot for the reason that they were prosperous or wealthy farmers (bourgeois), in Landau, in Karlsruhe and in Katharinental. Not satisfied with that, the Bolshevik robbers also set many of the nicest farms ablaze. In both of the last-mentioned villages, about 100 farms were burned down. The author himself was in a place which had been burned down. The sight was very sad. In Selz, in Landau, in Karlsruhe and in Katharinental the brutal bandits also raped defenseless girls and women. For days on end the men of Rastatt defended their native village against the wild attack of the neighboring Russian Bolsheviks who had coveted the fortunes of the German colonists for a

1. The robbers found a comrade who shared their views in a certain Reichert in Rastatt. This man murdered his own elderly uncle because the old man had tried to appeal to his conscience.

long time. When the ammunition ran out among the Germans, all of the inhabitants of the village at least attempted to save their lives by fleeing. Then the robbers attacked the empty village and literally robbed everything which was not tied down. As well, the 85 farms were reduced to rubble and ashes! The Bolsheviks did not even spare the sanctuary. They threw the tabernacle (May it be highly praised in eternity) to the ground, trampled on it with their feet, robbed the holy vessels and utensils from the church, the altar paraments, the liturgical robes for the mass from which they made saddle cloths for their pillaging raids. With his band the robber chieftain Machno brought the same evil to Heidelberg in the Molotschna and several other Catholic villages.

During one of his pillaging expeditions, the wild chieftain Machno, together with his horde, was also in close proximity to Georgsburg in the Molotschna. He immediately gave the "command" that for the following night the village should provide a girl for each one of his bandits. If there were not enough girls available then young women should be provided. The Catholic village administration informed the local curate of souls about this "command." He held a meeting with the girls and women in which, following an uplifting speech in regard to purity and an admonition to earnestly pray to God in order to remove the imminent danger, all unanimously stated and swore: better to die than to want to give themselves to the brutal robbers. This explanation was made known to Machno. Our dear Lord heard the prayer of the girls and women: the bands, under the leadership of their chieftain went in another direction with going to Georgsburg. All the women and girls in the village had prayed vehemently and been strengthened for endurance during this hard trial by the reception of the holy Sacraments.

During the persecution and suppression of the Germans, especially of the Catholics (there was much less terrorism in the Lutheran villages although they are more numerous than the Catholic villages), the murderous red assassins went so far that even Lenin, who was not afraid of the death of 40 million people, as we have read previously, had to command an end to the murders by the Bolsheviks! In order to suppress and subdue the "German insurrections" in the Volga region, the red despots had summoned the regiment from Tula (Tulskij Polk) which recruited its red army soldiers from the most uncivilized peoples of Russia. One probably feared sending Russian soldiers because these would perhaps have some sympathy with the unfortunate foe.

63. The great famine among the colonists

In such a large, expansive land such as European and Asian Russia, there are regions every year which are afflicted because of failed harvests as the result of drought or climatic conditions. One of the regions most prone to be afflicted by failed harvests is, without a doubt, the Volga region, which has served as a homeland for many immigrants for over 150 years.

The Black Sea region can also report bad harvests even if not to the same extent as the Volga region. Meanwhile, dire need sometimes grew so that there was a lack of food in the families of many diligent farmers. Yet there were generally so many provisions among the more prosperous and wealthy farmers that no one had to suffer from hunger or die of it. For the first time, Bolshevism's inhumanity and the lack of reason caused a famine to rage among the German colonists so that in the diocese of Tyraspol alone, which numbered 350,000 Germans; about 100,000 had to die of hunger. The Boshevik despots realized that their endless plundering among the German agricultural population and their perversion of all order were the reason for the famine among the Germans (also in regard to the death by famine of the other twelve million people). For this reason they tried to make the czarist regime responsible for the huge famine in order to justify themselves in the eyes of the world. As to that which pertains to the Germans and especially the Catholic Germans of the Volga and Black Sea regions, this accusation contradicts the facts. Bolshevism will never be able to cleanse itself from the crime of having mismanaged many millions of diligent and prosperous, yes even wealthy farmers so that they died of hunger. With all of its deficiencies, Russia under the regime of the czar was still the bread basket of Europe. For somewhat over two and a half years the country was at war with the central powers of Europe and had mobilized, fed, clothed and armed not less than twenty-five million men without in the least having felt, within its borders, even the smallest emergency or lack of foodstuffs such as bread and meat. In the entire black soil region the year 1919 produced an exceedingly rich harvest of all types of grain crops.

The harvest was especially good in the Volga and Black Sea regions. Here the author reports on a first hand basis. The stored provisions of grain should have been enough for the German colonists for a period of four years and this all the more as the Russian industry did not produce any wares as a result of the destruction of the factories by the proletariat and the demoralization which Bolshevism caused and foreign wares could not be purchased by the population because of a lack of Russian foreign reserves. The German people in the Volga region, who had experienced the "blessings" of Bolshevism first, despite the rich harvest of 1919, suffered because of famine during the following year 1. Many thousands of German farmers, among whom more than half were Catholic, forsook house and home and immigrated with the beggar's staff to those regions of Russia where they hoped to save their very lives from death by famine. Along the way, many traded clothing which they wore on their own bodies or the clothing of their children for foodstuffs so that many children arrived naked in Southern Russia! In their unspeakable distress, others remembered their old homeland Germany which their forbears had once left in order to seek their fortune or at least to find a good piece of bread in Russia. Because not a few started to flee while it was still winter, many were affected by serious illnesses and in their great distress, poverty and misery were snatched away to an early death. The way from Saratov to the Polish border to Minsk is sown with the graves of German and above all Catholic colonists. In Minsk, the unfortunate refugees received their first humanitarian aid from the German Red Cross.

1. The German farmers in the Black Sea region where first plundered in the year 1920, so that famine developed here somewhat later. Jewish tax inspectors (in many cases they

were women) caused the "requisitions" to be enforced with a terrible lack of consideration. They did not leave our unfortunate compatriots with even the most basic of necessities. In order to save their lives, the poor population exchanged its last livestock, its last horse, its last cow, kitchen utensils, even the most needed of clothing which they wore on their own bodies so that many could not cover their nakedness any more and could not go out in public. These are all the great "blessings" of Bolshevism!)

The Great Famine under the Bolshevik regime is probably the greatest history has ever known. According to the statistical reports it caused the deaths of ten to twelve million lives. Also, there had never been such a huge and extensive lack of crops· ever in Russia as in the year 1920. The Russian people had previously never suffered such great and terrible natural catastrophes as under the regime of the red tyrants. The words of the Book of Ecclesiastes seem to have been fulfilled by the Bolsheviks: "And the universe will march with him to fight the reckless" (Wisdom 5:21).

The Great Russian Famine caused most of the civilized world to do something. In Western Europe and in North and South America benevolent donations were collected in order to save the unfortunate from famine. It is known that there was magnanimous aid from the United States of America which earmarked twenty million dollars for the starving people. The aid workers sent by the Holy Father also stilled hunger among many thousands for years on end and also clothed them. And what did the unbridled Moscovite czars do in the meantime? They exported the extorted grain to other countries in Europe where they sold it! This is then the love of its subjects, this is the concern of the autocrats in Moscow that they take the last piece of bread out of the mouths of their starving comrades and exchange it for money! By this one fact the world can recognize and judge the entire spirit, the complete depravity of the Bolsheviks and their system of government.

Ten years have passed since the first great catastrophic famine in Russia but the hunger of those who ring bread from the earth among the Bolsheviks has not subsided. Ten years of misery, persecution, tyranny, enslavement of consciences, suppression of sanctified feelings among those who call themselves the government, ten years of no righteousness, no justice and no protection! Human strength cannot endure that. For this reason many have, in the last period of time, attempted to get out of this hellhole and left their possessions behind in order to simply save their own lives!

64. The value of the church assets which was stolen by the Bolsheviks

At the time when the German colonies were established, the Russian state granted the original churches in the Volga as well as in the Black Sea region 120 dessiatines of agricultural land each. The clergymen were to work this land and use it for their sustenance. Since the prospective income would not suffice, the congregations, on their part, were given the responsibility of additionally providing an annual wage of three hundred rubles. The land was to be exclusively for the benefit of the minister and the congregations had no right of disposition for it. Within certain perimeters, disposal of the property was the sole right of the spiritual authorities. The mother congregations of the Black Sea region were: Landau, Rastatt, Selz, K.leinlieb ental, Josephstal, Mannheim, Heidelberg, Eichwald, Jamburg; ancj Rosental in the Crimea. Both of the last-mentioned churches received much less: Jamburg got about 56 dessiatines, Eichwald as well as Rosental only received a few dessiatines (Translator's note: the original text is unclear here). As equalization, both parishes had to pay a higher salary to the minister. Apart from these parishes, the little church in Ponjatoflka/Ponyatovka (Potocki) was granted 50 dessiatines of parish land by the Polish Count Potocki. The church in Severinovka received 180 dessiatines of agricultural land from the owner of the estate. He was a

Catholic count. Of this, 100 dessiatines were determined for the support of the clergy in the parish and 80 dessiatines were to serve as support of the church and the church employees. In 1910 the Russian nobleman Suchomlinoff/Zuchomlinov, at that time a royal marshal of the county of Odessa, obtained the Severinovka estate without an agreement with the seller in regard to the church property. No document was found in either the episcopal chancellery or in the parish archive in which the ownership of the property by the church of the mentioned 180 dessiatines could be proven. In order to clarify this important situation, the Tiraspol diocesan wrote to the new proprietor of the estate. Mr. Zwchomlinov, despite the fact that he was of the Orthodox confession, replied that he had, together with the large estate, also purchased the so-called church land. He would, however, not lay any claim to it but would leave it to the church for its cultivation. The head shepherd kept this letter in the chancellery office as a legal document showing that the land belonged to the Catholic Church in Severinovka. In 1905, the great estate owner Jakob Dauenhauer built a church, school and priest's residence on his estate near Heikofka in the gouvemement of Cherson. At the request of the bishop's chancellery, he donated 200 dessiatines of fertile land to the church for the support of a curate of souls in the same. Beside this he deposited bonds worth 7,000 rubles in the Cherson agricultural bank from the interest of which an annual memorial mass was to be held for him and his wife.

In its decree, Bolshevism, as has already been mentioned, made all fixed and liquid assets of the churches the property of the state and thereby snatched the property of the church which was mentioned above. Spoken bluntly, it was stolen.

Since the Volga Germans already sensed a lack of land at the time of their settlement, they approached the government with the petition that it might give the church lands to them. The government approved their petition with the condition that a head tax of three and one-half kopecks be paid annually by the Catholic colonists for the support of the curate of souls, the twelve free spots in the pro-seminary and the consistory. In addition to this head tax, each priest in the Volga region received an annual contribution of 142 rubles and 90 copecks as was mentioned previously. While the Bolsheviks transferred the above property to the government, they were not able to requisition the additional contributions for salaries because they had caused a monetary devaluation on purpose in order to eliminate the bourgeois (middle class people).

After the red despots had completely expropriated the Church by issuing a decree on September 23, 1918 and had temporarily left the "use" of the churches to the religious societies as well as the holy vessels and things used for worship services, it was foreseen that they would demand rent for the same or would sell the holy vessels and valuable items. In the year 1921, that which was feared already proved to be true. If a religious society, that is a parish, could not pay the rent, the House of God was locked. The great famine of 1921 was used by the Bolshevik regime as an excuse to sell the silver, gold and other valuable church vessels with the pretense of feeding the starving but in fact to fill the pockets of the innumerable agitators and commissars. It was repeatedly reported in the daily newspapers that prominent commissars had moved items of great value and treasures to distant countries.

All of the assets which the Bolsheviks robbed from the Catholic Church in the diocese of Tyraspol have, according to an approximate and casual evaluation, a value of seven million gold rubles. 1

Apart from this, 202,000 rubles, which the two last head shepherds of Tiraspol had collected for a new seminary building, fell into the hands of the Bolsheviks. This included about 25,000 rubles of stipend capital for students at the seminary who were without means, 42,500 rubles and about 50,000 rubles of donated mass monies and finally 20,400 rubles for mass memorials. The latter funds were deposited in the city Bank of Saratov and the other funds in the Catholic Council Office in St. Petersburg.

The French have a proverb which states: "Whoever eats from the pope will die from doing so." The same can be considered true in even greater measure in regard to the stolen property of the church. God's curse is already consuming the property of the Bolsheviks. One only has to point to the continual economic disasters. Where actual facts are glaringly visible, no bragging and no lies from the mouths of several hundred thousand Bolsheviks in regard to "great economic successes" will change the situation one little bit.

1. The Houses of God are not included in this figure.

65. Directory of the bishops of the diocese of Tyraspol

1. Ferdinand Helanus Kahn, born 1787, consecrated as the bishop of Cherson responsible for Tyraspol on November 10, 1850, died on October 6, 1864.
2. Franz Xaverius Zottmann, born June 15, 1826 and consecrated as the bishop of Tyraspol on April 14, 1872, died November 29, 1901 in Ombau in Bavaria. He had resigned on December 18, 1889.
3. Antonius Johannes Zerr, born on March 10, 1849, designated bishop on March 3, 1883, suffragan bishop until December 18, 1889 when he was consecrated as the bishop ofTyraspol. He resigned from this position on August 1, 1901.

4. Eduard Baron von der Ropp, born December 2, 1851 and consecrated as the bishop ofTyraspol on May 27, 1902, transferred to Vilna on October 27, 1903. He was elevated as the archbishop of Mohilev in the year 1917.
5. Joseph Alqysius Kessler, born August 12, 1862, consecrated as the bishop of Tyraspol on April 7, 1904, renounced the diocese on November 27, 1929. Elevated by the presently reigning Holy Father Pius XI as the titular archbishop of the the Bosphorus on January 23, 1930.
6. Finally Suffragan Bishop Lipski oflonopolis, born on March 17, 1795; designated the suffragan bishop ofTyraspol on September 16, 1856, died in Odessa on December 11, 1875.
(Translator's note: Ionopolis is a city in presentd-day Turkey which is located in the province of Paphlagonia)

66. Directory of the parishes and filial congregations of the diocese

Deanery of Saratov
Saratov, cathedral and parish church: Number of souls 8,150
Chapels: in the bishop's palace, in the seminary for priests, at the cemetery, in the

bishop's villa
Filial congregations in Kosakenstadt (Pokrovsk)
Marienfeld, parish church constructed of wood. Number of souls 3,780
Filial congregation in Josephstal
Filial congregation in Kamyshin: prayer house constructed of stone.
Tsaritsyn, parish church constructed of stone. Number of souls 600
Astrakhan, parish church constructed of stone, built 1762. Number of souls 1,350
Kasizkoye (Brabander) parish church constructed of wood. Number of souls 4,248
Beresovka (Dehler) parish church constructed of wood. Number of souls 3,980

Deanery of Kamenka

Kamenka, parish church constructed of stone. Number of souls 3,467
Husaren (Jelschanka), parish church constructed of wood. Number of souls 2,300
Vollmar (Kopenka), parish church constructed of wood. Number of souls 1805
Schuck (Gryasnovatka), parish church constructed of wood. Number of souls 4,032
Filial Congregation in Degott, church constructed of stone.
Chapel constructed of wood.
Rothammel (Pamyatnoye), parish church constructed of wood. Number of souls ...2,185
Seewald, parish church constructed of wood. Number of souls 1,35 3
Pfeifer (Gnilnuschka), parish church constructed of wood. Number of souls ... .5 ,20 5

Hildmann (Panovka), parish church constructed of wood. Number of souls 3,60 8
Leichtling (Ilyovka), prayer house constructed of stone. Number of souls 2,100
Koehler, parish church constructed of wood. Number of souls 6,373
Chapel in honor of the discovery of the cross
Zemyonovk a, parish church constructed of wood. Number of souls 6,577
Chapel
Goebel (Ust-gryasnucha), parish church made of wood. Number of souls 3,738

Deanery ofKatharinenstadt (Marx)

Katharinenstadt, parish church rriade of stone, built in 1815. Number of souls 2,910
Chapel at the cemetery
Filial congregation in Boregard, prayer house made of wood.
Obermonjou, parish church made of stone. Number of souls 3, 052
Luzem, parish church made of wood. Number of souls 4,00 3
Zug, parish church made of wood. Number of souls .... : 3,744

Schoenchen (Paninskoye), parish church made of stone. Number of souls 3, 194
Solothurn, parish church made of wood, Number of souls 3,948

Deanery of Mariental

Mariental (Tonkoschurovka), parish church made of stone. Number of souls ... 8,000
Chapels on the grave of the Jesuit priest Aloisius Moritz, at the old cemetery, under the Kyrgyz Mountain (Kirgisienberg) on the other side of the Karaman River.
Rohleder (Rskaty), parish church made of stone. Number of souls 2,38 9
Chapel m honour of the Mother of God
Herzog, parish church-made of stone. Number of souls ....' 1,97 4
Chapels on the church grounds in honour of the Mother of Good Counsel
Graf, parish church made of wood. Number of Souls 2,153
Chapel in honour of St. Anthony of Padua
Louis (Ostrogovka), parish church made of stone. Number of souls 5,636
Chapel in honour of St. Anthony of Padua
Liebental, parish church made of wood. Number of souls 4,3 37
Filial congregation Neu-Obermonjou, church made of wood.
Filial congregation Neu-Mariental, church made of wood.
Filial congregation Urbach, prayer house made of wood.
Tschomaya Padina, parish church made of wood. Number of souls 1,072
Filial congregation Talovka, church made of wood.
Marienburg, parish church made of wood. Number of souls 3, 044

Deanery of Seelmann

Seelmann, parish church made of stone. Number of souls .... : 8,490
Chapel of the Perpetual Help of Mary
Neukolonie (Kustarevo-Kras:riorinovka) parish church made of stone
Number of souls ....3 ,526
Hoelzel, parish church made of stone and wood. Number of souls 2,360
Chapel on the church yard
Preuss, parish church made of wood. Number of souls 5,889
Chapel on the church yard
Marienberg, parish church made of stone. Number of souls 3,485
Streckerau, parish church made of wood. Number of souls 2,435

Deanery of Berdyansk

Berdyansk, parish church made of stone. Number of souls 726
Filial congregations: Neu-Stuttgart, Neu-Hoffnungstal, Waldheim
Yenakyevo, parish church made of stone. Number of souls 2,094
Filial congregations: David-Orloffka, Selieger, Sofieyeffka, Juliano.
Bachmut, parish church made of stone. Number of souls 3,200
Filial congregations: Konstantinovka, Druzkovka, Sodafabrik.
Yusovka, parish church made of wood (prayer house) Number of souls 1,890
Filial congregations: Marinska, Kremenoye, Delinterovo.
Lugansk, prayer house made of stone. Number of souls 2,500
Filial congregations: Konoplyanka, Nikolsk.
Mariupol, parish church made of stone. Number of souls 3,500
Eichwald, parish church made of stone. Number of souls 3,497
Filial congregations: Svytotrizkoye, Adamovka, Antonovka, Novodvorodovka, Blumenfeld.
Goettland, parish church made of stone. Number of souls 1,475
Filial congregations: Kaiserdorf, Kampenau, Myarau, Heitschule.
Grosswerder, parish church made of stone. Number of souls 858
Bergtal, parish church made of stone. Number of souls .... : ... 1,526
Filial congregation: Stepanovka, (Gruenfeld) Neu-Jamburg
Taganrog, parish church made of stone. Number of souls 1,315
Filial congregation Krinitschki
Gruental, parish church made of stone. Number of souls 1.361
Filial congregations: Novo-Vasilevka, Gross-Konstantinovka, Zolnzevo, Wagneropol.
Makeyevka, parish church made of stone. Number of souls 1,034

Rostov on Don, parish church made of stone. Number of souls 5,632
Chapel at the cemetery

Filial congregation Novoliyinka
Novocherkask, parish church of stone: Number of souls 4,231
Filial congregations: Gruenfeld, Gruenental, Liebental, Grosswerder, Kleinwerder.

Deanery of Yekaterinoslav

Yekaterinoslav, parish church made of stone. Number of souls 10,555
Filial congregations: Losovaya, Alexandrovsk, Grischino, Parlograd

Number of souls .... - 1,000
Jamburg, parish church made of stone. Number of souls 2,901
Filial congregations: Ekaterinovka, Rybalik, Marievka, Novoalexandrovka, Chortiztza, Zorotchino.
Kamenskoye-Fabrik, parish church made of stone. Number of souls 6,872
Georgsburg, parish church made of stone. Number of souls 1,300
Filial congregations: Dudnikovo, Y egorovka, Elisavetovka, Nikilayevka, Marislav, Moskovka, Kulymannstal, Katharinenfeld.
Heidelberg, parish church made of stone. Number of souls 3,576
Kostheim, parish church made of stone 2,461
Filial congregations
Leitershausen, Marienheim, Alexanderheim, Chechograd.
Konstantinovka, parish church· made of stone. Number of souls 1,798
Filial congregation: Novo-Petrovka
Nikolajevka, parish church made of stone. Number of souls 1,850
Filial congregations: Verchne-Torgayevka, Rubanovka.
Maryinskoye (Marienfeld), parish church made of stone. Number of souls 1;868
Filial congregations: Kotschubeyevka, Feodorovka
Maryanovka (Novo-Mannheim), parish church. Number of souls 2,776
Filial congregations: Neu-Landau, Neu-Kronental, Rosenfeld, Simonsfeld, Nikolaital, Michailovka.

Deanery of Simpferopol

Simpferopol, parish church made of stone. Number of souls 4,416
Chapel on the church yard
Filial congregations: Kronental, Aschaga-Dzamin, Turasch, Agodza, Franzfeld.
Rosental (Schaban Uba), parish church made of stone. Number of souls 1,205
Filial congregations: Altai, Dzajtschi, Pustarschi, Argin, Aila-Kaeli.

Perekop, parish church made of stone (without parish members/children), the priest resides in Grigoryevka, Number of members of the so-called parish church 2,387
Filial congregations: Preobrazenka, Belozerkovka, Michaelovka, Alexandrovka, Novokievka, Pavlovka, Dagmarovka, Novoalexeyevka.
Alexandrovka, parish church made of stone. Number of souls 1,770
FiJial congregations: Zerkovitch, Mirovka, Bohemka, Nogai-Toma, Kirej-Tabor, BertyBulat,
Ko,p-Kary, Attai, Baschbek and Komrat.
Karamin, parish church made of stone. Number of souls 413

Filial congregations: Dulat, Meschin.
Feodosia, parish church made of stone. Number of souls· 558

This church was changed from a Tartar mosque into a Roman Catholic Church. Empress In 1787, Empress Catharine II had donated this mosque, together with 20,000 rubles for the refurbishment to Archbishop Siestrzencevitch of Mohilev through Prince Potemkin. The archbishop specifically recorded this in his diary which he wrote in Latin and which Professor Godlevksi published in his monumenta historica (historical highlights). This House of God was illegally appropriated by the Armenian Catholics. Filial congregations: The Genoan Chapel in Sudak, which belongs to the Roman Catholic rite as well. In the year 1822, this was also transformed from a Tartar mosque into a Roman Catholic chapel by the Genoan Consul Soldai Golan Christian Mondiano.
Kertsch, parish church made of stone. Number of souls 1,065
Yalta, filial congregation, made of cut black granite. Number of souls 575
Sebastopol, parish church made of stone. Number of souls 3,209
Deanery of Nikolayev
Nikolayev, parish church made of stone. Number of souls 8,555
Filial congregations: Neu-Karlsruhe, Laryevka, Dobraya Kerniza.
Danilovka (Heikovka), chaplain's church made of stone, Number of souls 800
Belonging to this chaplaincy as well: Otschertino, Gosnovka ..
Krivoy-Rog, prayer house: Number of souls 1,334
Speyer, parish church made of stone. Number of souls 3,316
Katharinental, parish church made of stone. Number of souls 1,622
Chapel in the church yard
Karlsruhe, parish church made of stone. Number of souls 1,933
Chapel in the church yard
Filial congregation: Antonovka.
Landau, parish church made of stone. Number of souls 2,238
Schoenfeld, parish church made of stone. Number of souls ,.......................... 1,234
Filial congregations: Steinberg, Halbstadt, Petrovka
Sulz, parish church made of stone. Number of souls 2,051

Chapel in the church yard
Filial congregations: Votsche.
Blumenfeld, parish church made of stone. Number of souls 3,080
Filial congregations: Krasna, Sebastienfeld, Wilhelmstal, Eigengut, Lubyank:a, Neu-Petersburg, Kolopatino, Annovka, Kapustino

Christiania, parish church made of stone. Number of souls 2,636
Filial congregations: Felsenburg, Michaelovka, Novo-Alexandrovka, Kuhn.
Rastatt, parish church made of stone. Number of souls 2,450
Muenche n, parish church made of stone. Number ofs ouls ....1 ,7 3 7

Cherson, parish church made of stone. Number of souls ....2 ,245
Filial congregation: Zaredarovka
Klosterdorf, parish church made of stone. Number of souls 1,237
Kiselyevka, prayer house made of stone. Number of souls 1,440

Deanery of Odessa

Odessa, parish church of the Assumption of the Virgi☐ Mary made of stone. Number of souls 14,986
Filial congregation in honor of St. Peter
Chapel in the convent of the Sisters of St. Francis in the French Old Folks Home
Odessa, parish church of St. Clement. Number of souls 17,773
Mannheim, parish church made of stone. Number of souls 2,459
Filial congregations: Georgiental, Johannestal.
Elsass, parish church made ofs tone. Number of souls ....2 ,325
Yeremeyevka: Filial church made of stone. Number of souls ..... : ...... ?
Filial congregation Scherniott
K.leinliebental, parish church made of stone. Number of souls 2, 664
Chapel in the church yard
Josephstal, parish church made of stone. Number ofsouls ....1 ,162
Chapel
Mariental, parish church made of stone. Number of souls. 9 50
Franzfeld, parish church made of stone. Number of souls 6 72
Chapel in honour of the Mother of God
Kandel, parish church made of stone. Number of souls 2, 7 41
Chapel in the church.yard
Selz, parish church made of stone. Number of souls 2,537
Baden, parish church made of stone. Number of souls 1,842
Chapel in the church yard
Strassburg, parish church made of stone. Number of souls 3,643
Filial congregations:· Stepanovka, Andryaschovka, Mirolyubovka, Maryanovka. Prayer house made of stone.
Severinovka, parish church made of stone. Number of souls 1, 112

Ponyatovka, prayer house made of stone. Number of souls 1,500
Filial congregations: l<:-osc;hary, Bizilyevka, Simionovka.
Wolkov, parish church made of stone. Number of souls 2,510
Filial congregations: Neu-Baden, Kusakov, Bogunskoye, Kostkolovka.
Elisabethgrad, parish church made of stone. Number of souls 2,286
Tyraspol: prayer chapel in a rented building. Number of souls 100

Deanery of Pyatigorsk

Pyatigorsk, parish church made of stone. Number of souls 1,738
Timir-Chan-Schura, military parish church made of stone. Number of souls.360
Vladikavkasz, parish church made of stone .... Number of souls 550
Grozny, prayer house made of stone. Number of souls 5,800
Mosdok, parish church made of stone Number of souls 338
Stavropol, church made of stone. Number of souls in the parish 1,800
Yekaterinodar, parish church made ofs tone. Number of souls 2,500
Novorossisk, prayer house made of stone. Number of souls 3,580
Roschdestvenskoye, church made of wood. Number of souls 2,638
Semoinovka, church made of wood. Number of souls 2,700
Nikolayevka, church made of stone. Number of souls 500
Deanery of Thlisi
Tblisi, parish church of the Assumption of Mary: Number of souls 3,302
Tblisi, parish church of Sts. Peter and Paul: Number of souls 7,000
Chapel in the church yard of Kukuyev
Chapel at the second cemetery
Manglis, parish church made of stone. Number of souls (soldiers) 13,600
Gori, parish church made of stone. Number of souls .... .495
Chapel in the village of Betlemi
Kutais, parish church made of stone. Number of souls 2,087
Chapel in the church yard
Acbalzyck, prayer house made of stone. Number of souls 173
Batum, church made of stone. Number of souls 1,050
Baku, parish church made of stone. Number of souls 1,300

67. Directory of the priests who graduated from the Tyraspol Seminary

1. Albert, Johannes
2. Altmeier, Josef
3. Andreschejkowitsch, Boleslaus
4. Arasof, Johannes

1. Bader, Emmanuel
2. Back, Johannes
3. Baier, Georg Sen. Academic
4. Baier, Georg
5. Baranovski, Josef, honorary candidate
6. Baumtrog, Josef
7. Baumtrog, Augustin, Academic
8. Bach, Johannes
9. Bach, Peter
10. Beilmann, Josef
11. Beilmann, Johannes
12. Beilmann, Johannes
13. Bellendir, Adam
14. Becker, Philipp
15. Beratz, Gottlieb
16. Baechler, Valentin
17. Braun, Adolf
18. Brungardt, Andreas
19. Brungardt, Michael
20. Butsch, Kaspar
21. Burgardt, Johannes
22. Baczevski, Kaspar, prelate
23. Baier, Adam
24. Boehm, Otto, Academic Dr.
25. Bojarzynski, Stanislav
26. Berlis, Michael, Ac ademic Licentiate
27. Boos, Alexander, Cathedral Canon

1. Dittler, Eduard
2. Demuroff, Stephan
3. Dobrowolsky, Georg
4. Dobrowolsky, Jakob, papal prelate
5. Dovblis, Ignatius

6. Dornhof, Johannes
7. Dornhof, Alexander
8. Dorzweiler
9. Dechant, Georg

10. Dygris, Petrus
11. Doetzel, Georg
12. Desc☐ Adam
13. Duckart, Jakob
14. Duckart, Peter
15. Dietrich, Raphael
16. Dolongovski, Leonhard

1. Eberle, Leonhard
2. Ehresmann, Johannes
3. Ehrhardt, Raphael
4. Eberhardt, Alexander
5. Erk, Ludwig

1. Falkenstein, Johannes
2. Fauth, Michael
3. Feser, Jakob, Academic Dr.
4. Fix, Johannes
5. Fix, Martin
6. Fitterer, Nikolaus
7. Fleck; Raphael, Cathedral Canon
8. Fleck, Anton, Academic Dr. prelate
9. Froehlich, Anton
10. Froehlich, Raphael
11. Frison, Alexander, Acad emic Dr. (Bishop)
12. Fuchs, Johannes

1. Gabel, Augustin
2. Gareis, Adam
3. Gizycki, Johannes
4. Gibulski, Adam
5. Glassmann, Peter
6. Glassner, Robert
7. Glaser, Markus, Dr. Academic Cathedral Canon
8. Graf, Joseph
9. Graf, Alexius
10. Greiner, Valentin
11. Gibulsz
12. Gutovski, Adam
13. Gwaramadze, Gabriel
14. Guetlein, Josef

1. Hartmann, Valentin honorary candidate
2. Hatzenboeller, Michael
3. Haal, Jakob
4. Herrmann, Peter
5. Hermann, Johannes
6. Hein, Josef
7. Hilfer, Michael, Academic Dr.
8. Hirsch, Ferdinand
9. Hopfauf, Karl
10. Hopfauf, Eduard
11. Hoffmann, Johannes
12. Haas, Peter
13. Hellmann, Nikolaus, Academic
14. Heut, Peter

1. lhly, Josef
2. Ihly, Nikodemus
3. Ianski, Josef
4. Jaufmann, Philipp, Senior
5. Jau:fmann, Philipp
6. Jasenas
7. J aguloff, Michael

8. Ibach, Nikolaus
,9. Jaeger, Kaspar
10. Jungkind, Josef

1. Kayser, Jakob
2. Kessler, Joseph Academic Dr. Bishop
3. Kraft, Nikolaus
4. Klass, Georg, Academic Dr.
5. Kappes, Aloisius
6. Kapcinski, Adalbert
7. Kraft, Balthaser
8. Keller, Konrad
9. Keller, Andreas, honorary candidate
10. Koelsch, Josef
11. Klimaszewski, Xavier Academic Dr. Cathedral Canon
12. Koslowski, Leo
13. Koslowski, Franz
14. K.ruschinsky, Joseph, prelate
15. Kuhn, Franz
16. Kubik, Stanislaw
17. Koeberlein, Johannes
18. Krinicki, Aloisius, honorary candidate
19. Kniukszto, Johannes·
20. Kardasewicz, Stanislaw
21. Kistner, Friedrich
22. Kopp, Theobald

1. Liesel, Nikolaus
2. Lang, Johannes
3. Leibham, Georg
4. Leibham, Bernhard
5. Loran, Franz
6. Loran, Josef
7. Loran, Raphael
8. Loewenbrueck, Franz

1. Maier, Georg, Senior
2. Maier, Nikolaus
3. Malinovsky; Josef, Dr. of Philosophy
4. Marsal, Markus
5. Mikolajunas, Bartholomaeus
6. Mickiewicz, Ignatius
7. Mueller, Peter
8. Mitzig
9. · Mokelki, Emmanuel
10. Merklinger, Michael
11. Matery, Josef

1. Neugum, Josef, Cathedral Canon
2. Nold, Josef, honorary candidate

1. von Okupski, Josef
2. Oks, Aloisius
3. Oskierko, Stanislaw
4. Oborovsky, Georg

1. Pauer, Johannes
2. Potocki, Wladyslav
3. Paul, Josef
4. Porubsky, Stephan
5. Pieczuro
6. Pflug, Ferdinand, Lie. Juris Academic Candidate

1. Roether, Josef
2. Rauh, Franz
3. Rauh, Michael
4. Roth, Johannes, honorary candidate, apostolic administrator
5. Rohleder, Franz
6. Ruscheinsky, Kaspar, Candidate Professor
7. Riessling, Georg
8. Riessling, Ludwig
9. Riedel, Peter
10. Rollhaeuser, Peter

11. Rosenbacb, Jakob
12. Reichert, Rudolf, honorary candidate
13. Reichert, Cyriakus

1. Seewald, Andreas
2. Skwirecki, Vinzenz
3. Sokolovski, Kasimir
4. Schneider, Johannes Senior
5. Schneider, Johannes II
6. Schneider, Johannes III
7. Schoenfeld, Alo is
8. Schoenfeld, Jakob
9. Schoenheiter, Klemens
10. Sauer, Georg
11. Schamne, Johann von N. (Nepomuk?)
12. Sicard
13. Simon, Emmanuel
14. Stroemel, Georg
15. Schindler, Josef
16. Scherer, Franz
17. Scherr, Jakob
18. Schardt, Nikolaus
19. Schaefer, Raphael
20. Staub, Alexander
21. Staub, Konstantin, Dr. ofi>hilosophy
22. Schulz, Florian
23. Scherger, Franz
24. Selinger, Jakob
25. Stang, Alexander
26. Stang, Emmanuel, Academic Dr. Candidate
27. Stokrocki, Wladyslav
28. Schemberger, Johannes
29. Schoenberger, Andreas
30. Stein, Christian
31. Szczurek, Nikolaus
32. Count Szembek, Georg, Bishop and Archbishop
33. Szidagis, Matthias
34. Schoenfeld, Johannes

35. Szydlowski, Anton
36. Szewczynski, Josef

1. Thauberger, Johannes, Academic
2. Tomaszewski, Konstantin

1. Uselis, Johannes
2. Ullrich, Adolf
3. Ungemach, Johannes, honorary Candidate

1. Vondrau, Aloisius
2. Vetsch, Johannes
3. Veith, Josef

1. Weinmaier, Leo
2. Weigel, Peter
3. W alulis, Matthaeus
4. Weissenburger, Clemens
5. Wassinger, Johannes
6. Weber, Valentin
7. Wanner, Josef
8. Wolski, Stanislaw
9. Wolf, Willibald, honorary Candidate Professor Dr.
10. Wolf, Josef
11. Wolf, Laurentius
12. Wolf, Michael, Academic
13. Wolf, Jakob
14. Walter, Anton
15. Wagner, Adam
16. Walliser, Michael
17. Warzucyanski, Kasimir

1. Zerr, Antonius, Bishop of Tyraspol
2. Zimmermann, Andreas
3. Zimmermann, Johannes
4. Zimmermann, Johannes
5. Zerr, Jakob

6. Czerwinski, Anton, Academic Dr.
7. Cherniachowicz, Nikodemus papal prelate
8. Turczynski, Alexander
9. Rudnicki, Anton
10. Smolski
11. Puchalski
12. Szamostulski
13. Barski
14. Michalski
15. Szarturski

Explanations of some terms used in this book:

1. Riebelsuppe: In the Volga German dialect this is Riwwelsupp. It is a soup made with chicken broth and noodle dough that has been rubbed over a grater. The product is akin to Spaetzle, but the Riwwel can be and are often smaller, perhaps larger than kernels of rice. A Riwwelkuge is a cake which is sprinkled with small pieces of sweet dough mixed with sugar.

2. weliczko: grandeur, splendour. This must be a Polish word, and means something like "big" or "Great." The Russian word for Great Britain is Vieliko Britannia.

3. moltschaty: "to be silent" or "the silent one."

4. obysany and obyazyana (obyazyany is the plural form) and obesyany: The first word means monkey and the second means that someone is bound to something. "Ya obyasani tebe otvetit" means: "I'm bound to answer you."

5. one verst = 1.0668 kilometers = 3,500 feet = .663 of a mile